ESSEX
HUNDREDS & PARISHES

circa 1900.
Reproduced by courtesy of the Essex
Record Office

SWORN TO SERVE

Police in Essex
1840-1990

A Royal visit to Brentwood in the mid-1950s almost received some additional support from these sheep, which escaped from a nearby slaughterhouse.

SWORN TO SERVE

Police in Essex
1840-1990

Maureen Scollan

Phillimore

1993

Published by
PHILLIMORE & CO. LTD.
Shopwyke Manor Barn, Chichester, Sussex

ISBN 0 85033 999 5

Printed by
The Bath Press

Contents

List of Illustrations

Frontispiece: Royal Visit to Brentwood, 1950s

vi

Foreword

The publication in 1993 of this history of policing in Essex is particularly timely, as the police service is currently facing a period of significant and far-reaching reform. The changes will affect the accountability of the police, the size and structure of Forces and the conditions of service of individual officers; in addition, the report of the Royal Commission on Criminal Justice will also result in changes to police procedures and practice. It is therefore important that a record of policing in Essex is set down before these reforms take place.

In reading this story of what has gone before, future generations will learn and appreciate how the police men and women of Essex have created a tradition of service to the public in policing by consent. The rôle of these earlier officers in keeping the peace, in preventing and detecting crime, and providing support to the community in times of trouble and disaster is chronicled in these pages. It is a story which will not only interest, but inspire others to build upon this record of service; for whatever changes, or whatever reforms are made, the rôle of the Essex Police will remain the same—to serve the people of Essex.

I am most grateful to Maureen Scollan for her dedication in undertaking this task, and for her painstaking research and attention to detail which has resulted in this invaluable story of policing in Essex.

July 1993

JOHN BURROW
CHIEF CONSTABLE

Dedicated
to the Policemen and Policewomen
of Essex
Past, Present and Future

Preface

History, wrote Voltaire, is no more than the portrayal of crimes and misfortunes.[1] But the history of policing ought to be more than that: its facets touch so many aspects of life which can never be recorded in one volume.

This work seeks to trace the origins and subsequent development of the Essex County Constabulary, and the borough forces that amalgamated with it to become the present day Essex Police. It is not the first book on the subject, and I hope it will not be the last. The philosophy of policing is constantly being reappraised, and there can never be a definitive history of such a subject. There are other printed accounts of Essex Police and its constituent forces, ranging from Burnett Tabrum's outline published in 1911, to John Woodgate's book published in 1985. An official account of the former Southend-on-Sea Borough Constabulary appeared in 1964, and the 150th Anniversary of the Essex Police in 1990 generated Frederick Feather's commemorative booklet.

Recording and interpreting history depends largely on the availability of source material. Because official police policy has been to destroy documents after a comparatively short time, many potentially valuable sources of information no longer exist. Given these constraints, therefore, this work represents a selection of what I think have been the important trends—and some of the interesting incidents—in Essex police history over the past two centuries.

I hope this book will encourage more detailed research into particular aspects of force history, and with this in mind I have provided notes and references at the end of each chapter. There are also appendices recording the main changes in such matters as uniform and procedures, and 'potted histories' of the principal departments in the force. To give some idea of the variations in recruiting over the 150 years of the study, I have included details of those who joined Essex Police in the years 1840, 1900 and 1990, the year when the main study ends; however one or two later matters have been included.

The following abbreviations are used in the notes:
ERO	Essex Record Office
PRO	Public Record Office
VHM	Vestry House Museum, Walthamstow
BM	British Museum
BL	British Library
SJC	Standing Joint Committee

1. *L'Ingenu*, Voltaire, 1767

Acknowledgements

Many people have contributed in some way to the preparation of this work, but my primary debt of gratitude is to Peter Simpson, Deputy Chief Constable of Essex, October 1986— October 1993. Had he not actively encouraged and supported the writing of this book and the establishment of the Essex Police Museum, then it is doubtful whether either would have existed—other than in dreams!

I am grateful for the help of friends in the Essex Record Office, particularly June Beardsley, Ronald Bond and Janet Gyford; and to the librarians and archivists at the Police Staff College, Bramshill; the British Library; Chelmsford Library; Colindale Newspaper Library; Essex County Council's Local Government Library; and the Public Record Office at Kew and Chancery Lane. Malcolm White, Town Clerk of Saffron Walden, and Leonard Weaver, Harwich historian, allowed me to consult the borough police records in their care, and I thank them for their co-operation.

It is a pleasure to acknowledge the help of police colleagues and other friends. Those who provided specific pieces of information will find it acknowledged in the end notes to each chapter, and this also applies to retired officers who allowed me to tape record their recollections: sadly some of them have since died. I am particularly grateful to Elizabeth Sellers who generously shared with me numerous police references she found in local newspapers and quarter sessions records, and who later volunteered to read the draft chapters and suggest many improvements. Ann Turner allowed me to see her notes on the Colchester Borough Police, and provided introductions to the Colchester Recalled project; Graham and Gordon Oakley, Fred Winter and Frank Shepherd solved individual queries, and Martyn Lockwood gave me the benefit of his knowledge of the Gutteridge case, and was a useful sounding board during discussions on various points of layout. Peter Erskine applied his considerable knowledge of computer software and applications for my benefit; Mary Brassett patiently and accurately transferred my word-processed drafts into the final form for printing; Fred Feather helped with the cover, which was designed and drawn by Peter Rutherford, and David Pike drew the maps and charts. Ken Linge and the helpful staff of the Essex Police Photographic Department provided copies of many of the illustrations. Professor Clive Emsley and Dr. Arthur Brown kindly found time to read the draft chapters and make some constructive criticism, and Geoffrey Markham, Assistant Chief Constable (Operations), performed a similar service on the appendices. Any errors which remain are mine alone.

Lastly, but not least, I want to thank my parents—Elizabeth and Patrick Scollan—my brother Michael, and sister-in-law Sylvia for their continual support and encouragement, for always being interested in my researches, and for making many practical suggestions when passages of text were read to them at different times.

Royalties from sales of this book will go towards the financial support of the Essex Police Museum.

Chapter 1

Prelude

Birth of John McHardy, first Chief Constable of Essex, in Bahamas—his naval career—policing of Essex before 1840.

There is nothing more difficult to take in hand, more perilous to conduct, or more uncertain in its success, than to take the lead in the introduction of a new order of things.[1]

The Man

One fine Saturday in May 1812 HMS *Tartarus* dropped anchor in Nassau harbour, on New Providence Island in the Bahamas. Although only about 60 miles from Florida, the Bahamas had been a British colony since 1656, and its residents were British citizens. The islands themselves provided a convenient base from which to monitor the slave trade.

Tartarus was part of a British naval force assigned to tracking down slave ships, and dealing with smugglers and pirates. She needed fresh stores and new hands, and over the following days Captain John Pasco had the chance to observe those who joined his ship for the first time: including the 11 year old boy who was to become the first Chief Constable of Essex.[2] John Bunch Bonnemaison McHardy was born on 3 December 1801 in New Providence. Very little is known about his childhood, but there were several landowners with that surname in New Providence at the end of the 18th century. There is also some evidence that McHardy's father married twice, which may have been the reason why he left home.[3]

It was common for a boy to join the navy at 10 or 11 years of age, when he would be initially graded as boy third class. Anyone showing real aptitude could move into the first class in a matter of weeks, and thence to the position of midshipman. Progress thereafter depended on influence, on-the-job training and the passing of examinations in seamanship and navigation.

Naval captains were responsible for the welfare and training of their crews, and Pasco saw to it that McHardy quickly became a boy first class in *Tartarus*, and subsequently a midshipman in *Rota* which Pasco also commanded. McHardy spent most of his early naval career in the West Indies and South America, except when he was sent on courses to Portsmouth. By January 1828 he had qualified as a lieutenant, and assumed command of *Pickle*, which was employed in suppressing the slave trade. In June 1829 *Pickle* and her crew captured a notorious slave vessel called the *Bolodora* in a dramatic engagement. There were numerous deaths on both ships, and for the rest of his life McHardy was fond of talking about the incident. The capture of the slave ship earned him special promotion to commander.[4] On 11 October 1830 John McHardy married Horatia Victoria Elizabeth Atchison Pasco, daughter

1

of his first captain, and began a new career as inspecting commander of the Coast Guard which lasted until he became the first Chief Constable of Essex, almost ten years later. John McHardy's early naval career had a profound influence on him and his family, and on the police force that he led for more than 40 years. It seems appropriate, therefore, that the greater part of his life's work took place in a county also greatly influenced by the sea.

The County

Since time immemorial Essex has been deeply influenced by the North Sea, and the rivers and estuaries which flow into it. Battles against man and nature have been fought for its coastline, as periodically the sea has attempted to reclaim what was once its own.The sea itself has provided a wide range of activities.River estuaries made homes for oyster layings and refuges for wild fowl, while the remoteness of such areas as the Dengie peninsula encouraged smuggling. Ancient small ports like Harwich, Brightlingsea and Tilbury influenced the building of passenger vessels and naval ships: Essex men fought with Nelson in the Battle of Trafalgar, often in ships built within the county.[5]

When John McHardy and Horatia Pasco were married in 1830, Essex was still a mainly agricultural county, dominated by powerful landowners and their tenants. Most of the main roads from Essex to London had long since been turnpiked, and transport to the capital was relatively easy for those who could afford it; mass travel had to wait for the railways. The Eastern Counties Railway Company was formed in July 1836 to build a line from Shoreditch to Norwich through Romford, Brentwood, Chelmsford and Colchester. In the same year the Northern and Eastern Company began building a railway from London to Cambridge along the western border of Essex.[6]

The county had prospered during the Napoleonic Wars, but two decades of depression followed the peace. Agricultural labourers, fearing the loss of their jobs, rioted against the introduction of new machinery; there was also a spate of arson attacks near Witham, with machine breaking and incendiarism throughout Essex and in other parts of the country.[7] Law enforcement at this time depended on a system of local government which had been in use since the 17th century. Annually elected part-time parish constables had to combine official duties with their usual jobs, and work in conjunction with justices of the peace. Parish constables were supplemented when necessary by special constables, hiring a Bow Street runner, or—in extreme cases—calling in the military.[8] Discontent with such a system led to the formation in some areas of voluntary associations for the protection of property and the apprehension of felons.

Dissatisfaction with the archaic system of local government prompted some changes. The Metropolitan Police was introduced in 1829, and gradually took responsibility for policing geographical parts of Essex such as Waltham Abbey and Ilford; its men could also be hired by other areas. The Municipal Corporations Act of 1835 allowed corporate boroughs to appoint watch committees, some of which chose to appoint their own police.

By 1839 the piecemeal ways of enforcing the law clearly needed to be reconsidered.

Notes and References
1. Machiavelli, *The Prince*, 1532.
2. PRO ADM51/2876: Log of HMS *Tartarus*.
3. Government Archivist, Bahamas.
4. BM Add. MS. 38047: manuscript copy of questionnaire completed by McHardy in 1845 for his entry in W. O'Byrne's *Biography of All Living Naval Officers*, published in 1849.
5. A. C. Edwards, *History of Essex*, published by Phillimore, 1978. Between 1804 and 1807 eleven ships for the navy were built at Brightlingsea.
6. *ibid* An Act of Parliament of 1838 [1 & 2 Vic. c.80] allowed railway companies to employ special constables to deal with problems caused by railway labourers.
7. A. F. J. Brown *Chartism in Essex and Suffolk*, published by Essex Record Office and Suffolk Libraries and Archives, 1982.
8. In 1837, for example, quarter sessions paid £6 6s. for special constables to keep order at Fairlop Fair [ERO Q/FAb 103/6]. The following year the cost was £13 14s. 6d. to hire Sergeant Havard and 12 constables from the Metropolitan Police to keep order at the fair [ERO Q/FAb 1042]. As late as November 1837 George Sperling of Halstead hired a Bow Street runner to trace those responsible for arson attacks in the area [HO 60/3].

Chapter 2

How the Force Began

Setting up borough forces under 1835 Act—arrangements for county forces—Capt. McHardy appointed first Essex Chief Constable, 1840.

Was trying to prevent crime better than dealing with its effects? Prevention of crime was one of the philosophies behind the establishment of the Metropolitan Police in 1829, and the Whig government, which came to power three years later, promised to improve the state of policing in the rest of the country.

In 1833 the Lighting and Watching Act allowed ratepayers to start their own police forces independently of magistrates: Braintree and Walthamstow are two examples of Essex parishes which did so. Braintree's force was little more than a system of part-time watchmen, whereas Walthamstow's officers were well-organised, with uniforms and established beats.[1] The Municipal Corporations Act of 1835 required boroughs to establish watch committees which could appoint their own police officers, and arrangements for the Essex boroughs will be described in later chapters.

In the English counties justices of the peace sitting at quarter sessions tried criminal and civil cases. Their administrative responsibilities included licensing alehouses and regulating weights and measures, as well as providing prisons and repairing roads and bridges. The county police bill introduced into parliament in July 1839 was a voluntary one: each group of county justices of the peace could decide whether or not to adopt it. Once a favourable decision was made, a chief constable could be appointed, and the number of constables decided upon. The Home Secretary's responsibility was limited to giving or withholding approval of their arrangements, and amending their rules if he wished to do so.[2]

During the bill's progress some subtle changes were made. By the time the bill reached the statute book it was the Home Secretary who framed the rules: justices could only make local variations with his approval. A superintendent was to head each division, and one was also to act as deputy chief constable, but not for more than three months at a time.[3]

Nowadays every chief constable has to make an annual report to his elected police authority. Such a requirement dates from 1839, when a chief constable had to attend every sitting of the quarter sessions and make reports on his force and the offences it had dealt with. The requirement for each chief constable to make an annual report was included in successive police Acts to ensure local accountability. The justices in every petty sessional district were also entitled to receive a report from the superintendent in charge, and he had to attend every sitting of the petty sessions.

On 15 October 1839, all the Essex justices of the peace met in the Shire Hall at Chelmsford. They received a request from the inhabitants of Dunmow to adopt the Constabulary Act which had received the Royal Assent on 27 August 1839. Chief constables were already being appointed in Gloucestershire and Wiltshire. The Essex justices arranged a special meeting for 25 November, and in the intervening month they canvassed opinion from other parts of Essex and neighbouring counties. Hertfordshire JPs decided not to introduce the Act, because they said paid police had not stopped crime in London. Norfolk took the opposite view, although its chief constable later observed that he could not find enough candidates for the superintendents' posts at the pay Norfolk justices were offering.[4]

How did public opinion in Essex view the proposals for a full-time paid police force? The editor of the *Chelmsford Chronicle* noted that he had found no serious objections, as 'the want of an efficient police is widely and deeply felt'.[5]

After what was described as 'a very animated five hour discussion', Essex justices decided to introduce the Act in all parts of Essex not already covered by the Metropolitan Police which had been in existence for 10 years. By 31 December 1839 the Home Secretary had approved the employment of one chief constable, 15 superintendents and 100 constables, and supplied a copy of his rules for setting up police forces. Once official approval had been given, the chief constable's post was advertised, and a committee appointed to select and interview the candidates.

On the day appointed for interviews—Tuesday, 11 February 1840—more magistrates crowded into the Shire Hall than the *Chelmsford Chronicle* reporter had ever seen. Nineteen of the original 31 candidates were interviewed, many being military or naval officers. Several with what were considered exceptional qualifications could not be considered because they were too old—over 45.[6]

Captain John Bunch Bonnemaison McHardy was elected as the first Chief Constable of Essex. His acceptance speech made it plain that he was proud of his lack of influence or sponsorship; he made a point of saying that until the previous week he had never set foot in Essex. Details of McHardy's appointment appeared on an inside page of the *Chelmsford Chronicle*, because the wedding of Queen Victoria and Prince Albert filled most of the issue.

Although Captain McHardy was one of the earliest county chief constables to be appointed, those already in post—including Worcestershire, Durham, Gloucestershire and Wiltshire—had found important omissions in the Constabulary Act. No one had thought far enough ahead about superannuation, or whether justices had the power to increase county rates to pay for the new police. An amending bill was promptly introduced in February 1840, and received the Royal Assent in August that year.[7]

The amended Act allowed a police rate to be set in each petty sessional area, and gave borough forces the chance to amalgamate with neighbouring counties, provided that the county chief constable was in overall command. County justices were allowed to use police rates to pay for building station houses and strong rooms in every petty sessional area with at least 250,000 inhabitants. Each petty sessional area was indirectly responsible for financing its own constables, and allocating their areas of work, although they could be deployed anywhere. County rates funded general expenses; salaries and clothing costs were paid for by rates in each police district.

The 1840 Act created a superannuation fund, but a pension was not to be received as an automatic right: only men recommended by the chief constable and approved by the justices received one. To be eligible for a half-pay pension an officer had to serve for between 15 and 20 years; a two-thirds pension meant working for 20 years or more. The superannuation fund was to be created from wage deductions, selling cast clothing, and fines imposed for disciplinary offences. If a man's health broke down he might get a pension earlier—as long as there was enough money in the fund.

Right from the beginning some people objected to the cost of having a full-time, paid police force. Parliament acknowledged the objections by giving local justices the power to disband a force if enough of them wanted to do so. The only proviso the Home Secretary made was to demand six months' notice of the justices' intention.

Any individual or organisation who could prove the need, and was able to pay most of the expenses, could ask for what the Act called 'additional constables' for specific responsibilities. Such officers were additional to the agreed numbers of men in a force. The earliest additional constable in Essex was Andrew Rome, a 22-year-old former Scottish tea dealer, who joined the force in August 1840. He was transferred to the detachment of men financed by the Burnham Oyster Company, was promoted inspector in 1848, and remained at Burnham until his retirement in 1897. There are many other examples of additional constables in Essex, but Andrew Rome holds the record for the longest service.[8]

Who else was eligible to join a county force? Applicants had to be literate, and willing to devote their whole time to policing—unlike the parish constables who usually combined their policing duties with full-time jobs. Joining the police force meant ex-servicemen could retain their half-pay pensions; and all policemen were exempt from jury duty and militia service. Any intending policeman who already had the right to vote was not allowed to exercise it while in office, or for six months after leaving.

Notes and References
1. VHM P8/3/27-29. The force continued until the area was taken over by the Metropolitan Police in 1840.
2. An Act for Establishing County and District Constables 1839 (2&3 Vic. c.93). For more details of the work of Quarter Sessions, see *Essex Quarter Sessions Order Book 1652-1661* edited by D. H. Allen. Edited Texts Vol. 1, published by Essex County Council 1974.
3. For details of all who held the rank of deputy chief constable and (later) assistant chief constable, see Appendix III.
4. *Chelmsford Chronicle* 22 November 1839.
5. *ibid.*
6. These included Lieutenant Charles Greaves and Lieutenant Colonel William Cartwright. Greaves had been a candidate for Chief Constable of Wiltshire, and later became an Essex superintendent. Cartwright was a prominent magistrate in Northamptonshire who became one of the earliest of Her Majesty's Inspectors of Constabulary in 1857: he had to inspect Essex. The other candidates interviewed were: Lieutenants Lamphier,* Charles Greaves+ and John Manby; Major William Sperling, James Waller,* C. Townley; Captains Joseph Cripps, H.W.S. Stuart, E. Leveson Gower, Hawker, J.J. Grove, E. Hawkins, William Williams, James Leckie; Lieut. Cols. W. Cartwright, Willson and J.M.A. Skerrett,* F. Roper* Esq, R.J. Hill Esq,+ H. Walford, H.W. Riom, J.H. Hatton,* John Rose, R.J. Gregg, William H. Hemsworth, and Capt. McHardy. Those marked * were soon on the short list for chief constable in Suffolk; those marked + had been candidates for Wiltshire in November 1839. [Sources: *Wiltshire and Gloucestershire Standard* 23 November 1839; and *Policing the Victorian Community* by Caroline Steedman, Routledge and Kegan Paul 1984].
7. An Act to Amend the County and District Constables Act 1840 [3&4 Vic. c.88].
8. ERO J/P 2/1.

Chapter 3

Appointing the First Men, 1840

*McHardy appoints first constables, superintendents and inspectors—first police
headquarters occupied—backgrounds of men joining in 1840.*

Essex had its first chief constable; now he needed somewhere to work and a job description.
Both were soon resolved: a temporary office was set up in Springfield gaol, and quarter
sessions appointed a committee of justices to help with the initial organisation of the force,
following the Home Secretary's guidelines. The minimum height for all candidates—except
chief constables—was to be 5 feet 7 inches; they had to be less than 40, and able to produce
character references from two people who had known them for at least five years.[1]

Although it is known that the chief constable's post was advertised nationally, no
advertisement for the initial intake of constables has been found in the two principal local
papers, the *Chelmsford Chronicle* and the *Essex Standard*. There must have been other ways
of seeking applicants; the most likely method would have been through the justices in each
petty sessional area.[2]

Although he was elected as chief constable on 11 February 1840, Captain McHardy
did not start work straight away: presumably he had to find somewhere to live. When the
census was taken in April 1841 the McHardy family was living in King Street, near the
present railway station in Chelmsford.[3]

Because the whole force was to be supervised by superintendents, these posts were
filled first. McHardy's first batch of interviews was carried out on 26 February, two of the
candidates having been applicants for the chief constable's job. Both men were appointed as
superintendents, but neither stayed long in the force. By the end of 1840 Henry William
Riom had been dismissed for misappropriating county funds, and Lieutenant Charles Greaves
had resigned. The third successful candidate was solicitor Edward Davies; he remained in the
force until October the following year, but the records do not show what happened to him
afterwards.[4]

The Chief Constable intended to apply consistent standards to all applicants for the
force, but anyone failing to meet the age and height criteria could still be appointed if the
Home Secretary approved. Several of the original Essex superintendents needed Home Office
approval for appointment because they were over forty. They included John McInnes and
John Hawkins, who had been sergeants in the 2nd Battalion of the Scots Fusiliers; Charles
Cooke, a former lieutenant in the 1st Royal Regiment; and Thomas Coulson, who had been
a corporal major in the Life Guards.[5]

Not every potential superintendent was accepted, however. Captain Tyner appealed to the Home Secretary in March 1840 when McHardy refused to appoint him, although the Captain had made two trips to Chelmsford and produced satisfactory testimonials. Further enquiries showed that he had been stationed in Spain, and because McHardy did not like the country or trust people with his sort of service background, Tyner had been turned down. The Home Secretary accepted the prejudices, and Captain Tyner went elsewhere.[6]

As the county town, Chelmsford was the division where the first officers were trained for a probationary period of two months, before being posted to other places as accommodation became available. Although the local papers liked the idea of men having a probationary period, there was criticism of the force for apparently neglecting rural areas while Chelmsford appeared over-policed. Public opinion wanted the constables spread throughout the county, but McHardy wanted all the men in each division living together in one station, as soon as such a building could be provided. That would mean they were always available for duty, and the divisional superintendent could make sure that each man was taking his proper rest.[7]

The first batch of 13 men took the oath before Chelmsford magistrates on 13 March 1840, and over the following weeks further small intakes were 'sworn in' every few days, e.g. on 20 March, 31 March, 3 April, 10 April.[8] By 10 April the *Chelmsford Chronicle* was able to report that the first recruits were on duty in Chelmsford, being trained by their superintendents of whom there were currently ten out of the establishment of fifteen. 'They are a fine body of men', continued the *Chronicle,* 'and their selection reflects credit on Captain McHardy.'[9]

It must remembered, however, that because the county force was experimental, the old methods of policing continued to work in parallel. Constables were still appointed by parish vestries and manorial courts, or under Lighting and Watching Acts. The 1839 County Police Act also gave a chief constable power to supervise the duties of local constables; e.g. the county justices ordered McHardy to instruct local constables to report anyone selling coal without scales and weights.[10]

Three constables who had been dismissed from the Metropolitan Police were turned down when they applied to Essex, but later—in October 1840—James Fowler was accepted without revealing he had been dismissed by the Metropolitan Police: he stayed until August 1842. It appears that the Home Secretary had good reason to complain that his procedures were not being followed, so later transferees were required to produce a certificate of good conduct from their previous force in order to be considered for Essex.[11]

The *Chelmsford Chronicle*, a local paper allegedly 'neutral in politics and independent of party',[12] maintained its interest in the embryo force, reporting in detail the quarter sessions meetings where its progress was discussed. Captain McHardy's need for a non-police secretary prompted comment: he was sure it would cause jealousy amongst the other men if he used one of the superintendents. As McHardy wanted a man who could also deal with his private letters, the justices allowed him to appoint Walter Burke, a retired naval purser. Walter Burke started work on 1 March 1840 and remained for eight years: he can therefore be regarded as the first civilian member of the Essex Constabulary.

By the end of April the increasing numbers of new police had outgrown the Chief Constable's temporary office in Springfield gaol. The justices in quarter sessions decided that the force should take over the stores depot of the West Essex Militia in Arbour Lane, Springfield: it was known as 'Old Court'. There was strong objection from the military authorities, who protested that 'if the government thought fit to have a new species of force then they must find a proper place for them'. Commitment to the new force was such that the military authorities were overruled.[13]

ESSEX

to wit.

THESE are to certify that *John B.D. McHardy*

having been duly appointed a SPECIAL CONSTABLE *to act as Chief*

Constable ——————— under the provisions of the

Act 2nd and 3rd Vic, c. 93, for the County of Essex, has this day been by

me sworn into the said Office, and that the oath prescribed by the Statute

1st and 2nd W. 4, c. 41, has been administered to him.

Given under my hand at Chelmsford, this *19* Day of

May   184 *0* – being one of Her Majesty's Justices of the

Peace for the said County.

Jas Boggis.

1. Officers employed under the 1839 Police Act were sworn-in in batches before Chelmsford magistrates as they were appointed. Each one was attested as a special constable under an Act of 1831, because the 1839 Act did not cover such matters. Although Captain McHardy was appointed on 11 February 1840 he was not sworn-in by James Boggis until 19 May, after most of the first hundred constables had been given their powers.

By 8 May 1840 the *Chelmsford Chronicle* reported that the force was nearly complete, with 99 out of the 100 men initially approved having been 'sworn-in' as special constables. The oath they took was provided by the Special Constables' Act of 1831.[14] McHardy himself was not sworn-in until 19 May.

Around 200 men joined the force during its first year. They came from a variety of occupational backgrounds, with many having been involved in agriculture. Pay may have been one incentive for some men to try police work, for the average wage of a farm labourer in parts of Essex was around eight shillings a week: the first constables received 19 shillings. Some candidates had previous experience in a police force—usually the Metropolitan Police— or one of the armed services. Eighty-three of those joining in 1840 were born in Essex, 18 had birthplaces in London or Middlesex, 15 in Suffolk, nine in Ireland and six in Scotland. Interest in the new police was such that Captain McHardy's first set of orders and instructions were published in full in the *Chelmsford Chronicle* of 5 June 1840.[15]

The difference in status between the ranks was clearly made by Captain McHardy. Constables were all supposed to be intelligent and trustworthy men, capable of reading and

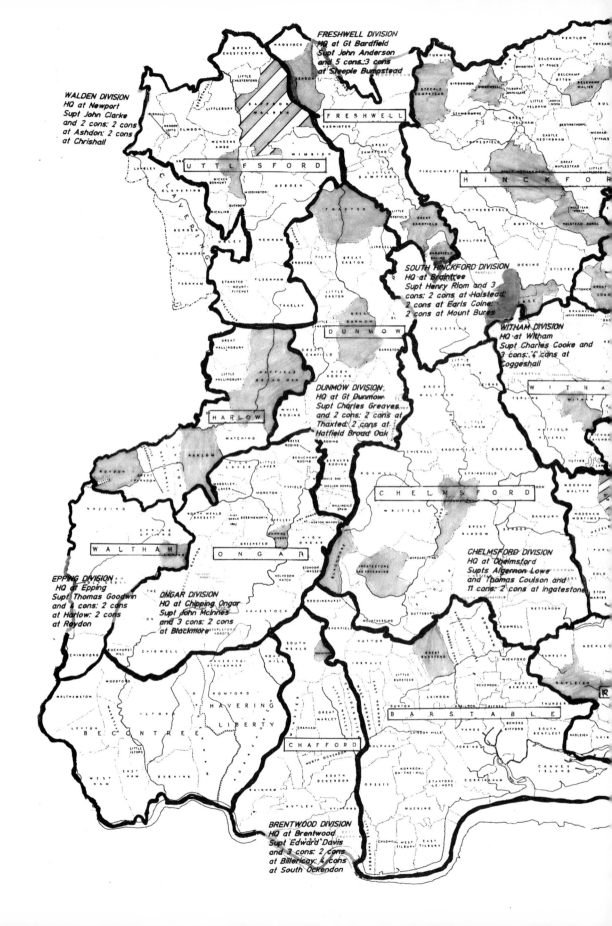

WALDEN DIVISION
HQ at Newport
Supt John Clarke
and 2 cons: 2 cons
at Ashdon: 2 cons
at Chrishall

FRESHWELL DIVISION
HQ at Gt Bardfield
Supt John Anderson
and 5 cons: 3 cons
at Steeple Bumpstead

SOUTH HINCKFORD DIVISION
HQ at Braintree
Supt Henry Riom and 3
cons: 2 cons at Halstead:
2 cons at Earls Colne:
2 cons at Mount Bures

WITHAM DIVISION
HQ at Witham
Supt Charles Cooke and
3 cons: 4 cons at
Coggeshall

DUNMOW DIVISION
HQ at Gt Dunmow
Supt Charles Greaves
and 2 cons: 2 cons at
Thaxted: 2 cons at
Hatfield Broad Oak

CHELMSFORD DIVISION
HQ at Chelmsford
Supts Algernon Lowe
and Thomas Coulson and
11 cons: 2 cons at Ingatestone

EPPING DIVISION
HQ at Epping
Supt Thomas Goodwin
and 4 cons: 2 cons
at Harlow: 2 cons
at Roydon

ONGAR DIVISION
HQ at Chipping Ongar
Supt John McInnes
and 3 cons: 2 cons
at Blackmore

BRENTWOOD DIVISION
HQ at Brentwood
Supt Edward Davis
and 3 cons: 2 cons
at Billericay: 4 cons
at South Ockendon

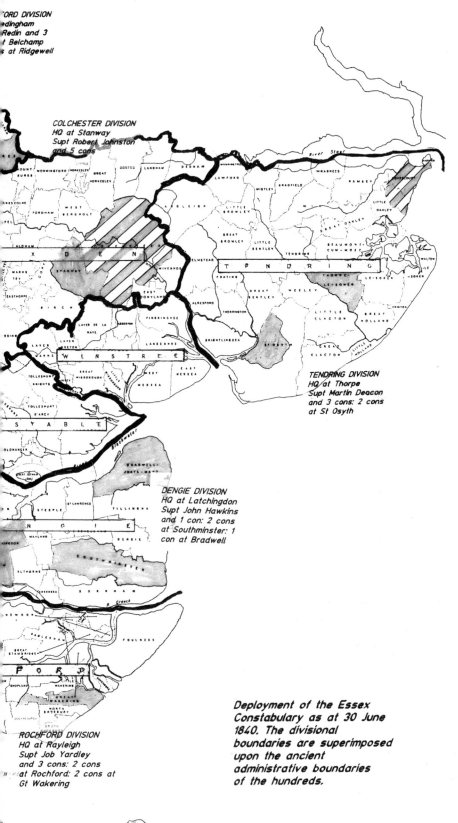

COLCHESTER DIVISION
HQ at Stanway
Supt Robert Johnston
and 5 cons

TENDRING DIVISION
HQ at Thorpe
Supt Martin Deacon
and 3 cons: 2 cons
at St Osyth

DENGIE DIVISION
HQ at Latchingdon
Supt John Hawkins
and 1 con: 2 cons
at Southminster: 1
con at Bradwell

ROCHFORD DIVISION
HQ at Rayleigh
Supt Job Yardley
and 3 cons: 2 cons
at Rochford: 2 cons at
Gt Wakering

Deployment of the Essex
Constabulary as at 30 June
1840. The divisional
boundaries are superimposed
upon the ancient
administrative boundaries
of the hundreds.

⬭ = Borough Forces

2. The 14 divisions of Essex Constabulary in June 1840 showing the names of their senior officers, and where constables were based. With no police stations having yet been built, officers either worked from their lodgings, or from buildings temporarily leased to the county.

writing, and of a class much above the common labourer. A superintendent's responsible situation needed some knowledge of legal proceedings, with a variety of other qualifications.

It was the superintendents on whom McHardy depended to carry out his instructions; he prepared written orders for them on an almost daily basis, and they were expected to visit him whenever they were in Chelmsford. Each divisional superintendent was issued with a journal and a letter book, and he had to record all details of his correspondence and send the Chief Constable copies of all the letters written.

It seemed that the gulf between the ranks of superintendent and constable was too great—even without modern connotations—for within a few months the Chief Constable sought approval to introduce the intermediate rank of inspector. Captain McHardy thought that an inspector should be at least a degree above a constable, but not of a station in life to need superior accommodation. One of an inspector's jobs was to copy out McHardy's frequent written orders and pass them on to the constables.[16]

In August 1840 the amended Constabulary Act was passed, and the justices increased the establishment by 20 men, which allowed McHardy to promote 10 of his constables to the rank of inspector. The 100 constables were divided into two classes, 50 to receive £1 1s. per week and the remainder to have 19s. The amended Act introduced superannuation, and deductions were made according to rank: superintendents paid 6d a week, inspectors 5d. a week and constables 4d.[17]

By the end of 1840 a total of 204 men had served in the Essex Constabulary, and of these 40 had been dismissed and 26 had resigned.[18] Some of those who resigned probably went to other forces, but the records do not always indicate why they left. Inspector Charles Bailey is an exception—he became a superintendent in Hertfordshire.[19] Thirteen of the 1840 recruits were promoted, but only 10 stayed long enough to be superannuated. The two who served longest were McHardy himself, who retired when he was 80 in 1881; and Inspector Andrew Rome who remained until 1897 when he was 79.[20]

Sometimes the detailed reasons why men were dismissed appear in the force staffing records: being drunk was a common reason, but in 1840 one man was dismissed for drinking with improper characters, and another for drinking and gambling in a public place. A third man was either brave or foolhardy: he had been insolent to the chief constable!

Notes and References

1. For an edited transcript of the guidelines see Appendix II.
2. ERO Q/FAb 105/3, accounts passed by quarter sessions. On 19 February 1840 the Clerk of the Peace wrote to every justices' clerk in the county (18), telling them that a committee of local justices had been appointed to liaise with the new chief constable.
3. ERO microfilm of 1841 census enumerators' notebooks.
4. Force records give details of Riom's dismissal. Lieutenant Greaves, formerly of the Royal Irish Fusiliers, had been a lieutenant since 8 June 1840 and on half-pay since 9 May 1834 [Source Army List for 1839].
5. PRO HO65/4, Home Office letter book 1839-54. At the same time, some neighbouring counties were also adopting the 1839 Act. In March 1840 Suffolk was seeking a chief constable, and five of those who had also applied for McHardy's job were interviewed. None was successful.
6. *ibid.*
7. *Chelmsford Chronicle*, 1 May 1840.
8. ERO P/CP 54, Chelmsford Petty Sessions bundles.
9. *Chelmsford Chronicle*, 1 May 1840.
10. A search through the Chelmsford petty sessions records revealed names of those being sworn-in before the justices in 1840: several do not appear in the surviving records of county police. They may

possibly have resigned before their details were recorded (this did happen in some cases), or else they were paid constables appointed by the parish but supervised by McHardy. Chelmsford appointed constables under the Lighting and Watching Act, and in October 1840 McHardy took over responsibility for their duties; he assumed responsibility the previous month for the duties of the parish constables in Chelmsford. With the co-operation of the Lighting and Watching commissioners, he also took control of the watchmen who still walked in the town. Some men who seem to have begun as parish constables did later join the county force [ERO Q/SO 37, quarter sessions order book and information from the late Hilda Grieve].

11. *ibid.*
12. BL *Newspaper Press Directory*, 1846.
13. *Essex Standard,* 3 July 1840: described by the press directory as 'conservative in politics and strongly attached to the Church of England'.
14. The words of the oath, as written in the 1831 statute 1&2 Wm IV c40, are: 'I do swear that I will well and truly serve our Sovereign Lady the Queen in the Office of Special Constable for the parish of **, without favour or affection, malice or ill will, and that I will to the best of my power cause the peace to be kept and preserved and prevent all offences against the persons and properties of Her Majesty's subjects.'
15. ERO J/P 2/1 and *Meagre Harvest* by A.F.J. Brown, published by ERO. See Appendices for names of recruits in 1840, and pp.10-11 for a map showing where they were based in June that year.
16. ERO Q/ACp 2A and D/DZ 129.
17. It was 5 November 1840 before final approval was given for the first 10 inspectors to be promoted, all of whom had joined between March and June: their former occupations are given in brackets. John May, Francis Knock, Stephen Francis and Abraham Hindes (all clerks); Edward Evans (watchmaker); James Holby (labourer); John Haydon (glover); Charles Fletcher (constable); Charles Bailey (army), and Joshua Radley (printer). James Barker and William Alford (soldiers), and James Nix (butcher) were direct entrants on 13 November; Robert Berwick (soldier) and Samuel Mayling (clerk), were direct entrants on 17 November; and John Tull was promoted on 3 December, possibly to replace Stephen Francis who had been demoted to constable. Appointments to inspector continued to be a mixture of promotions and direct entry for several years.
18. Between 1840 and 1850 32 men held the rank of superintendent. Of this number 3 were dismissed or absconded; 19 resigned; 8 were superannuated; 1 was reduced in rank; 1 was promoted. During the same decade, 70 men held the rank of inspector. Of that number 19 were promoted; 7 dismissed; 35 resigned; 5 superannuated; 1 reduced in rank and 3 died in post.
19. Inspector Joshua Radley joined as an inspector in November 1840, and in February 1843 resigned to join the Eastern Counties Railway Police. He twice rejoined Essex, and resigned again during the next few years, before finally resigning in 1848. Superintendent Martin Deacon served from April 1840 until January 1842 and then resigned;in May 1842 he was sworn into the Wiltshire Constabulary, still as a superintendent. ['A Chief Constable's Diary' by Supt. C. E. Turner, in *Police Journal* volume XXXIV, 1961, p.395.]
20. ERO J/P 2/1.

Chapter 4

Policemen at Work in County Force and Boroughs

*Arranging divisional boundaries 1840—equipping the force—first court appearances—
borough forces at work.*

Supervision of the force must have been relatively easy while all the constables were based in Chelmsford, but once they moved out to other towns and villages McHardy had to find different ways of keeping control of his men.

The county was partitioned into divisions and detachments, and subdivided into guards—what would today be called 'beats'. The guards were supposed to link-up, so that officers on adjoining guards could meet and patrol in pairs, a practice thought to improve their moral and physical efficiency. Justices of the peace sitting at petty sessions often met in a public house as there were few court houses. Captain McHardy wanted each divisional superintendent to have an office as near as possible to the petty sessions meeting place, and he tried to ensure that such a divisional headquarters building was large enough to hold the inspector, and at least some of the constables as well: the remainder often had to work from their own lodgings. It was important for members of the public to be able to communicate with the police, and McHardy wanted a constable on duty in the divisional headquarters at all times.[1]

In July 1840 superintendents were warned against neglecting the rural parts of their divisions. A horse and cart was provided in each division for the conveyance of prisoners, and for the use of constables who were being posted. Each horse cost around £20 to buy, and it took some while for the whole county to be equipped. On many occasions horses had to be hired, and there were strict rules against driving an animal at more than six miles an hour. Some superintendents had to hire horses for particular reasons, such as the superintendent who claimed 7s. 6d. to survey the ancient boundary of Chelmsford Hundred, which formed the basis of the Chelmsford police division. When the first four constables were posted to Bardfield, it cost the county 18s. 6d. to hire a horse and cart to move the men and their families.[2] In order to be exempt from excise duty, county carts had to be open, drawn by one horse, and have less than four wheels.[3]

Unfortunately a practical system of photography did not exist in 1840; but we can get some idea of what the first officers looked like from the descriptions of their uniforms on the invoice from the supplier, Charles Hebbert and Company of Pall Mall. The force provided the basic uniform, including a blue dress coat with an embroidered collar bearing a crown and numerals; a pair of dress trousers and a pair of 'undress' trousers; a waterproofed greatcoat, cape; hat; pair of boots; pair of shoes; and buttons marked 'Essex Constabulary'. Each recruit had to provide himself with a knapsack and a notebook, two pairs of white drill

14

trousers, two pairs of white gloves and a decent suit of plain clothes; the white trousers were to be worn between 1 May and 1 October on days decided by the superintendent.[4] Each man also had a rattle, a lantern, and a baton painted with the county arms. A constable's uniform and equipment in 1840 cost £8 9s. 8d. per set. Anyone who resigned had to pay five shillings to have it altered for the next recruit: that practice caused much discontent over the years.

A Metropolitan Police superintendent's uniform was comparatively ornate. The Essex version cost £10 15s. 3d. and consisted of a frock coat with silver buttons and braid on the collar; the cuffs and skirt lining of the coat were silk. Dress trousers, a tall hat, silk cravat, and a brass truncheon completed the picture. Every superintendent had to provide his own boots and shoes, for which he was given an allowance, and every officer was issued with an embroidered badge. The force also bought 81 pairs of handcuffs and 41 swords in 1840.[5]

Once officers were posted outside Chelmsford, they began to deal with incidents which went to court and were reported in local papers. One of the earliest police reports concerns Halstead and Braintree fairs in May 1840. Superintendents Henry Riom and Thomas Redin, and their constables, were said to have prevented the 'disgraceful scenes, robberies and outrages' which usually took place: only a couple of minor thefts were reported. A few days later Riom and his men kept order when the Earl of Essex laid the foundation stone for an extension to Rayne church.[6]

An early prosecution for furious driving seems to have been carried out at the end of May on the initiative of Superintendent Riom. He had been travelling from Chelmsford to Braintree, when his gig had almost been run off the road at Great Leighs by two stage wagons coming from the opposite direction at 10 miles an hour. When brought before the magistrates, the two drivers excused themselves by saying their masters had ordered them to get some perishable commodities to London as quickly as possible, so time had to be made while going down hill. The maximum fine for furious driving was £5, but each man was only fined five shillings.

Superintendent Riom dealt with a theft on 5 June, when he took three boys before Halstead magistrates on suspicion of stealing some silver spoons. The boys had offered them for sale to a jeweller at Sudbury, but, because Riom failed to identify the spoons conclusively, the case was dismissed. Captain McHardy himself was present at the hearing, taking the opportunity to tell the Halstead bench that his officers needed a proper station house. They agreed; within a year the house of correction was closed, for it to become the first Halstead police station.[7]

Police officers were not supposed to enter licensed premises except in the course of their duty, and any licensee who allowed an officer to do so could be fined up to £5. Several prosecutions at Dunmow were reported in June 1840, because they raised procedural questions. Had police the right to enter licensed premises to detect offences? The Chief Constable was present in court, and able to tell the justices that Epping magistrates had experienced similar problems; they were seeking the opinion of the Excise Commissioners. The Dunmow licensees' solicitor was adamant that the officers had exceeded their authority, but although the magistrates disagreed, they dismissed the case because of lack of evidence of an actual sale of alcohol.

The same solicitor wrote to the *Chelmsford Chronicle* again a few days later. He had been defending the alleged father of a bastard child, and found to his disgust that Police Constable George Sams had walked the four miles from Braintree to Pattiswick to serve the notice of prosecution. Mr. Lane, the solicitor, felt that civil process should not be a job for a policeman. Captain McHardy pointed out that his men were already on duty and receiving wages; it was therefore cheaper to use them, rather than parish constables who would have been entitled to claim expenses.

When quarter sessions met at the end of June, satisfaction was expressed at what the force had done so far. Constables had been involved in a variety of duties, including a major railway accident at Brentwood, where carriages had piled on top of each other at the bottom of a hill. Hundreds of sightseers had flooded into the area, and Brentwood officers earned favourable comments for the way they had removed the injured from the wreckage.[8]

By October 1840 there had been enough court cases for some thought to be given to professional training and support; legal help was promised for prosecuting more complex cases at quarter sessions and assizes. McHardy suggested to the justices at quarter sessions that the police should be given authority to capture smugglers and seize contraband; he had been corresponding with the Controller General of Coastguards, and they both thought it would: 'promote the morality and good order of some districts of the county if the men had these commissions'. Although Captain McHardy believed the power would hardly ever be used, he thought the men would consider themselves more of a preventive force if they had such a power. Several justices strongly objected to McHardy's proposal; one retorted that if the suggestion was adopted it would be giving the government a power over the force which they might afterwards exercise, and it was approaching the system of centralisation which he detested. McHardy's proposal was dropped. [9]

It seemed as if the force was beginning to make some impact. A certain amount of favourable publicity in some newspapers led to interest from towns which had been slow to take up the option of full-time police. One Coggeshall resident wanted to see more than its three officers on patrol. The *Chronicle* was realistic, pointing out that there were 350 parishes in Essex and only 100 men to guard them; Coggeshall had more than its fair share.

The older forms of policing did not change over night when the county force was formed; most of them remained for many years, although their powers were gradually eroded. While it was acknowledged that full-time paid policemen had their uses, they were expensive, and there was an initial reluctance to have many. In 1842 Parliament sought to revitalise the old system of parish constables and put them on a more regular basis. They were to have a 'cordial co-operation' with the county police, and be entitled to claim fees and allowances for carrying out such activities as executing warrants and serving summonses; they could also be used to escort prisoners, and to act as a reserve force under the control of a chief constable.[10] Some counties, which had not voluntarily adopted the 1839 Act, saw local constables as a means of saving themselves expense. McHardy had to submit lists to justices of everyone qualified and willing to serve as a local constable, but it is not clear whether they made any major impact in Essex. The borough forces were a different matter.

The earlier Municipal Corporations Act of 1835 required the creation of watch committees comprising the mayor and other councillors. Within three weeks of being appointed, watch committees were supposed to appoint 'a sufficient number of fit men ... to act as constables', but not necessarily on a full-time basis. The four ancient Essex boroughs—Harwich, Saffron Walden, Colchester, and Maldon—duly established police forces of varying quality and efficiency. None of them had full-time police, so the watch committees continued to appoint parish and special constables and reimburse them for their expenses; watch committees had the same legal powers as a county chief constable. One clause in the 1839 County Police Act allowed borough forces to amalgamate with their nearest county force. The ratepayers of Saffron Walden wanted to take up that option, but the watch committee chose to retain its independence by continuing to operate its own police force.[11]

Colchester's watch committee records show it to have been organised quite efficiently from the start. At its first meeting to discuss the appointment of constables, members realised just how imprecise their instructions were and decided to seek advice from the Attorney General. When no reply had been received at the next meeting they decided to go ahead. The only requirement for appointment as a borough constable was to be between 25 and 40, and at least 5 feet 6 inches tall; the ability to read and write was not a requirement. The watch committee appointed one man for each of the 16 parishes within the borough, plus three sergeants for the town, with a superintendent in overall charge; the sergeants and the superintendent all held ceremonial office within the borough. Before the constables could begin work on 25 February 1836 seven of the original 16 had either declined to serve or had been found medically unfit.

The original intention in Colchester had been to have two sections, made up of day and night police. The 16 night police were under the command of a constable termed 'superintendent of police', while the day police consisted of three constables. The superintendent was responsible for the general good conduct and order of the night police. He had to ensure that all rules issued by the watch committee were obeyed as well as attending every fire by day or night, and taking control of the constables. The superintendent had to ensure the way was clear 'for free scope for the firemen's exertion'; and he then had to safeguard property and ascertain the cause of the fire.[12]

The newly-formed watch committee of Harwich met in the Guildhall on 4 June 1836 to appoint William Burton as chief constable at £20 a year. He seems to have been full-time, having been given instructions to supervise the three part-time constables of Dovercourt, and the nine part-time constables of Harwich. One of their main jobs was to prevent the town's narrow streets from being blocked, especially by sailors.[13]

Maldon's watch committee met for the first time on 1 January 1836, when it swore in 11 men who were to be paid for specific duties; the chief constable's post was combined with that of gaoler. The main duties of the part-time force seem to have been watching the town on Saturday nights and ensuring the beershops were closed during church services. Some of the later Maldon constables were quite prominent citizens with other jobs, e.g. Joseph Beale, who was governor of the workhouse in 1847.[14] Could it perhaps have been envisaged that his inmates might form the main clientèle of the new force?

Notes and References

1. ERO D/DZ 129: manuscript copy of McHardy's memos, 1840.
2. ERO Q/FAc 7/2. In March 1841 Superintendent Edward Evans at Thorpe had his bill returned by McHardy asking why he was claiming forage expenses when he had not yet been given a county horse. The superintendent explained that he had been obliged to borrow a horse in order to do his job.
3. ERO D/DZ 129. To comply with an Act of 1833 [3 & 4 Wm IV cap. 39] carts had to have painted on them in white letters or Roman characters at least one inch long, the Christian names, surname, and occupation of the owner. Rails at the back of Essex carts were painted, 'John Bunch Bonnemaison McHardy, Chief Constable, Chelmsford, Essex'.
4. ERO Q/FAc 7/2. For details of uniform through the ages see appendix IV. Messrs. Hebberts were sent an impression of the county arms on 28 February 1840 [Q/FAb 105/3].
5. ERO Q/FAc 7/2.
6. *Chelmsford Chronicle*, 1840.
7. Halstead's purpose-built station opened in 1853; its interior has been modernised but it is still in use.
8. ERO D/DZ 129. In March 1841 McHardy extended the idea of good press relations by ordering his superintendents to send details of all offences and detections in their divisions to the *Essex Standard* and *Chelmsford Chronicle*. That was in addition to incidents reported as part of petty sessions business.

9. *Chelmsford Chronicle,* 3 April 1840.
10. Page 45 of *The English Police: A Political and Social History* by Clive Emsley, published by Harvester Wheatsheaf, St. Martin's Press, 1991.
11. Saffron Walden borough records, in custody of Town Clerk.
12. ERO Colchester Watch Committee minutes.
13. Harwich Watch Committee minutes, in custody of Town Council.
14. ERO D/B 3/3 Maldon Borough Records.

Chapter 5

Extra Duties for Police

Building police stations 1841-2—the London to Colchester railway workers cause problems—ways of making police more cost effective—extra jobs for police, 1844.

In 1840 the Essex Constabulary cost £9,330 10s. to operate, although only a small part of this covered building work. Police stations were needed, however, for in order to be cost effective policemen needed to be spread throughout the county and working from purpose-built premises; the force could not continue to run from rented buildings and private houses.[1] How could this be achieved without causing the county's ratepayers to revolt?

The answer has a modern ring to it—private enterprise. Individuals and companies were invited to lend money to the county, in return for interest on their investments. The Essex Provident Society, for example, loaned £1,500 at 4.5 per cent interest to pay for building the original Witham police station. One of the earliest stations to be completed was at Latchingdon. Tenders had to be submitted before 3 August 1841; and the work was to be carried out under the county surveyor's supervision with a penalty clause of £1 per day after the agreed completion date.[2] Stations were also needed at Castle Hedingham—to cover the vast rural area south and east of the Suffolk border; Epping—to cover the area adjoining the Metropolitan Police and Hertfordshire, and Brentwood to cover the division which included Romford.[3] Some existing buildings were rented by the county, to act as police stations; they included Billericay market house, and the houses of correction at Newport and Halstead.

In April 1842 McHardy asked for a further increase in establishment, which provoked a debate at quarter sessions. Complaints were received from residents of parishes that they never saw a policeman and yet were paying excessive police rates. There were also several petitions from parishes which wanted the county force to be abolished. One magistrate considered the whole force unconstitutional, and 'if extended over this kingdom, would place unlimited power in the hands of those who ought not to have it'. He also objected to the men not being known by name 'but by numbers like soldiers for action'. The Chief Constable argued forcefully, pointing out that the constabulary was in its infancy, and there were difficulties in getting men of the right material because their qualifications could not be proved until they tried to do the job of a policeman. He won his argument, and the increase was granted.[4]

Other forces were having similar debates. In November 1842 two thirds of the parishes in the largely agricultural county of Bedfordshire petitioned for removal of the police force which was considered 'expensive if not inefficient'. Nottinghamshire reduced its police from 42 to 33 at about the same time. The Lancashire justices voted for abolition, but compromised by reducing the size of their force.[5]

Between 1837 and 1843 the Eastern Counties railway was under construction from London towards Colchester. The labourers who built it were known as navigators—hence 'navvies'—and were renowned for their violent behaviour and heavy drinking. Although many parts of the line did not go directly through villages, local residents often experienced problems from the unruly behaviour of navvies. Railway legislation instructed directors of the company to protect property in the vicinity of the line, and the company appointed its own police who worked in conjunction with the county force and parish constables in villages like Writtle, Baddow, Moulsham and Springfield. At least two of these parish constables—James Otway and George Sams—later joined the county force. Perpetual troublemakers amongst railway navvies were usually dismissed, but there were still occasional outbreaks of rioting, such as that which occurred at Ingatestone over a weekend in July 1841 when county police and railway constables joined forces to bring the situation under control. A report prepared by the Railway police inspector suggested that the men had been fighting amongst themselves: they had no antagonism to the Ingatestone inhabitants. It seemed the men were from Yorkshire, Lincolnshire and Sussex and 'when they got a little drunk they fell out more about the counties than anything else'.[6]

As the Eastern Counties railway progressed across Essex, and the line from London to Cambridge reached Great Chesterford, there were similar public order problems. A number of 'additional constables' were appointed to the force, and paid for by the railway companies, so that McHardy's men had to spend less time sorting out fights.[7] They were, however, expected to attend a church service every Sunday, religious observance being an integral part of police life, partly due to the Chief Constable's example. Other sections of the working population increasingly treated Sunday as a normal working day, and in May 1841 the home secretary introduced a bill to suppress such practices. Policemen in the Roothings near Dunmow were told by their justices to prevent horses and wagons, cattle drovers and coal sellers from working on Sundays.[8]

The Chief Constable and local justices were always looking for ways to make the force more cost effective: this usually involved policemen taking on additional tasks. In January 1844 the High Sheriff asked for police constables to keep order at assizes, but the request was refused as it was thought it would interfere with their police duties. However, their presence while waiting to give evidence probably ensured order in court. Officers giving evidence at assize courts had to wear best frock coats and caps, reporting to Old Court by 9 a.m. on the day of the court, to hand over to the Chelmsford superintendent any article needed as evidence.[9]

Cases of arson had been a problem in Essex for many years, since the end of the Napoleonic wars and the social upheaval which followed. As the county's economy began to include more than just agriculture, there were outbreaks of disorder involving farmworkers in Essex and elsewhere; the Witham area suffered particularly badly.[10] Dealing with fires was one of the responsibilities given to both borough and county constables. In December 1843 eight county policemen were at the scene of a farm fire at High Roothing where arson was suspected. The Dunmow parish fire engine attended under the direction of Superintendent Thomas Redin. Most of the farmer's furniture was saved by the police, and they had hoped to save many of the buildings. Unfortunately someone cut the water hose on the fire engine and the buildings were destroyed.[11]

In 1843 all the county's weights and measures inspectors were dismissed so that police superintendents could become weights and measures inspectors: Norfolk justices had saved £600 a year by taking such a step. The superintendents who were appointed had to attend at prescribed places according to a rota published in local newspapers. No extra pay was given at first, and one justice thought that if policemen had time for such duties then there were too many of them.[12] Weights and measures was a police responsibility in some areas until well into the 20th century.

The Poor Law Act of 1834 had required groups of parishes to unite in poor law unions, each of which had to provide a workhouse for those unable to support themselves. Casual wards were also provided for vagrants. Poor relief in each union was administered by a board of guardians made up of important local residents, and from the mid-1840s some policemen began to be appointed as assistant relieving officers with particular responsibility for vagrants: it was not a popular duty. Epping guardians complained that policemen took no pains to execute their warrants for vagrancy offences, and other people thought that the police already interfered enough in the lives of poor and destitute people.[13]

Despite increasing daytime workloads, superintendents were still expected to work at night. The weekly journals kept by all ranks had to be submitted to the Chief Constable who often commented that superintendents did not make many visits between midnight and 4 a.m. to their constables on patrol![14]

Throughout the first decade of the force there was still a good deal of suspicion about a body of men with so many extra powers who were expensive to maintain. Captain McHardy enthusiastically suggested that many extra responsibilities be given to his men to justify the continuation of the force. It was still considered expensive, however, and in 1850 there was a cut-back in spending; the Chief Constable's expenses were reduced from £160 to £120 a year, and each constable had 1s. 6d. a week deducted from his wages.[15] But the next decade was to bring some dramatic changes in the way that police forces were organised.

Notes and References

1. ERO Q/ACp 2A: McHardy's 1841 report to quarter sessions. In 1849 the *Chelmsford Chronicle* noted that Witham justices had asked for a police station and court room, because they had to meet in public houses to hear cases, and witnesses were often tipsy. Witham was on the road to Springfield gaol, so prisoners had to be lodged in a public house, and the officers guarding them could not go out on patrol.
2. ERO Q/ACm 15. The bricks for Latchingdon police station were made locally. In a contract between H.H. Hayward of Bank Building Colchester, and Richard Solly of Mundon Hall Farm, Hayward agreed to pay 9s. per thousand, including the transportation from Solly's yard to the station house site. Additional bricks cost 6s. per thousand [Information from Stephen Potter of Purleigh].
3. *ibid.* In 1841 suitable sites were being sought for police stations at Braintree, and Dunmow. In 1843 Epping and Brentwood justices found suitable sites, and in March 1844 Orsett Union offered land on which a station house and cart shed could be built. Once plans were underway for stations at Coggeshall and Rochford, it was decided there was no immediate need for any more, except at Halstead (the house of correction having proved unsuitable), and in the Harlow and Tendring areas.
4. *Essex Standard,* 8 April 1842.
5. Emsley *op.cit.* pp.43-44.
6. ERO P/CP 53: Chelmsford Petty Sessions records.
7. *ibid.*
8. ERO D/Z 129.
9. *Essex Standard,* 22 December 1843.
10. See *Men of Bad Character* by Janet Gyford, published by ERO 1991.
11. *Essex Standard* 30 June 1843.
12. ERO Q/APp5. The first police weights and measures inspectors were Superintendents Thomas Coulson, John May, John Brown, Francis Knock, Thomas Redin, Thomas Godwin, William Oakley, John Hoy, Samuel Malings, John McInnes, Algernon Lowe, Richard Steer, John Clarke, and Charles Cooke.
13. ERO G/EM 5—Epping Guardians' minutes 1843.
14. ERO Q/APp 5.
15. *ibid.*

Chapter 6

Investigations from 1850 Onwards

Policing experiments in other counties 1841-52—Colchester special constables—criminal investigations—two police officers murdered—Great Exhibition 1851—Select Committee on Police 1852—introduction of Her Majesty's Inspectors of Constabulary 1856.

Although the Essex Constabulary was 10 years old in 1850, county forces were not yet compulsory and experiments were still being made with a variety of policing models. Between 1841-52 five schemes were put before parliament suggesting the appointment of professional police superintendents to supervise parish constables: all of the plans originated in Kent which refused to adopt the county police act. Thirteen other counties decided to employ those 'superintending constables', some of them being Essex men who were able to gain promotion. When county forces were made compulsory in 1857, the practice of having superintending constables was abandoned.[1]

A borough force like Colchester only had a handful of officers, and needed special constables to help meet policing obligations. At the annual meeting for appointing special constables in November 1850 the *Essex Standard* reported that one of the men had asked for his expenses for the day, commenting that as they were called upon to do dirty work he thought they ought to be paid for it. The justices were disgusted at his attitude; they said he ought to feel pleasure in doing his duty to Queen and Country, especially as the swearing-in only took 15 minutes, and special constables were not often called out.

Local newspapers are a rich source of information about policing matters. The fortnightly meetings of the petty sessions courts in each area were reported in detail, as were the sittings of quarter sessions and assizes; the names of policemen who attended are frequently given. Few original records of a policeman's daily work are known to have survived, however one exception are the notebooks of Pc James Gates, who was sworn-in on 9 April 1847 when he was 27 years old.[2]

Gates was born in High Ongar, and after an initial period at headquarters was sent to Latchingdon, then on to Tillingham where he seems to have stayed for two years. He then served at Rayleigh, North Benfleet, Bowers Gifford, and back to Rayleigh just before his retirement in 1870. Pc Gates had to provide his own duty notebooks, so they contain a mixture of official and private entries. The books include offences he dealt with and the sentences imposed; deaths of his relatives, and recipes for such delights as bread, and onion soup. Pc Gates detained a number of women offenders who received various terms of hard labour for stealing items varying from ducks to a petticoat. On 26 December 1849 he arrested Hannah Thomas of Prittlewell for stealing 76 hares and rabbits. The three months hard labour she received were obviously not hard enough, for three years later she was in trouble again. Pc Gates had to attend quarter sessions to prove the previous conviction, and Hannah received 12 months' hard labour. Modern attitudes towards juvenile criminals are also revealed in the case of a Thundersley girl who stole a pair of stockings. She was tried the following day at Brentwood under the Youthful Offenders Act 1854, fined 2s. 6d. and cautioned as to her future behaviour. The fine was paid on the spot, by an unknown benefactor.[3]

Investigating serious crime was a superintendent's responsibility, and Superintendent Algernon Lowe investigated the murder of an illegitimate child in April 1849; such cases were not uncommon. Superintendent Lowe had been called to the home of Elizabeth Evans in Union Lane, Rochford and, because of what he had already been told, he asked one of the household to open the privy; from the pit was taken the dead body of a female child. Elizabeth Evans was arrested for murder, but she denied having anything to do with the matter, until the surgeon who examined the baby's body found that Elizabeth had recently given birth. Only then did the woman admit that she had killed her illegitimate baby because she did not want to go into the workhouse, her only means of obtaining financial support.[4]

By the 1850s there is evidence of a more investigative approach to other serious crimes, including murder. After the suspicious death of a Tollesbury woman in 1851, Superintendent Charles Cooke from Witham took the suspect's trousers to Professor Taylor at the London Hospital, to see if he could establish whether the blood stains on them really came from a pig as was alleged, or whether they were made by human blood. The differences could not be proved, so the suspect was found not guilty.

In mid-November 1850 Mr. Viall of Manningtree had a fire in his hairdresser's shop and, despite a fire engine attending, the contents were destroyed. Mr. Viall told the police he had been in bed and heard noises downstairs. Finding his door fastened from the outside with a cord tied to a gimlet, he had been forced to escape from an upstairs window. Police enquiries showed that Mr. Viall had recently taken out insurance and over-valued some of his goods; he had made the gimlet holes himself from the inside.[5]

In the early years of the new decade there were several severe assaults, one of which resulted in the death of a police officer. On 21 November 1850 Inspector John Rough of Billericay instructed Pc Robert Bamborough to walk to Brentwood escorting a convicted poacher named William Wood who was attached to the officer by the single handcuff used at that time; Wood would then be picked up by the county cart which would take him to Chelmsford gaol. Two children, one of whom raised the alarm, witnessed what happened on the journey. In a pond near Hutton House, John Langridge saw the policeman and his prisoner struggling, with both of them going into the water. Twelve-year-old Sarah Hatch had also seen the fight, but she was baby sitting and afraid to leave the baby on its own, so had told no one.

Pc Bamborough was beaten with his own handcuff by Wood, and while trying to draw his truncheon, fell onto his back. Wood then jumped on the policeman, and while pushing black mud into his eyes and mouth threatened he would be drowned if he didn't let go of the handcuff: when he was obliged to do so, Wood ran off. When help came to Pc Bamborough he was pulled from the pond, and taken to the nearby *Chequers* public house where a 'dying declaration' was taken.

The officer's condition was so serious that he died on 30 November 1850, despite nine days of daily medical treatment and the careful nursing by his wife and her retired policeman brother Thomas Smith, who had served with Bamborough in the infantry. Pc Bamborough was buried in Great Burstead churchyard.[6]

William Wood was eventually arrested at Chatham and tried for murder, but in March 1851 was found guilty of manslaughter and transported for life. Inspector Rough resigned in December 1850, but in the 1851 census was living in Billericay High Street.[7]

The Metropolitan Police had a detective department from 1842 but, before detectives were appointed on a regular basis in county forces, it has previously been mentioned that conducting enquiries into crimes was part of a superintendent's responsibility. Superintendent John Clarke from Newport was involved in some interesting criminal cases around 1850. In one of them, a deposition from his wife Jane shows how much policemen relied on their wives to maintain proprieties in cases involving women. Sarah Chesham, who lived at Clavering, had the dubious distinction of being tried and found not guilty of poisoning her two sons in 1847. In 1850 Sarah's husband Richard died after a long illness: people suspected he had been poisoned. From their house Superintendent Clarke took a bag of rice for analysis, which was found to have been 'liberally mixed with white arsenic'. Sarah Chesham was arrested on 2 September 1850, and lodged in Newport lock-up where Mrs. Clarke searched her. The policeman's wife later gave evidence of what Sarah had said: 'I have no more to do in poisoning my husband than you have mam. Dr Brown told me that he had no more arsenic in his body than had been given to him by his medicine'. Protestations of innocence did no good; the technical evidence was too strong, and Sarah was hanged in March 1851.[8]

Two years before, Superintendent Clarke had been less successful in his enquiries into the murder of William Campling, the chief (or high) constable of the Saffron Walden borough force. Late in the evening of 31 October 1849, William Campling, aged 53, was going home after an evening's drinking. As he opened the front door of his house, Campling was shot in the legs, and his daughter and a neighbour found him 'weltering in his blood', suffering from what were later found to be 136 gunshot wounds. The principal inhabitants of Saffron Walden immediately searched the town looking for a local man named Benjamin Pettitt who had previously been heard to make threats against Campling: he had been seen that afternoon cleaning a single barrelled gun. Although Pettitt was quickly remanded on suspicion of shooting the high constable, there was a lack of firm evidence against him.

With no full-time professionally organised police force in the town, the part-time borough constables needed help. Although Pettitt's house had already been searched by one of them, the watch committee invited Superintendent John Clarke to try to get direct evidence of Pettitt's involvement. The following day the superintendent found footmarks in the shrubbery opposite Campling's house, and nail patterns in the footmarks matched a pair of shoes taken from Pettitt. The superintendent was also present when Thomas Brown, the surgeon, extracted a number of shotgun pellets from the high constable's legs. When the pellets were weighed on a pair of silversmith's scales, they were found to be of four different sizes, and tallied with some taken from a pouch in Benjamin Pettitt's house.

William Campling died on 9 November 1849, and was buried in the parish cemetery a week later. Enquiries into his murder continued, but the watch committee members were jealous of their independence, and declined further professional help: they had apparently made up their minds that Pettitt was guilty. However, in January 1850, the committee made another approach to Captain McHardy asking for a policeman to search for evidence. McHardy declined any further assistance, so in February 1850 Inspector Lund of the Metropolitan Police was invited to visit Saffron Walden and make enquiries. With such a time lapse since the shooting, it is not surprising that he failed to find any further evidence. Benjamin Pettitt was tried at the assizes in March 1850, and despite the circumstantial evidence against him was found not guilty.[9]

Campling's death—and the investigative problems which followed—may have helped to prove the necessity for a more professional body of police in the town. In August 1852 a William Redhead of Saffron Walden purchased a quantity of police uniform from tailors named Smart in Cambridge. It included two uniform suits comprising coat and trousers, and a frock coat with a silver collar, plus capes, stocks, belts and buttons; the order for clothing was repeated the following year. Few original records survive of the Saffron Walden force, but those which do suggest that the borough force had several more head constables before it was absorbed into the county in 1857.[10]

Although Superintendent Clarke's work at Saffron Walden did not result in a conviction, the thorough manner in which he appears to have approached most of his enquiries was recognised. In April 1851 the justices praised him and one of his constables for having brought to court several serious offenders; they wanted to make the officers a present, but thought they ought to consult the Chief Constable first. Under normal circumstances McHardy would not allow any officer to receive a reward for doing his job, except where he had put his life in danger, but because Clarke and his men had always acted with 'zeal, energy, intelligence, and sagacity' they were allowed to receive the financial proof of the magistrates' approval.[11]

In Manningtree at about the same time, Pc Samuel Duce had what was considered a miraculous escape when he was attacked by two men he found burgling a shop. The knife thrust at him hardly touched his skin thanks to his flannel waistcoat, but the items found at the scene after the men escaped led to their capture. One of the items was a wooden hand with a glove on; it led to the arrest and conviction of a one-handed poacher called Holden![12]

Captain McHardy expected his policemen to be able to use their initiative when necessary, and in November 1851 the *Essex Standard* reported a smart piece of detective work at Great Coggeshall where initiative had been used. Having failed to arrest a man they wanted, Constables Smith and Oakley dressed as distressed labourers, and went from door to door selling matches. As their suspect opened his door to buy the matches, he was arrested.

While the old styles of policing still ran in parallel with the county force, there continued to be some opposition to the expense of a permanent full-time constabulary. However, by the year of the Great Exhibition, *Punch* commented that: 'The blue coats—the defenders of order are becoming the national favourites ... everyone has been charmed during the Great Exhibition by the mode in which this truly civil power has been rendered effective ...[13]

The Great Exhibition was held at the Crystal Palace in London, being open to the public between May and October 1851. One of its objects was to educate the working classes, and for 80 of the 141 days the exhibition ran the entrance fee was only one shilling: well within the price range of most people. Special trains ran from all over England, including at least one from Colchester, and it is likely that many officers attended. There was at least one exhibit on display from a member of the Essex Constabulary, and the *Essex County Standard* reported in detail on the work of Pc Henry Fitch, stationed at Stebbing, who spent

> more than 500 of his leisure hours making an exceedingly clever model of Stebbing church on a scale of one inch to five feet ... with columns, arches, organ, pulpit, reading desk, clerk's desk, pews, mural tablets and floor tombs in the utmost accuracy as to proportion and position ... When illuminated by a candle inside the effect is striking and splendid...[14]

In 1852 the government convened a House of Commons select committee to find whether police forces were proving satisfactory. Several former Essex officers appeared as witnesses, as well as the chairman of quarter sessions and a number of landowners. Captain McHardy was something of a star witness when he gave his first evidence on 27 May 1853. He told the committee that his force consisted of 202 men, and that its example had encouraged most neighbouring counties—except Kent—to start their own forces. He expounded his ideas on several other topics including the possibility of what amounted to a national police force divided into four areas. The select committee was also told that many Essex policemen had been appointed as assistant relieving officers of vagrants, and had therefore been able to reduce the level of applications for poor relief. Over-zealous Essex officers had to be reminded in July 1854 that the Poor Law Board had issued instructions to ensure that 'women and children', and those with 'an enfeebled and sickly appearance', were to be treated humanely. Superintendents were 'cautioned most strongly against deviating from the humane directions of the Board'.[15] Much of McHardy's evidence to the select committee concerned ways of reducing the cost of policing.[16]

McHardy told the select committee that there was insufficient co-operation between existing forces, although the Essex borough forces quickly turned to him when they were in trouble. At a recent parliamentary election Colchester had been policed by around half of the Essex force. County constables were also jealous of the borough constables' powers to make an arrest outside their area; county constables' powers could not be exercised in boroughs.[17]

Perhaps the evidence McHardy had given to the select committee set him thinking even more deeply than usual, for in 1854 he submitted a detailed report to quarter sessions with his plans for the future of the force. Amongst the many proposals was one to reduce the numbers of superintendents and inspectors, and introduce a rank which provided more general supervision. Holders of the new rank of sergeant were to receive two shillings a week more than first-class constables, a practice which McHardy hoped would encourage men to qualify themselves for promotion.[18]

The deliberations of the select committee eventually contributed to the County and Borough Police Act of 1856. Many of its recommendations were based on what was already happening in Essex, and a number of Essex officers achieved promotion by joining newer forces, including the North Riding of Yorkshire.[19] The main point of the Act was the central supervision vested in the two (later three) government inspectors of constabulary (often abbreviated to H.M.I.) who were appointed. They had to inspect each force and, if they regarded it as efficient, then a percentage of the running costs could be reclaimed from the government. The inspectors were working in an advisory capacity for several months before the Act took effect on 1 January 1857.

Essex was part of the area inspected by Major General William Cartwright of North-amptonshire. He was not a police officer, but was interested in policing and had been one of the original applicants for the Essex Chief Constable's post. Essex earned special praise in the government inspector's second report:

> This force has long been known as one of the most efficient in England, and has been most valuable in leading the way with a few other forces when police organization was but little understood ...

Cartwright liked the Essex practice of appointing police officers as weights and measures inspectors, because they had nothing to gain by falsifying scales. It was good public relations for the poor to see policemen taking their side in that way.[20]

At the time of the HMI's second report in 1858, Harwich and Saffron Walden borough forces had decided to consolidate with the county. Colchester and Maldon remained independent, but were still as inefficient as ever. Saffron Walden made a last stand for the independence of its police force by protesting against the 1856 Police Act, even though many of the townspeople were in favour of the county force taking over the policing of the town. Facilities in Saffron Walden were so limited that anyone who was arrested had to be taken to Chelmsford—27 miles away—leaving only one policeman on duty. It is little wonder that the HMI was strongly in favour of such small forces amalgamating with county forces.[21]

The HMI's activities had an immediate effect on officers of all ranks. In the divisions he visited everyone had to parade before him, and on one occasion men of the Rochford division were inspected at Southend railway station. There was also an increase in the orders and memos from headquarters after his visits. More notice was taken of prisoners' rights, although Superintendent Thomas Rogerson was reprimanded by McHardy for not having 'sufficient sagacity' to remove a female prisoner from his station, rather than putting five male prisoners into one cell! [22]

An additional police responsibility after 1864 was the supervision of convicts on licence. This was made easier by greater use of photography; two copies of a convict's photograph were sent to the appropriate police station. Photography was not then practised in all prisons: and in 1866 it had still not been introduced at Chelmsford, which made matters difficult when a prisoner escaped.[23] There is no evidence that Essex officers were ever asked to make checks on the credit worthiness of individuals, but it had happened in some areas, and McHardy warned his men against such practices which would—it was said—lead to a loss of public support.[24]

It appears that Essex pay scales were not keeping pace with those of other forces or other trades. A standard procedure was recommended for every force, where a recruit spent six months as a third-class constable on probation, and then moved into the second class as a matter of course; it was eventually approved by the Home Office in 1871. The HMI felt that if pay was increased and the height regulation dropped to 5 feet 7 inches, then young men around the age of 20 might be more attracted to police work, rather than 'older men antagonistic to the life and discipline'.

A system of promotion examinations was mentioned for the first time in the HMI's report for 1861. McHardy's early attempts to encourage his men in self improvement had generally been confined to advising them to read more, and getting them to copy out his written orders to improve their handwriting. The HMI commended a system introduced in Lincolnshire, where constables were examined in writing, spelling and arithmetic; sergeants took another examination in the higher rules of arithmetic, making up pay sheets, charge sheets and summons returns, and the classification of different crimes under appropriate headings. Eventually a variation of this system was adopted in Essex.[25]

Notes and References
1. Emsley, *op. cit.* p.56. Several ex-Essex men gave evidence to the 1853 Select Committee which was considering the effectiveness of police forces. They included Thomas Redin (Essex superintendent between 1 May 1840-21 October 1845); David Smith, Essex inspector between 20 July 1841-14 March 1843, William Oakley, of Bath (superintendent in Essex between 11 May 1842-19 February 1849); and John Dunne who joined Essex as a constable on 20 August 1842, was promoted inspector on 31 December 1846, and superintendent on 9 September 1849. He became the Head Constable of Cumberland and Westmorland in December 1856, having been Head Constable of Newcastle since 8 August 1854.
2. ERO TS 558.
3. *ibid.*
4. PRO ASSI 36/6.
5. *Essex County Standard* 28 November 1851 and 22 November 1850.

6. ERO D/P 143/1/4 Gt. Burstead parish register and PRO ASSI 36/6. A 'dying declaration' is a statement taken from an injured and dying person as to the circumstances of his death. For the statement to be acceptable as evidence in court, the person who made it has to believe he is dying.

7. Pc Bamborough's medical charges cost the force a total of £3 13s. 6d. The itemised bill from William Carter, surgeon, included eight days charges. Apart from two journeys each day the surgeon had bled the patient at least once and sometimes twice a day; and there were charges for boxes of pills, six powders a day, cough mixture and several pints of lotion [ERO Q/FAc 7/2]. A total of £4 13s. was paid to Mrs. Bamborough for her husband's funeral, including £1 16s. for a lined coffin, 7s. 6d. for three pairs of gloves; 5s. for fees to the clerk and grave digger and 10s. for a pall. Of the seven men who had assisted at the scene by lifting the injured man or taking messages, five were paid 2s. 6d. each and two one shilling each [ERO Q/FAc 7/2].

8. PRO ASSI 36/6. The case of Sarah Chesham led to moves to restrict the sale of arsenic. Lord Carlisle introduced a bill in 1851 to oblige anyone who wanted to buy arsenic to sign their names in a book. A letter to the *Chelmsford Chronicle* on 4 April 1851 suggested that it would be more appropriate if they obtained certificates of suitability from their neighbours! That was because Mrs. Chesham's boasting had led to her arrest.

9. Saffron Walden borough records (at Town Hall), and *Essex Standard,* 2 and 16 November 1849. No surviving records show when William Campling became high constable, but he does not appear to be the same man who served in the Essex force between 7 February and 3 April 1843 and was dismissed for incapacity; that man was only 23 years old.

10. Information supplied by Chief Superintendent Les Waters, Cambridgeshire Constabulary.

11. *Chelmsford Chronicle*, 18 April 1851.

12. *Essex County Standard,* 4 April 1851.

13. Emsley *op. cit.* p.59.

14. *Essex County Standard*, 7 February 1851.

15. ERO Q/APp 5.

16. The force was continually being given extra jobs to make it more cost effective. From October 1853 policemen arranged most coroners' inquests to save the fees charged by parish constables; all cases of sudden and violent death had to be reported immediately to the Chief Constable. Police officers were also given powers under customs law to seize contraband, and as an inducement to the public to give information about smuggling, McHardy was prepared to consider any who were also suitable in other ways for employment in the force. In September 1852 the government ordered a further enrolment of militia, and officers were canvassed by their superintendents to see if they would be prepared to find recruits; however they were not supposed to go into public houses or beer shops to get volunteers. The five shilling fee the government donated for each man who volunteered could be kept by the police division which enrolled him. McHardy suggested the money went towards a library in each division to remedy deficiencies in general knowledge 'amongst the subordinates ... who evince little desire to acquire it'. McHardy's proposal received 'almost unqualified negative comment', so he stopped interfering, commenting that it was sad to disappoint those who had wanted to raise themselves [ERO Q/APp 5]. Police were also expected to be fire fighters, even though fire brigades were provided by a mixture of parish funds, insurance companies and boards of health. When a fire brigade was formed in Chelmsford in 1860 with a professional superintendent and assistant and 10 firemen, McHardy agreed that police should be trained to operate the fire escape that was bought by subscribers and handed over to the local board of health [Information from Hilda Grieve].

17. *Report of the House of Commons Select Committee on Police and Minutes of Evidence*, 1853 [Facsimile edition by Arno Press 1971.] McHardy had some fairly extreme ideas that he was never allowed to implement fully. One of them was presented to the committee as a 'Scheme for an Efficient Constabulary and Defensive Force throughout England and Wales' which organised the Essex force as the basis of a volunteer defensive force which would make the calling out of the local militia unnecessary in times of crisis. The proposal gives some idea of the unsettled climate in which mid-19th-century police worked [Steedman *Policing the Victorian Community* p.22]. Excluding the Metropolitan Police, McHardy wanted there to be one constable per 1,000 head of population in order to make a defensive force of 14,000 men. McHardy had also given evidence to the 1850 Select Committee enquiring into the beer acts. He told them how difficult it was to get evidence of

disorderly conduct in beer houses as 'they watch us in every way; they shut the doors and resort to all sorts of schemes to defeat us' [ERO Q/CM 3/10].

18. ERO Q/APp 5.

19. For example, Sergeant George Howard who served in Essex from 15 April 1850 - 31 December 1856 resigned in order to become an inspector in North Riding. He would undoubtedly have been promoted had he stayed in Essex, for McHardy gave him a 'highly exemplary testimonial' which recommended him to the special notice of his new chief constable. In November 1856 two other Essex inspectors, John Jones (who served from 22 April 1842-30 November 1856), and Henry Seers, (from 27 March 1840 -15 April 1857) also resigned, but force records do not say where they were going.

20. HMI printed Reports of HM Inspector of Constabulary.

21. *Essex Standard*, 23 March 1856. Harwich amalgamated with Essex on 1 February 1857 and Saffron Walden on 1 November 1857.

22. ERO Q/APp 5. McHardy issued a circular of management guidance on 12 January 1855. Commenting on the long service of some of his inspectors and superintendents, he still felt the need to remind them that they must follow his instructions and display more energy and ambition. 'I must insist upon suppressing the disposition which I have observed in many officers to keep their respective Divisions distinct and isolated from each other ... and I am convinced that the effectual operation of the constabulary has been greatly retarded by the unwillingness of some officers to communicate with me and with each other...' Superintendents were particularly reminded that their authority depended on being aware of the needs of their men as 'some superintendents have improperly deprecated inspectors in the estimation of the constables...'

23. *Essex Standard*, 6 July 1856. The 1851 census for Saffron Walden shows a retired Metropolitan police officer who gave his occupation as 'photographer' [Information from Elizabeth Sellers].

24. ERO Q/APp 5.

25. Printed Report of HMI, 1861.

Chapter 7

The Force at Work, 1870-1881

State of force in 1870—new legislation—farm labourers join police—introduction of merit star for distinguished conduct 1871—Maldon borough force better organised— Colchester borough force and the army—railways affect Southend.

At the start of the third decade Captain McHardy was still in command, but now there was a new HMI, Colonel Cobb. At his first inspection he found that Essex had 20 police stations, 53 cells and police accommodation for 63 officers and men: the remainder of the force lived in private accommodation—either rented houses, in lodgings with other officers, or with civilian families.

A great deal of new legislation extended the activities of the police in the 1870s. The Pedlars Act and Prevention of Crime Acts of 1871, Licensing Act 1872, Explosives Act 1875 and the Customs and Revenue Act 1878: the latter introduced dog licences.[1] Police work was becoming more complex, and it was felt that some of the older men would not be able to cope with the new responsibilities. Moves to lower the average age of entry for constables were considered helpful, but there was already a good deal of discontent. Captain McHardy complained that the force was underpaid and unpopular. Officers complained about the pay scales, the uncertainty of superannuation, the high rents they had to pay in police stations, and having to pay their own doctor's bills.[2]

At least they were better off than most farm labourers, for whom joining the police became a way to better themselves. Attempts were being made to establish the National Agricultural Labourers' Union in north Essex in 1872, and local leadership was assumed by Charles Jay of Codham Hall in Wethersfield. One of the union's objectives was to encourage badly paid Essex labourers to migrate—either to northern England or Australia—where places were found for them in industry, and the Liverpool police. Some of those who joined the Liverpool police wrote to Charles Jay with their impressions:

> ...On Tuesday we were swearing in as constables and 2 suits of good clothes, and then the drill came. We can do that better than hopping over clods all day. We get a lb of beef every day and a good bed to lie upon... We seem to like it so we are your truly Policemen.[3]

Constable Walter Burrows came from an agricultural labourer's family at Cold Norton, and he too fell under Charles Jay's influence. Pc Burrows was stationed at Dunmow in April 1871, where his pay was £4 4s. 1d. a month plus allowances of 10s. 11d. He already had children, and the wage was not enough for him. In August 1873, with three years' service, he resigned; the personnel register is endorsed 'Australia Mr Jay'.[4]

One temporary solution to discontent about pay was extra recognition for men already serving. Although a merit star system had been introduced in some other forces much earlier on, it was not introduced into Essex until January 1871. Ten sergeants were granted two shillings a week extra, and 20 constables one shilling a week extra for 'highly distinguished and discreet conduct in the discharge of duty particularly when accompanied with risk of life'. The Chief Constable was authorised to issue each officer with a special star to be worn on the collar and, although the badge was retained on promotion, the extra pay ceased. At the same time in 1871, there was an increase of 40 in the authorised establishment, and a reduction in the height limit from 5 feet 8 inches to 5 feet 7 inches. The increase in establishment numbers, plus improved recognition for officers, helped to raise the annual recruitment figures from 20 in 1869 to 34 in 1872; a total of 42 men joined in 1871.[5]

The first constable to earn the merit star was Constable John Street of Foxearth, who in the early hours of 7 January 1872 saw three men leaving a farm with 17 fowls they had killed. Seizing the thief carrying the largest sack, the constable was then attacked by the other two thieves who tried to escape. The officer managed to give chase, capture one man, and recover the fowls. Pc Street became the first holder of the merit star, and was ordered to display it on a new uniform jacket when the case came to court.[6]

The two remaining borough forces were gradually becoming more efficient. Maldon decided to have full-time policemen for the first time in 1853, when there were 17 applicants for the two advertised posts; Frederick Chilvers, an Essex inspector, was appointed as Chief Constable of Maldon, with John Rye from Colchester as second officer. When the HMI made his first report for 1857, he recorded the strength of the Maldon force as only two men who were of equal rank and status: they took day and night duty by turns. No records were kept except a charge book, the station house and cells were bad, and the force was considered inefficient in numbers and discipline. It remained so until 1871. By that time the borough's population had risen to 5,362, and the HMI suggested that the authorities might find it useful to increase the size of its force. With more officers the force could be considered efficient, and thus qualify for a government grant. The HMI suggested that they appoint one head constable, one sergeant and three constables at different rates of pay; they should also have a merit class with a distinctive badge and 2d. a day extra pay.

Following the advice of the HMI the borough authorities advertised for constables. William King a warder at Springfield gaol was appointed as head constable. Alfred Clark, a Great Eastern railway worker, was invited to apply, but he wrote declining as he did not feel himself capable of taking on a policeman's responsibilities. One of the successful candidates was William Dudley of Terling who had served in the Metropolitan Police. The standard of some applicants was not high. James Ford, aged 20, was obviously conscious of his lack of education for his application is endorsed: 'he who has done this as well as he possible can as this is about the second time of his trying to write and asked me to tell you that he is not a very good scholar'.

In the HMI's report for 1872 the Maldon force of five men was considered efficient for the first time, and surviving records give more details of their duties. There is an interesting example of communication between the forces in December 1877, when Superintendent George Rutledge of Latchingdon sent a telegram to Maldon describing a large silver watch and chain that had been stolen that morning. The Maldon head constable sent an officer to stand at Wantz Road to wait for the suspected thief. He was detained, taken to Maldon police station in the town hall, and a return telegram sent to Latchingdon. By 5 p.m. Pc Pennock from Latchingdon had collected his prisoner.[7]

At Colchester, where evening fights between soldiers and civilians were quite common, the borough officers had close contact with military authorities. In September 1869 a Colonel Bourke of the 4th depot battalion complained that two of the borough constables had failed to arrest a drunken half naked man who had later committed a serious assault on a soldier. Another constable had held the cap and belt of a soldier involved in a fight, rather than arresting the participants. The appointment of head constable Coombs in 1883 led to better cooperation, as he established a direct link with the brigade major, rather than dealing with a variety of officers.

In 1870 the efficiency of the Colchester force was discussed by the watch committee, and the head constable was asked for his views on each officer. He considered two worn-out and four not effective; they got warning letters from the town clerk. The whole affair threatened to turn into a scandal when information was received that several members of the force were involved in gross immorality and misconduct. Rather than deal with the allegations, the watch committee decided that everyone would start again with a clean sheet.[8]

The development of the railway system made it much easier for people to travel out of London into parts of Essex such as Southend. Although the force made use of railways— senior officers regularly travelling by rail—horses were still used. They were, however, increasingly difficult to buy for the £30 that quarter sessions had authorised for each one; £40 was nearer the current price.[9]

By 1870 'excursionists' were already a problem in the seaside town of Southend, and in October 1872 a meeting was held at the *Royal Hotel* to discuss policing in the town. Residents complained that there were insufficient officers in the area, and Captain McHardy produced a scheme to combine the parishes of Prittlewell, Leigh, Southchurch and South Shoebury into a separate police district.

A new police station with every modern convenience was completed by 24 June 1874 in Alexandra Street. One of its admirers was an American lady who signed herself 'Olive Harper' in a letter to the *Essex Weekly News* on 25 December 1874.

> I find Southend-on-Sea too dull for anything, especially of a Sunday ... I like to see the inside of everything that is shut up ... and in that laudable spirit I went to see the police station ... I shall tell you how I found it ... There might be a few armchairs and velvet sofas added to the cells, and a small parlour organ for each, to while away the hours that might otherwise be wearisome [but] the station is really everything that could be desired and a decided improvement on any I have seen in even go-ahead America. The beds are comfortable, and so arranged that fresh straw is added for every fresh prisoner, and the bedding ample and clean. The cells are warmed by hot water pipes and there is no unhealthy smell. They are well ventilated, and ... the prisoners are well fed and are given exercise in a large iron cage... The station is under the control of Inspector Hawtree who seems to conduct all his affairs like a Christian man, never forgetting while in the function of his official duties that he has also duties to his fellow men...[10]

Admiral McHardy was 79 in 1880 and had been Chief Constable for 40 years. He had actively campaigned for police officers to take on a variety of jobs to justify their existence, and the government had added to them. For example, policemen had to report parents who would not let their children be vaccinated, check whether children were still sweeping chimneys, and regularly examine telegraph wires to see if the insulators had been destroyed. Anomalies continued in the pension regulations, and superannuation payments could be reduced at the discretion of the Chief Constable.

3. This is Superintendent Samuel Hawtree who was born on 3 April 1834 in Aldenham, Hertfordshire. He transferred from the Metropolitan Police to Essex on 22 March 1864, was promoted to second class inspector on 1 October 1866, and superintendent on 1 November 1880; there is no reference to his having been a sergeant. Much of Hawtree's service as inspector and superintendent was in the Rochford and Southend areas where he was active in public life, including acting as census enumerator for both towns between 1871-91. Superintendent Hawtree was well-respected as a man, for when he remarried in 1888 after the death of his first wife, all his men subscribed to a handsome clock in a marble case as an expression of 'the great esteem and respect we have for you ... whom we honour as a man, respect as a friend, and to whose kindly guidance and courteous manner we owe more than we can express'. He died in 1918.

Another ancillary duty acquired by some police officers was as inspectors under the Food and Drugs Acts. On 18 January 1881 this involved Superintendent Samuel Hawtree in a nightmare journey after he had taken some sweets to the London Hospital for analysis. At Thames Haven, on the return journey from Fenchurch Street, the train ran into six feet of snow and was stranded. When he eventually arrived home, Hawtree wrote a report to the Chief Constable, asking for approval to claim what was known as special service allowance for his expenses:

> I have the honour to inform you that I conveyed samples to the analyst on 18 January last and on my return home the train became 'snowed up' and I had to remain fourteen hours in the carriage and had only got 9 miles from London on the 19th. I returned to

London, and there followed behind a group of men as they cleared the snow away reaching Grays at 1am on the 20th. I left Grays at 8am on the 20th and walked 13 miles through the snow to Pitsea, and from there to Southend by train. I reached Southend at 6pm 20th having been three days and two nights performing the journey and at considerable expense, also spoiling a pair of shoes, and under these exceptional circumstances I must respectfully solicit your permission to crave special service for the three days and two nights.

He was granted an allowance of £1 4s.[11]

At the April 1881 sitting of quarter sessions, Admiral McHardy gave notice that he intended to retire on 1 July. His retirement ended a long period of stable leadership in the force, and reconsideration of his life in the next chapter will demonstrate the effect of his personality and experiences on the development of the Essex Constabulary during its first four decades.

Notes and References

1. Printed HMI Reports.
2. ERO Q/SO 48.
3. A. F. J. Brown, *Meagre Harvest,* p.48 (published by ERO 1990).
4. ERO J/P 2/2.
5. ERO J/P 2/7.
6. *ibid.*
7. ERO D/B 3/3.
8. Colchester Watch Committee minutes. When the soldiers had to be back in barracks at night it was easy to control them, but changes in army regulations in 1902 allowed soldiers to stay out all night provided they reported for duty at 6a.m.: the Colchester police were not pleased!
9. ERO Q/SO 48.
10. *Essex Weekly News,* 25 December 1874.
11. ERO Q/FAb 146/3. Samuel Hawtree joined the force in 1864 after serving in the Metropolitan Police. He was promoted inspector in 1866 and superintendent in 1880. While inspector in charge of the Rochford division he was a census enumerator for the 1871 census. As a superintendent he was also employed in numerous crime enquiries in and around Essex. After a major scandal in the Metropolitan Police the whole of its detective division was reorganised and placed under the command of a specially appointed barrister, Mr. C. E. Howard Vincent, who was keen to establish good relations with Essex. In July 1881 he wrote to thank Superintendent Hawtree and Southend officers for the way they had co-operated with the Metropolitan Police in the arrest of Percy Lefroy Mapleton for a murder committed on the Brighton railway.

Chapter 8

McHardy—A Man of this Time?

Summary of early lives of John and Horatia McHardy—births of children—drowning of Mary Malvina McHardy 1844—influences from county families—Admiral McHardy's retirement in 1881—his funeral 1882.

On 31 October 1881 a major period in the history of the Essex Constabulary ended with the retirement of Admiral McHardy. Many generalisations have been made about the values of the Victorian age, and it may be appropriate to ask if McHardy was a man of his time?

The reign of Queen Victoria saw the rise of the middle classes, who followed the philosophy of self-help expressed by writers like Samuel Smiles. Marriage was seen as an economic and social building block, and demographic evidence shows it to have been a step often taken by men in later life, with younger wives. Such families might have many children over a period of 20-25 years.

John McHardy can be described as belonging to the professional middle classes. His family originated in Scotland, but how or why his father Robert McHardy came to settle in Nassau in the Bahamas we do not know. Robert owned land and slaves, and married twice, producing children by each wife. We may conjecture that rejection by his stepmother led the young McHardy to join the navy, but we know next to nothing about his very early life.[1]

Nothing is known of John McHardy's courtship with Horatia Victoria Atchison Pasco, daughter of John Pasco his first captain, but McHardy was 29 and Horatia 22 when they were married on 11 December 1830.[2] On 20 March 1835 he joined the Coast Guard service, and from census entries giving birthplaces of their children it can be seen that he served in Norfolk and the Isle of Wight. On his appointment as Chief Constable of Essex, Captain and Mrs. McHardy lived in a house in King Street, Chelmsford before moving to police headquarters at Old Court. In June 1841 the McHardy family had five children at home: Mary Malvina (born 1833), James (born 1834), Emily Lees (born 1836), Coglan McLean (born 1838), Hardy (born 1840). Two other children—Malvina (born 1834) and John (born 1835)— were away from home on census night.[3] The family also employed three female servants.

Deaths of infants and children from a range of possible illnesses were not uncommon in the 19th century, but the tragedy which hit the McHardy family on the evening of Thursday 2 May 1844 was an unusual death for a Victorian child. Mary Malvina and her younger sister Malvina had been seen by some village children walking along the river with their governess, Emily Fanny Gace. The girls were throwing sticks into the river, when Mary fell in and Emily Gace tried to rescue her. Their screams brought a group of railway labourers to the scene, but the water was deep and none of them could swim. John Terry, working in a field near Springfield railway bridge, sent for two creepers (hooked instruments for dragging deep water). Before these arrived 10 minutes later, the two bodies had been recovered, and all attempts at resuscitation by Captain McHardy and the local doctor had failed. The inquest recorded a verdict of accidental death. [4]

Captain McHardy commissioned a memorial window for Emily Gace from a well known stained glass artist, Thomas Willement of London. The subscription list was headed by Queen Charlotte and prominent county families, and included members of the force. The memorial window was placed in the north wall of Holy Trinity Church in Springfield, but was almost totally destroyed when the church was badly damaged in a bombing raid in 1941. Dr. Badeley—who had tried to revive the girls—wrote a poem which formed part of the memorial:

> Lost where yon Chelmer winds his way
> Two fond companions here united lie.
> One met alas an unsuspected grave,
> the other plunged to save her or to die ...[5]

At the time of Mary's death the Chief Constable's wife was recovering from the birth on 19 April of her sixth son, Wallace Bruce. However, it was not customary for middle-class women to attend funerals, even of close family members. Because childhood mortality was so common Christian names were often used again: four years later the McHardy family named another daughter Mary.[6]

Captain McHardy was proud to be appointed Chief Constable on his own merits[7] but once in post he built up a network of friends amongst influential county families. Robert Peel's fears that his new Metropolitan Police would become a 'jobbing opportunity for the upper class ... if gentlemen's servants and so forth are placed in the higher opportunities' has been interpreted to mean that police work was regarded as a lower-class occupation.[8] There was encouragement for the lower classes to rise to a certain level in the police if they were seen to be helping themselves, and many men of humble origin achieved high rank by their own efforts. A few early Essex policemen did come from 'the upper classes' and wealthy family backgrounds; among these was William Pattisson.

When Jacob Pattisson, a wealthy Witham solicitor, went bankrupt, it was left to his wife Charlotte to help find jobs for their children. Their son, William Henry, withdrawn from Cambridge in 1859 before completing his degree, refused an offer to be a sheep farmer in New Zealand in order to go 'into the police force under our old ... friend ... Admiral McHardy, with many prospects of living as useful a life as can possibly be desired'.[9] William Pattisson's parents thought his physical strength, active energy and organisational skills would fit him for a police career. Pattisson was sent to work initially in Epping, but socially he had close links with the McHardy family, and often escorted Mrs.. McHardy and her daughters to social functions after he became deputy chief constable in 1867. Pattisson seems to have been popular in the force, and might well have achieved high rank even without his friends in high places.

Others were not so fortunate. Someone signing himself 'A discontented ex-policeman' wrote a caustic letter to the *Essex County Standard* in 1859, in support of Constable John Maguire who had been dismissed without a testimonial. The writer complained that he had joined with good testimonials and had been told that he would rise by merit if he exerted himself. Despite praise by his superiors and local gentry he had not been promoted, and yet he had watched a 'very young Scotchman scarcely out of his teens rise in three years from lowest to highest grade; and never heard of him having detected a thief during the whole time ... if this is rising by merit I am ignorant of the word merit.'[10]

McHardy, by now promoted to admiral, extended his period of notice to 31 October 1881 and on 1 November 1881 his former deputy, Superintendent William Bridges, led a deputation of policemen who presented gifts from the force of a black marble clock, ornamental

4. The panel at the base of the window in Holy Trinity Church, Springfield, reads, 'Emily Fanny Grace aged twenty two years drowned while attempting to save Mary McHardy aged eleven years May 2 MDCCCXLIV'.

Although the bombing did not destroy the commemorative plaque, installation of heaters in the church obscured most of it. The inscription reads: 'Emblems expressive of a Christian's hope are placed in this window to commemorate the self devotion of Emily Fanny, daughter of Captain Gace of Louth, Lincolnshire, who lost her life in the attempt to save Mary daughteer of Captain McHardy R.N., Chief Constable of this County, who perished in the river Chelmer on the second day of May in the year of our LORD 1844. This Tribute of respect is paid to her memory by Her Majesty Queen Adelaide, The Lord Lieutenant, The Vice Lieutenant, the High Sheriff, And others the Nobility. County and Borough Members of the Commissioners of Parliament, Clergy and Gentry of Essex, The Chief Constable, Officers and men of the County Constabulary force: and many private friends of both bereaved families who have committed their dead to an adjoining grave in sure and certain hope of a resurrection to normal life through OUR LORD AND SAVIOUR JESUS CHRIST'.

[Photograph by permission of the British Library.]

vases and a silver tea service. The county justices and the parish of Springfield also made their own presentations.[11] Many other testimonials to Admiral McHardy's long service were arranged, and the following appeared in the *Essex Chronicle* in response to a proposal made by the justices in quarter sessions:

> Complaints are often made that in these days we are over taxed, over talked and over populated ... William Cobbett used to declare that no man was entitled to special respect unless he did something beyond the bounds of his well-known duties, but nowadays testimonials are showered among people like medals at a coronation, and it is not often they get into hands that deserve them. But there are exceptions to the rule ... Admiral McHardy is to have a testimonial on his retirement ... after a service of 41 years. It ought to be a good one, and there is promise that it will be.[12]

All McHardy's surviving sons achieved high professional status in their chosen careers. Three of them followed their father into the Royal Navy where John George Graham died in Lagos in 1865. Hardy and Wallace Bruce then joined different police forces, Wallace being appointed an Essex superintendent on 23 March 1874. He became his father's deputy before moving on to become Chief Constable of Lanarkshire in May 1876. Wallace's acknowledged skills in anticipating and dealing with problems seems to have affected his mental health. His police authority gave him leave of absence and enough money to visit one of his brothers in South Africa, but the break only gave a temporary respite, and he died in post in January 1896. Hardy McHardy became Chief Constable of Ayrshire in October 1876, and retired when he was 71 in May 1911; he died in October 1919.[13]

Admiral John McHardy died at the home of his married daughter in Bath after less than a year in retirement. There were many lengthy tributes in the press, and references to his descriptive powers and enjoyment of telling stories: 'He brought every timber and every rope of a ship before your eyes, and you fancied that you could see the sailors moving about the deck and hitching up their trousers'.[14]

McHardy was buried in his old church at Springfield on 22 December 1882. The funeral procession included his male relatives, most of the force, and many county dignitaries.[15] Horatia survived for almost two years longer, and is buried in the same tomb as her husband, seven of their children, and Emily Gace. It still stands in the grounds of Holy Trinity church.

Notes and References
 1. Government Archivist, Bahamas.
 2. BM Add. MS. 38047.
 3. ERO microfilm of 1841 census.
 4. *Chelmsford Chronicle*, 10 May 1844.
 5. BM Add MS 52413.
 6. D/P 211/1 Springfield parish registers.
 7. Acceptance speech, quoted in *Chelmsford Chronicle*, 14 February 1840.
 8. Quoted on p.466 of *The Age of Reform* by Sir Llewellyn Woodward, Oxford 1985.
 9. Information provided by Janet Gyford, quoting original letters in Dr. Williams' Library, London, between the Pattisson family and Henry Crabb Robinson.
10. *Essex County Standard*, 18 March 1859.
11. *Essex Chronicle*, 21 October 1881.
12. *ibid.*
13. Strathclyde Record Office—Minutes of Standing Joint Committee.
14. *Essex Chronicle*, 22 December 1882.
15. Although Mrs. McHardy and two McHardy daughters were all living, they did not attend the funeral as it was not customary for middle-class women to be mourners until later on in the 1880s. McHardy's status as an admiral and chief constable dictated the funeral etiquette, and only his sons and son-in-law could be official mourners. (Written information from Julian Litten, Victoria and Albert Museum.)

Chapter 9

Major Poyntz makes Changes, 1881-87

*Major Poyntz becomes Chief 1881—new ideas in action—murder of Inspector Simmons
1885—public order problems involving Salvation Army and Guy Fawkes festivities—
Major Poyntz's accident 1887*

After 41 years under one Chief Constable, new ideas were inevitable when McHardy's
successor was appointed. Major William Henry Poyntz was only 43, the Chief Constable of
Nottingham and had served in the Royal Marine Light Infantry, mostly in the Far East. A
branch of his family had owned estates at North Ockendon, but Poyntz himself was new to
Essex.

The new Chief Constable wanted to broaden his police experience by taking charge of
a county force, but there are hints of just how challenging he found his new post. He seems
to have found difficulty in taking charge of senior officers who had served for most of their
working lives under McHardy. One of his first actions was to 'get rid of a large number of
worthy old officers whose age and weakened physical powers were their only fault'. Seventy
men of various ranks were speedily superannuated. They included Superintendent James May
who had served since 1842 and was then 67; Constable David Scarfe, who had joined in 1841
and was then 66; and Constable William Hubbard, who was 60 and had 35 years' service.
Many others retired in the following months.[1]

As Chief Constable of Nottingham, Poyntz had been keen on welfare. He had given
his men more opportunities for promotion, increased their leave, re-established the force
band, encouraged the cricket club, and done his best to make the superannuation system
fairer.[2] What was he going to do in Essex?

Within a few days of becoming Chief Constable, Poyntz started to issue a new series
of written general orders. The first, dated 13 November 1881, suggested that he was not
satisfied with the standards of his new force, particularly about uniform. Officers were told
to wear belts on uniform jackets and greatcoats, and linen collars which showed above the
collar were forbidden. Hair was to be a 'reasonable length', boots were to be worn in
preference to shoes, and decorated staffs were to be scraped clean and varnished.

The language used in writing reports was also modernised. Use of the word 'crave' was
forbidden, and officers were ordered to 'make application' or 'beg to make application'. The
word 'beat' was officially recognised rather than the previous 'guard'. Information likely to be
of interest to other officers was to be recorded in the newly introduced occurrence books.

Major Poyntz dealt severely with men who drank on duty, and officers were often
dismissed or moved at their own expense: quite severe punishments. Had standards really
dropped so far in McHardy's last years, or was Poyntz playing the proverbial new broom?

The Chief Constable seems to have been keen on establishing links with what he called the respectable classes of society, and officers of all ranks were reminded to call on important members of the community when they changed station. Poyntz enjoyed hunting as he thought it gave him an opportunity to see the countryside, and visit members of his force unexpectedly. He would often appear unannounced when cases were being heard by local justices, and sometimes commented unfavourably on the way his officers gave their evidence.

Major Poyntz was constantly reminding the superintendents of their responsibilities, and their need to check everything from the renewal of pedlars' certificates to the health of their men. They were even ordered to inspect the drains and water closets in their stations at regular intervals after an outbreak of diphtheria at Dunmow. The outbreak was caused by 'a great want of attention to sanitary matters', and the Dunmow Superintendent, William Ackers, his wife and family were taken ill. Three of their children died from the disease; and when the superintendent later tried to claim £141 11s. 8d. for medical expenses payment was refused; he only received a contribution of £50 from county funds.[3]

In August 1884 the county authorities were more generous after Sergeant William Gifford of Orsett died from smallpox at the police station. Inspector Freeman was paid £3 for attending to the sergeant, and Mrs. Gifford received a pension of £75 12s. 1d. As a result of the death all members of the force not vaccinated in the previous seven years were encouraged to be protected against 'the terrible scourge of smallpox'. Recruits were not admitted unless they could produce a vaccination certificate.

It was decided to dispose of Orsett police station by auction, and put the money into a fund to provide police cottages at Grays. Four years later the building was auctioned, and a journalist on the *Essex Standard* in October 1888 wrote a satirical editorial about the sale.[4]

Until 1883 officers used horses and county carts to convey prisoners, but with the passing of the Cheap Trains Act of 1883 officers could be issued with rail warrants. This practice only lasted a few months, because the railway companies failed to send in their accounts on time; officers were then ordered to buy their tickets in the normal way and claim expenses.

When twice-yearly superintendents' conferences were introduced in January 1885, the participants were expected to attend and to travel by train: one hopes the service was punctual! Criminals, of course, could also make use of cheap train services to travel out of London and commit crimes in rural areas. Two such men—James Lee and David Dredge—were responsible for the murder of Inspector Thomas Simmons at Romford.

Thomas Simmons had been inspector at Romford for four years when he set out on 20 January 1885 to tour the Romford area, part of Brentwood division, accompanied by Pc Alfred Marden. On the road between Romford and Hornchurch they saw three men, and Simmons recognised one as a well-known burglar named David Dredge. Marden was dropped off to keep observation, while the inspector drove on in a vain attempt to find some help. Marden continued to track the three men, but lost sight of them (it seemed later that he may have gone for a pint!). On the return journey to Romford the men were seen again and Simmons decided to stop them. 'Where are you chaps going ?' he called. 'Home', came the reply. The taller of the trio then turned round with a revolver in his hand and fired at Inspector Simmons, hitting him in the stomach. Marden gave chase, until one of the three shot at him also, but missed.

Inspector Simmons was carried home while the hunt began for his attackers. All stations in Essex and the Metropolitan Police were alerted by telegraph, but it was feared the culprits had fled to the East End. Havering petty sessions offered a reward of £150 for information leading to the arrest of one or all the attackers.[5] The *Essex Weekly News* deplored what had happened to the officers:

The experiences of policemen amongst the daring and reckless burglars of London have been painfully experienced in Essex. The use of firearms by these desperadoes has been too frequent of late to be at all comfortable to the guardians of the peace, in whose trust the public place the safekeeping of their property, their lives and their homes. It would be well if some severe check could not be put upon this lawlessness ... We have grown too humane lately in dealing with some of the worst class of offenders ... [6]

Inspector Simmons died four days later on 24 January 1885. David Dredge was arrested at Limehouse on 6 February on suspicion of threatening to murder Pc Marden, and was taken by train to Romford. The tall man, said by Pc Marden to have fired the fatal shot, had disappeared. All pawnbrokers in London were circulated with his description in case he tried to pawn the murder weapon, and on 10 March a man calling himself James Lee was detained as he tried to pawn a revolver in Euston. He was arrested and taken to Romford by train, where Pc Marden identified him. Lee objected strongly, commenting that after being dragged through the streets of the town and viewed by half the population, neither Marden nor anyone else could fail to recognise him.

Superintendent Dobson thought Lee's objections were valid, and he went back to the railway platform to see if anyone visiting Romford would help with an unofficial identification parade. He had no luck, and later commented that suitable people were like angels—few and far between. Eventually Lee was formally identified at an identification parade held outside the gates of Chelmsford Prison.

On 27 April Lee and Dredge appeared at the Central Criminal Court in London, having insisted

5.   This is William Raven who joined the Essex Constabulary on 15 May 1844, aged 26; he was already married with two children, and had previously been a gardener. Constable Raven was stationed at Great Chishall and West Bergholt, before being posted to Elmstead in September 1855; he retired from there as sergeant in 1879. The photograph illustrates the style of uniform approved from 1875, and illustrates how the top hat of the original constables evolved into the helmet. Sergeants did not wear numbers on their uniform until after 1907.
[Photograph taken from an original in the possession of Dr. James Raven.]

that a fair trial would be impossible in Essex. The evidence of identification was strongly contested, but Lee was found guilty of shooting Inspector Simmons and hanged. Dredge was found not guilty, but was re-arrested and tried for the attempted murder of Pc Marden. The third man John Martin, was eventually tried in Carlisle in 1886 for serious offences, including the murder of one policeman and the shooting of three others.[7]

The circumstances of Inspector Simmons' death led to the provision of revolvers which could be carried at night by officers on beats adjoining the Metropolitan area; after a series of armed burglaries in London in the 1880s some Metropolitan officers also patrolled with revolvers in holsters on their belts.[8] Shooting practice was allowed on new rifle butts at Romford, but officers had to undertake to draw weapons only in 'extreme cases of self defence'. The *Essex Chronicle* supported the use of weapons, pointing out that, while it might not deter dangerous characters away from the county, it would at least put the police as far as possible on equal terms with the desperate men they had to deal with.[9]

Inspector Simmons was succeeded at Romford by Inspector Thomas Cooper. One of his most persistent problems was the Salvation Army, which had been re-organised on military lines in 1878. The self-styled General William Booth encouraged his Salvation Army's gatherings and marches to be rousing; hymns sung to drinking songs were a reminder of the dangers of excessive drinking. The Salvation Army was persecuted by all sorts of communities. Some banned the marches: others gave them the minimum of attention and picked up the pieces if rioting occurred. There were numerous prosecutions in various parts of the country, such as Hampshire, Warwick and London.[10]

Harwich was one of the first towns in Essex to have trouble with the Salvation Army. During 1882 the Salvationists paraded in the narrow streets, and one local man was charged with assaulting a Salvation Army corporal.[11] In 1882 Colchester also experienced problems with the Salvation Army, and in 1885 tried to introduce a bylaw to stop their parades. Complaints had been received that one of the borough constables was guarding the Salvation Army processions, rather than doing general patrol on his beat. Borough officers were told to escort processions only on their own beats; if the Army wanted further protection it must pay for it.[12]

The Romford branch had its headquarters at Holm Lodge, and the commanding officer strongly objected to marches being forbidden under the Riot Act: she demanded adequate police protection. Inspector Cooper had to report on each march to the magistrates: 'With one carrying a banner, one beating a drum very loud, three singing and throwing their arms up in the air in a frantic manner, and a boy playing a triangle ... they were always followed by large numbers of the lowest classes and roughs in the town.[13]

The *Essex Chronicle* was scathing about the Salvation Army, commenting that aggressiveness was its leading policy; the small corps in Romford had incurred hostility because of its disregard for local sensibilities. 'The irrepressible enthusiasts, headed by their inharmonious band, continue to take to the streets ... and to retaliate an impromptu band even more incongruous and discordant ... started to play ... the Salvationists and their police escort retreated. [14]

Police officers also had long-standing obligations to deal with different kinds of disorder linked to Guy Fawkes celebrations. Guy Fawkes celebrations in Chelmsford had their origins in religious discontent as far back as 5 November 1641 when a mob broke the stained glass windows in the church.[15] The *Essex Weekly News* for 11 November 1881 reported that Guy Fawkes Day gave Witham some notoriety, as 30 men in disguise and armed with sticks and bludgeons broke windows and pulled down fences before setting fire to them in Newland

Street. Despite reinforcements from Colchester, and a baton charge ordered by the Chief Constable, there were no arrests at the time, although warrants to arrest offenders were later drawn up by local magistrates.

One of the two officers assaulted had to be taken home to Harold Wood on the 2 a.m. mail train the following morning. There was similar trouble in later years and, in November 1885, 40 constables, some in plain clothes, were deployed all over Witham. On that occasion a tar barrel was set on fire, and a blacksmith's shop in Maldon Road was partly demolished to provide wood. The owner's solicitor later made an unsuccessful attempt to prove the police had been negligent in protecting his client's property.[16]

The *Essex Weekly News* in November 1888 refers to the

> dreary anniversary being on its last legs in the Borough of Chelmsford, with guys being taken to each door accompanied by old doggerel, 'a penny to burn the old Pope, a penn'orth of cheese to choke 'um, a pint of beer to make him drunk, and a jolly good faggot to burn 'um'. If the coppers received were in proportion to their shouting a very good business must have been done.[17]

It was common practice for guys to represent local people, occasionally in a complimentary way, such as when one of the four guys in Chelmsford represented a candidate for the position of mayor in 1888. More usually the guy represented an unpopular member of the community. The people of Stebbing celebrated Guy Fawkes day:

> by making an effigy of a gentleman in Her Majesty's employment who has rendered himself unpopular by doing his duty. The effigy of Pc Enoch Raison was borne through the village in the afternoon and again at night in a torchlight procession before being hanged and burned at Bran End.[18]

The procession obviously caused Pc Raison and his family great distress, and led to his hurried removal from Stebbing. Mrs Harriott Raison wrote to the *Essex Weekly News* thanking the people who had supported her and her family in their 'terrible and undeserved mental affliction', caused by the persecution of Pc Raison for 'doing his duty'.[19]

What sort of other jobs was a constable of the 1880s likely to be doing? Enforcing the Contagious Diseases of Animals Act was one responsibility imposed by government, but it could be lucrative for the constable concerned. Whoever laid the information before the local magistrates received a proportion of the penalty finally imposed on the offender. In one division the Chief Constable found that it was always the superintendent who laid the information—whether or not he had discovered the case—and presumably claimed the penalty. Major Poyntz decided that whoever discovered the offence would submit a report to him, via their immediate supervisor. The reporting officer would then get the summons drawn and receive his share of the fine.[20]

Constables were also given greater discretion in dealing with gipsies who let their animals stray on the highway. Where speed was of the essence they could apply for a summons themselves and tell the inspector afterwards. Many police officers continued to be inspectors under the Sale of Food and Drugs Acts, and because of the increasing amount of work involved they could appoint a deputy—not a police officer—to collect samples.

Poyntz tried to encourage the cultural life of his men, wanting them to read; partly for pleasure and partly for professional advancement. He promoted the formation of a force library—something which McHardy had proposed unsuccessfully. This provided such varied reading matter as copies of *Justice of the Peace*, and magazines like *Sunday at Home*. The library ran on a divisional basis until well into the 20th century.

In January 1887 Poyntz was granted several months' leave of absence for health reasons; perhaps his service in the tropics had weakened his health, or the strain of the job was too much. Then in September 1887, back on duty and apparently in good health, he drove himself to Chelmsford railway station to meet Colonel Cobb the government inspector. On the way back to Old Court the pony bolted into the yard of the *Saracen's Head* hotel, throwing Colonel Cobb onto the ground, and knocking down and killing the mother-in-law of the licensee. Major Poyntz was not physically injured, but the incident broke his health, and he resigned on medical grounds in July 1888. Colonel Cobb recovered from his injuries and remained as HMI for another four years. One of his retirement gifts was a signed copy of Major Poyntz's autobiography, *'Per Mare Per Terram'*.[21]

Among the officers who transferred from Nottingham at the time of Major Poyntz's appointment was Raglan Somerset, who became the Chelmsford superintendent; he was promoted deputy chief constable on 1 July 1883, and was in charge of the force during Major Poyntz's sick leave. Raglan Somerset was able to smooth the transition between Poyntz and his successor, Captain Edward Morgan Showers. The relationship between them was destined to be close and long-lasting:: as Somerset's sister Georgina became Captain Showers' second wife.[22]

Notes and References

 1. Major Poyntz's autobiography, *Per Mare Per Terram: Reminiscences of Thirty Two years Military, Naval and Constabulary Service*, published in 1892.
 2. *Essex Chronicle*, 4 November 1881.
 3. ERO Q/ACm 17. Could this have affected his mental health? W. H. Ackers was admitted to Brentwood Asylum on 6 September 1889 after disappearing from home [ERO G/DM 17, Dunmow Guardians' Minutes 1889].
 4. The editorial begins,
    ... Here is a chance, not to be met with every day, for any person with a fancy for picking up police stations. For the Orsett police station is to be assuredly knocked down under the auctioneer's hammer, if indeed it does not fall down of its own accord before... We do not know the exact nature of the accommodation but for a small society of hermits, each desiring a cool secluded cell, in which perfect retirement from the world might be secured, what could be more suitable? Or for fathers and mothers with refractory children how convenient such a residence might be! Might not the premises be even adapted for a preparatory school? And to any ordinary private individual, the honour and dignity of living in a disused police station ought to be worth something. Possibly the burglariously inclined and shady characters of the district might be supposed to know the inns and outs of such a residence rather too familiarly; but on the whole we imagine that the fact of living in such a place would strike terror into the hearts of evil doers, especially if 'Police Station Villa' were painted up in large letters... This police station had been going from 'bad to worse' which shows the demoralising effect of association with criminals. Let us hope, however that the old building may take a new lease of life, or that at any rate when it is knocked down it may bring a substantial sum for the benefit of the County of Essex.
 5. 'An Inspector Dies' by Maureen Scollan in *Essex Police Magazine*, Winter 1977.
 6. *Essex Weekly News*, 23 January 1885.
 7. Written information from David Garner of Penrith.
 8. Emsley, *op. cit.*, p.236
 9. *Essex Chronicle*, 6 November 1885. The revolvers bought in consequence of the Simmons case remained in use until December 1912, when the Chief Constable asked for permission to replace them with 20 Webley Scott automatic pistols at 35s. each, 20 holsters, 20 pouches and 20 extra magazines, because the weapons 'have become obsolete and unserviceable' [ERO C/MSj;4/3].
10. *Riotous Victorians* by Donald C. Richter, published by Ohio University Press, 1981.
11. *Crime and Criminals in Victorian Essex* by Adrian Gray, 1988.
12. Colchester Watch Committee minutes.

13. ERO Q/HZ 5/3.

14. *Essex Chronicle*, 13 November 1885.

15. Information supplied by Hilda Grieve.

16. ERO Q/ACm 17.

17. *Essex Weekly News*, 9 November 1888.

18. *ibid.*

19. *ibid.* Pc 180 Enoch Raison originally joined in 1851, working at Ashdon, Coggeshall, Saffron Walden and Helions Bumpstead. He was superannuated for two years between 1880-82, but then reinstated, being posted to Stebbing on 24 November1885. He retired after the incident referred to [ERO J/P 2/2].

20. The HMI Report for 1885 records 17 Essex police officers holding various sorts of extra inspecting duties; 17 weights and measures, 1 common lodging house, 12 assistant relieving officers, 22 diseases of animals, 19 explosives, 16 petrol, 17 food and drugs, 11 hackney carriages and 1 conservator of Shenfield Common.

21. One of the Royal Marine mottoes, meaning 'On land and Sea'. The copy is owned by Pc Laurence Pipe.

22. Gravestone in Holy Trinity church, Springfield.

Chapter 10

County Councils to the First World War

Capt. Showers becomes Chief Constable 1887—County Councils created—Maldon borough force amalgamated 1889—Colchester river police—1890 Police Act introduces pensions—murder of Acting Sergeant Eves 1893—telephones introduced—bicycles and hired cars—Basildon and Moat Farm murders—new HQ—beginning of Southend borough force 1914—strikes of farm workers.

At the time of the new Chief Constable's appointment, major administrative changes were in the final stages of preparation. The structure of English local government was reorganised under the Local Government Act of 1888, and many responsibilities formerly undertaken by quarter sessions were transferred to the newly-created county councils. Ordinary ratepayers had more influence, now they could elect county councillors every three years. The changes also affected police forces. Instead of being responsible to a body of justices from influential families, police became accountable to a powerful standing joint committee of elected county councillors and non-elected justices.

Captain Edward Morgan Showers—like his predecessors—was appointed in 1887 when the justices still had sole responsibility for the police. He was thus able to oversee the changes made by the Local Government Act when it took effect on 1 April 1889. Every borough with a population of less than 10,000 was obliged to amalgamate its police force with the neighbouring county. The five men of the Maldon borough force therefore joined their 310 Essex colleagues, and their head constable became an inspector.[1]

The abolition of Maldon borough police left only one independent force in Essex, that in the rapidly growing borough of Colchester. In 1890 the size of the beats had grown so large that the town centre was left unattended for too long. Damage and public order problems occurred, so additional patrol officers had to be appointed. In the same year Colchester Council fishery committee asked for a permanent sergeant and three constables to protect the oyster fisheries on the River Colne. The Essex Chief Constable was asked to recommend one of his men to be the sergeant, and Thomas Poole transferred to the borough's river police. The constables appointed were Edward French, a former West Mersea fisherman; Charles Absalom, a Southend waterman; and Cornelius Simmonds.

Accusations were sometimes made that river police officers stole oysters, and the fishery board had to remind them that their job was to keep the shores free from trespassers and not take sea food for their own consumption. Sergeant Poole pointed out that they had no need to steal as oysters were easily obtained: he had frequently been offered some but had, of course, refused them![2]

In June 1892 the river constables complained that one of their boats was unsafe; a Colchester councillor went out on the vessel with the head constable and 'considered her so cranky as to be unsafe in a breeze even with the light air'. The report led to the eventual purchase of a sailing boat called the *Raven*, and two lightweight boats called *Alert* and *Brisk*.

By 1899 the river police establishment had been increased by extra constables and an inspector. When two of the constables and acting sergeant Absalom resigned, constables French and Simmonds both applied to be acting sergeant. French was promoted and began to keep a journal combining personal entries as well as official duties. The second entry has a human touch: 'Pc Simmonds was very abusive to me on account of my promotion': the following day Pc Simmons apologised.[3]

In August 1899 a young constable disappeared after being in the river police for only three months. Henry Ernest Wright came from Lowestoft and when he failed to sign off duty one evening, a search resulted in the patrol boat containing his uniform being found in Pyefleet Creek. The borough Chief Constable told the inquest that it was a rule for every officer to be a competent swimmer, so they were allowed to swim on duty if nothing else was happening. A fellow constable gave evidence that Wright had previously complained of cramp; so the coroner recorded a verdict of accidental death.[4]

Responsibility for public health, drains and sanitation at local level had been divided among a number of authorities, with few of them showing any great concern about the arrangements in individual buildings; even policemen acted as sanitary inspectors in some parts of Essex. One of the earliest meetings of the standing joint committee—on 3 May 1889—was concerned with the state of drains in county police stations. From then onwards there seems to be more concern with such conditions: perhaps reflecting the influence of more ordinary people on the county council? The first Braintree station was in Rayne Road and had cells which 'rendered them offensive to the occupants of the station'; the water had twice been described by the public analyst as dangerous, and there was no drainage. Conditions at police headquarters seem to have been as bad, and Captain Showers was reimbursed £60 for having his own drains at Old Court repaired.[5]

One other event in 1889 affected the daily life of Essex police officers. The London dock strike was organised by the embryo dockers' union fighting for a standard wage of 6d. an hour: the 'dockers tanner' as it was dubbed by the press. When the violence of the strike spread to Tilbury docks, policemen from all over Essex were drafted in to assist the docks police: this cost the docks administrators more than £190 to pay for Essex officers' time.[6]

General conditions of the time helped to justify the Police Act of 1890 which brought improvements in pension regulations. Although things were probably no worse in Essex than elsewhere, policemen in general were beginning to see themselves as a group. It could be asked how they might make their collective views known? Trade unionism amongst skilled craftsmen had achieved legal recognition, but the isolated nature of rural policemen in such counties as Essex made organisation difficult. There were strikes in some borough forces and the Metropolitan Police, and there could be one piece of evidence indicating union sympathies in Essex. In 1886 Pc 134 Walter Tuffin was fined 4s. 6d. and moved to another station— possibly Coggeshall—for presuming to write on behalf of himself and eight comrades directly to the Chief Constable. Unfortunately the nature of the complaint is unknown.[7]

Until Lloyd George's National Insurance Act of 1911 introduced a general pension scheme, few working men could expect a pension when they retired. Policemen were an exception. Superannuation had been in operation since 1840, but it was dependent upon a chief constable's recommendation and could be withheld or reduced at his discretion. The

1890 Act gave a pension for life to every officer of 50 and over who completed at least 25 years' service. Any man who became incapacitated after serving for at least 15 years could also receive a pension. Officers forced to retire before qualifying for a pension could receive a gratuity—at the discretion of the police authority—and the widow and children of a man killed on duty could also be compensated.

Doubtless a pension was poor consolation to Elizabeth Eves, widow of Acting Sergeant Adam John Eves. Eves joined the force when he was 20 and like many officers fell victim to the harsh disciplinary procedures. In 1884, while stationed at Witham, he failed to report the finding of a bracelet. For such an offence he was fined 10s. and not allowed to accept the reward that had been offered. Redeeming himself by his study of first aid, Eves appeared in general orders several times for the way he exercised his first aid skills, and for his ability in detecting crime. On 29 April 1892 he was commended at quarter sessions for splinting the fractured ankle of an accident victim. That led the chairman to say how useful it was to have so many policemen qualified to render first aid.[8]

On Saturday 14 April 1893 Acting Sergeant Eves—then stationed at Hazeleigh— called into the *Royal Oak* pub to deliver a notice about poisoning rooks. Much later it was established that on the way home he had challenged four men in possession of stolen grain; they turned on him, beat him to death with heavy sticks, cut his throat, and dumped the body in a ditch. Local information soon led to the detention of six men who had made threats against Eves, and two brothers named Richard and John Davis were subsequently hanged for his murder.

Members of the force were horrified by his murder. At the time of death Eves earned around 30s. a week, and his widow was given a pension of £15 a year. Colleagues in the force subscribed to a headstone for his grave, but over the years it became overgrown and forgotten. It was not until March 1989 that the present constable on that beat—Graham Ferris— instigated the restoration of Adam Eves' grave and its headstone.[9]

The introduction of a telephone system between Chelmsford, Brentwood, Romford and Chadwell Heath police stations from March 1894 helped to improve communications. In 1897 a telephone link was installed between Chelmsford police station in the Shire Hall and the National Telephone Company's offices in the High Street; Chelmsford officers could then speak direct to other police forces. Soon the sergeants at Ingatestone and Widford were paid one shilling a week for allowing a room in their homes to hold a county telephone.[10] Privacy could not be guaranteed, however, and within a few years the Chief Constable was complaining to the standing joint committee that the instruments were worn out, and that when he rang a particular station, everyone else along the line could eavesdrop.[11]

The police were beginning to be seen more as a corporate body, rather than as groups of individuals. To provide them with a forum in which to express their views was the objective of a magazine then called *The Police Review and Parade Gossip*, which began in 1893. The first editor believed that society treated policemen as machines, while he saw them as 'citizens in need of healthy sources of information'. The *Police Review* campaigned for better conditions of service, and for policemen to have the right to vote.[12] It also allowed the anonymity of pen names for officers who thought their views could get them into trouble. That included many Essex men who wrote to the magazine in its early years.

Some complaints about living conditions were made to the standing joint committee, and there were several requests for reimbursement of medical expenses, particularly from residents at force headquarters at Old Court where the drains were appalling. When it was estimated that at least £9,000 needed to be spent on Old Court, it seemed more cost effective

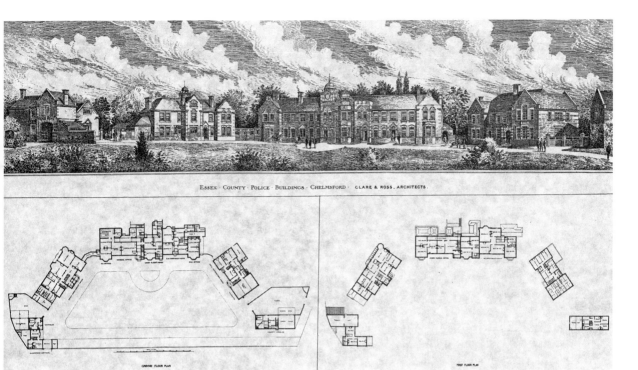

Essex · County · Police · Buildings · Chelmsford ·   Clare & Ross, Architects.

6.   Eight tenders were obtained for the building of police headquarters in 1900, and this is the winning design submitted by George E. Clare. Although the buildings were considered 'the most complete of their kind in the country, with every care taken for the health and comfort of the staff and recruits', there was no library or money for books. Burnett Tabrum of Billericay, chairman of the police stations sub-committee of the standing joint committee, started a public fund so Essex policemen could have reading matter.

to plan a new building. Three acres of land near Springfield gaol were bought for £1,250, and local architects were invited to design suitable buildings, the estimated cost being £14,500. The winning designer was George Clare, but by the time the buildings were opened in August 1903 costs had risen to well in excess of £18,000. A woman cleaner was paid five shillings a week to clean the new buildings: an innovation as cleaning had usually been done by constables.

In the course of his tour of duty a constable might have to walk anything up to 20 miles. The introduction of bicycles therefore had an effect on policing in Essex. Some officers had their own machines, and a greater number were able to ride. For a time the force hired bicycles as a cheaper and quicker alternative to hiring a horse and cart when they were needed; men authorised to use their own bicycles on duty were paid a penny a mile. Cycling became very popular throughout the country, and the problems caused by 'scorchers'—those who rode at a furious rate—were discussed at conferences of chief constables as well as locally. 'If we touch them we commit an assault, and if we ride after them we are ourselves liable to be prosecuted', complained Captain Showers to the standing joint committee.[13]

At one committee, members heard about some of the methods of control adopted by other forces, including the Metropolitan Police. One constable used a rolled up cape to knock cyclists off their machines: other forces instructed mounted policemen to run them into a hedge. One force kept a flock of sheep waiting at a particularly troublesome point, and stopped the cyclists that way.[14]

At the start of the 20th century there were no national pay scales, and Essex decided to revise its conditions of service for the first time since 1884. Recruits after 1901 had to be single, and were not allowed to marry until they had at least one year's service.[15] All officers were granted 24 hours' leave once a month if they could be spared; except for officers working in seaside towns who had to save their days off until the end of the season.[16]

Even though the horse was still in general use, a discussion on the 'modern juggernaut' took place at the county council meeting on 6 October 1900. Councillor Belsham of Maldon wanted more regulations to control motor cars after Maldon had seen three accidents in one week; cars were driving at 20 miles an hour when the maximum speed was twelve. Regulations for cars did exist, but neither police nor public had the chance to study them, and with six more cars being 'launched onto the roads of Chelmsford',[17] councillors wanted the regulations to be advertised and to include a prohibition on turning corners at more than five miles an hour.[18]

At 3.40 one Sunday afternoon in August 1904, Mr. Hatherley Page Wood was stopped while driving along Lexden Road in Colchester. He had passed over a measured quarter mile in 29 seconds, from which two police officers, Detective Hammond and Sergeant Ball, estimated, with the aid of two stopwatches, his speed at $31\frac{1}{2}$ miles per hour. The maximum allowed was 20 miles per hour, and Mr. Page Wood subsequently appeared at Colchester magistrates' court giving evidence that his car had four speeds, and under very favourable conditions going downhill might reach 28 to 30 miles per hour. On the day in question he was going at third speed which meant the car would not do more than 20 miles an hour. As he reached the measured quarter mile: '... he saw two very excited gentlemen and thought they might be friends of his. He stopped and came back, thinking they wanted to tell him something—perhaps a tramway wire was down—and he then found they were policemen'.

Mr. Page Wood's barrister alleged that the officers could not possibly have got the correct calculations, and the case was dismissed.[19]

Two years after the adoption of the Motor Car Act of 1903, the Chief Constable tried to get a car for the force, but permission was refused. The murder of a married couple named Watson in August 1906 prompted the *Essex Weekly News* to campaign for the force to have a car, because the shootings occurred in Honeypot Lane, Basildon, 'in one of the most inaccessible districts of Essex'. Richard and Robert Buckenham (20 and 17 years), neighbours of the Watsons, were arrested the following day by Superintendent Alfred Marden and Sergeant Richard Giggins, so lack of a car did not delay detection to any great extent. Captain Showers made another request for a car in 1909, and on that occasion he was authorised to hire a vehicle, provided it cost no more than £100 a year. The hiring arrangements continued for another seven years.

Published details of the 'Basildon Murder', as it became known, set some precedents. It had been suggested that the Watsons had committed suicide, but after experiments carried out by a Home Office examiner on sheets of cardboard and breasts of mutton this was found not to be the case. It also seems to have been one of the first Essex murders to have photographs of the scene published in local newspapers. The photographs were taken on Captain Showers' instructions by Fred Spalding, the well-known Chelmsford photographer.

There is no suggestion that use of a motor car would have led to an earlier arrest in the notorious Moat Farm murder case. It is a story with all the ingredients of a Victorian melodrama, and as a result has been the subject of several published articles. Samuel Herbert Dougal became involved with Camille Holland—a 56-year-old spinster—and they lived together in Bayswater and Sussex before buying Moat Farm at Clavering (then known as Coldham's Farm). The couple had lodgings in Saffron Walden between January and April 1899 while Moat Farm was being prepared but, three weeks after they moved in, Miss Holland disappeared.

Much later on it transpired that Dougal had tried to seduce a servant named Florence Havies at Moat Farm, and Florence had complained to Miss Holland. On the evening of 19 May 1899 Miss Holland went out with Dougal saying she would not be long. Dougal returned alone, telling Florence that the mistress had gone to London and that he would collect her later from Newport railway station. During the evening he left the house several times, but returned each time without Miss Holland. Florence was collected by her mother and left her job at Moat Farm the following day.

A succession of other women began to appear at Moat Farm, one of them Dougal's real wife. Servant girls came and went, but were later able to give evidence of letters arriving at the farm addressed to Miss Holland; her bankers and stockbrokers believed they were still conducting business with her. Her family later explained that they thought her failure to get in touch was due to her reluctance to explain her behaviour.

About three years after Miss Holland's disappearance the local beat officer, Pc James Drew, reported local gossip about Dougal to the Chief Constable. Captain Showers could see no obvious excuse for police interference, but ordered Detective Inspector Alfred Marden to make discreet enquiries into the financial affairs of Dougal and Miss Holland. Miss Holland's signatures on a number of cheques were found to be forgeries and an arrest warrant was issued for Dougal. He was apprehended in London, and detailed financial enquiries were made which resulted in the decision to have Moat Farm thoroughly searched. By that time Florence—the first servant girl—had been contacted, and the account of her last sighting of Miss Holland led to a search of the house and grounds. The moat was drained and exploratory digging took place over several weeks. Eventually Detective Sergeant David Scott uncovered a woman's tiny button boot attached to the remains of a body with a bullet hole in its skull. The clothing was identified by Miss Holland's former landlady, and the boot maker identified the unusually small boots he had made for her. Dougal was eventually charged, convicted and hanged at Chelmsford Prison on 14 July 1903.[20] During the protracted enquiries into the murder of Miss Holland, Essex officers had frequently liaised with both Metropolitan Police and City of London officers. Three years later, in 1906, the Metropolitan Police offered all county forces the services of its experienced detectives for any particularly complex cases.[21]

By 1903 the number of police in Southend had been increased to one superintendent, one inspector, six sergeants and 25 constables. In 1906 five extra constables were posted there, and by 1911 there were three inspectors, eight sergeants and 52 constables. Such an increase in numbers prompts a question as to the reason. The borough was becoming a popular seaside resort frequented by day-trippers described as 'excursionists' who took advantage of the cheap railway fares from London. In 1911 the Chief Constable was authorised to hire a horse for mounted patrol in Southend but, despite that, still more constables were needed to control the crowds of excursionists. Who would pay for the extra police? It was then found that the rateable value of Southend properties had increased so rapidly that the borough could easily pay for its own police. Captain Showers was reluctant to sanction such a move, but when Southend was being considered for county borough status in 1913 the whole question of police funding was reopened.

For several years prior to 1914 Southend Corporation had increasingly demanded more control over the local Police, demanding that the Chief Constable consulted its members on matters which were traditionally his to decide. They demanded that the town became a separate police area under a superintendent of their choice; insisting on fixing his salary, and dictating who should work in the town. No more than ten constables in Southend could have less than one year's service, and the bulk of officers were to be experienced men with more than three years' service. The corporation even insisted on selecting who could be drafted in for emergencies.

No self-respecting Chief Constable would accept such limitations on his traditional authority. As a result, when Southend was granted county borough status on 1 April 1914, it set up a separate police force. Henry Maurice Kerslake from Dewsbury in West Yorkshire was appointed as Chief Constable in December 1913, and was able to select the 101 men he wanted in the new force. County policemen already working in the Southend area were given the option of transferring to the new force; seventy-three did so, their uniforms being sold to Southend corporation at £3 a time. The remainder transferred into Southend from outside forces.[22]

Essex County policemen were already discontented, and the existence of the new borough force with its more generous pay scales helped to focus discontent. A group of superintendents led by Raglan Somerset, the deputy chief constable, reported to Captain Showers that Essex officers were underpaid: a fact which was having a serious influence on recruitment and leading to general dissatisfaction. As a result small pay rises were recommended by the standing joint committee.[23]

In north Essex agricultural labourers were still only earning around 13s. a week, and a new agricultural labourers' union was trying to build up strength. In March 1914 members of the union at Helions Bumpstead were involved in a lockout which led to a district strike. By June 1914 farming had practically stopped in the Saffron Walden area; the village of Ashdon was virtually in a state of warfare. Superintendent John Boyce at Saffron Walden promised farmers that his men would protect them and their volunteer labourers, so police officers had to remain on guard in the hayfields. Some must have had conflicts in loyalties if they came from villages in the area; and at least one policeman helped to bring in the harvest. The strike went on for almost a month, and many men were sent to prison for infringements of public order.[24]

The First World War was declared on 4 August 1914, and the whole fabric of society started to change as the population was subjected to restrictions never before encountered. Shortages of manpower and increased regulations gave the police even greater responsibilities, and some of these will be illustrated in the next chapter.

Notes and References

1. HMIs printed report. *Essex Weekly News* for 22 March 1889 had little to say about the amalgamation of Maldon police, merely observing that it hoped policing would continue to be adequate, and that from 1 April 1889 parishes in the borough would be assessed at the county rate. Sergeant Colt and Pc Parrott were allowed to keep their appointments as town hall keeper and clock winder, provided the duties did not interfere with police work. Pc Parrott was soon posted to Writtle, and thence to Upminster after promotion to sergeant. He retired in 1911 from Mistley.
2. Colchester Watch Committee minutes.
3. Copy of Acting Sergeant French's journal in the Essex Police Museum.
4. Inquest report in *Essex Standard*, 7 August 1899.
5. ERO Q/ACm 17. After Sergeant Galley died of typhoid at Southend in 1892 the medical officer ordered the building to be vacated while the drainage system was relaid. The problems were caused

by partly-buried carcases of dogs, buried without enough soil and lime to decompose them properly so the soil around them was contaminated. Captain Showers' annual salary was £600 less £100 for rent, rates and taxes. A bill of £60 to repair the drains of his house would therefore have been a substantial part of his income.

6. Glyn Hardwicke: *Keepers of the Door*, published by Peel Press.

7. Mutual aid allowed officers power to act in forces which had made previous agreements. Hertfordshire and Kent had agreements with Essex, but Nottinghamshire's request in 1895 was refused because it was too far away. Walter Tuffin joined the force when he was 20 on 14 December 1855. He served at Walton, Gt Oakley, Coggeshall and Kelvedon, from where he was pensioned on 3 June 1891.

8. It is not clear whether study of first aid was initially an individual initiative, as men appear to be qualifying from May 1888. Later the SJC paid 1s. 6d. for each constable to take St John's ambulance exams.

9. For more detailed accounts of Adam Eves' murder see *Country Copper* by George Totterdell, *Essex Headlines* by Stan Jarvis and The Murder of Sergeant Eves by Martyn Lockwood (Essex Police History Notebook Number 1).

10. SJC minutes.

11. ERO T/P 181/17 .

12. The right to vote was given in the Police Disabilities Removal Act, adopted in Essex in 1892. Officers whose names appeared on the voting register had to be given the chance to vote. [Source: General Orders.].

13. ERO T/P 181/17.

14. *ibid*.

15. This may have been prompted by the shortage of accommodation and attempts to standardise rent allowances. Married sergeants and constables whose rent exceeded 3s. 1d. a week automatically qualified for rent allowance. The *Essex Chronicle* also campaigned for improved police housing, suggesting that the county authorities should build or buy suitable cottages exclusively for the police in every parish, because of the difficulty of finding suitable police accommodation. 'Everybody of good sense knows that he cannot have a good pig without providing a proper cote for it' [*Essex Chronicle*, 19 April 1895]. Any houses that the county hired had to be in the Chief Constable's name from 1885 onwards.

16. The Police (Weekly Rest Day Act) of 1910 was not implemented in Essex till 1914, although one rest day in seven had been granted since 1913. The Essex system allowed two days' extra annual leave (making 16) and three rest days a month, instead of one in seven; a variation which needed less manpower.

17. ERO T/P 181/10/3.

18. The speed limit was raised to 20 m.p.h. in 1903 and to 30 m.p.h. in March 1935. The AA was founded in 1905 to protect motorists, and patrols in some areas were reported for warning their members of police speed traps [Critchley p.177]. In 1913 the 200 members of the Essex Motor Club threatened to get their licences in another county if police around Chelmsford did not stop persecuting them. After the 1903 Motor Car Act 357 motor cars were registered in Essex and 433 motor cycles. 1,053 drivers licences were issued [ERO T/P 181/17].

19. *Essex Weekly News*, 12 August 1904.

20. *The Truncheon* and sources in the Essex Police Museum.

21. The Home Office circular does not appear to have been formally rescinded but fell into disuse as detective training and experience became standardised. The Metropolitan Police was last called in to help Essex Police after the Tony Maffia murder in 1966.

22. For a detailed history of *Southend Borough Police* see the jubilee booklet prepared by Doxsey and Williams and published in 1964.

23. The other superintendents were George Hastings, William Cowell, Henry Mules and John Lennon. In the Metropolitan Police the maximum pay of a constable was between 1s. 4d. and 4s. 10d. more than the pay of an Essex sergeant.

24. A. F. J. Brown, *Meagre Harvest* and editions of *Essex County Chronicle* and *Essex Observer*, June 1914.

Chapter 11

Keeping the Peace in Wartime

Complaints about Essex pay rates before and during First World War—Captain Unett becomes Chief Constable in 1915—Organisation of Special Constabulary—war duties— Zeppelins crash at Burstead and Wigborough 1916

When the war began in August 1914 many policemen joined the military services. Superintendents had to decide the minimum number of men needed to run the force, and everyone else was encouraged to join up. Those who were left had to police a vulnerable county, as members of a force that was stretched to its utmost limits.

An Act of Parliament passed in 1910 had allowed chief constables the discretion to give their men a weekly rest day. The fact that it was not introduced in Essex until 1914 was a source of discontent, as was the fact that Essex pay scales had fallen well below those of other forces. A committee of superintendents had been asked to consider what could be done, and had recommended pay rises. Some sergeants and constables objected to the way the members of the committee had operated without consultation in recommending a pay rise of £25 a year for their own rank, £15 for inspectors, and £3 0s. 8d. for sergeants and constables. As the protesters dared not criticise openly, they wrote letters to the *Police Review*, which printed them under pen names. Essex writer 'One of Em' complained that sergeants needed at least £10 and constables £6, as they were all affected by the increase in living costs:

> What is wanted in Essex is more unity and no cliques. A proper proportion of all ranks should be represented on committees, and until this is done dissatisfaction will continue to the detriment of the service, and we shall always have the inner circle looking after themselves at the expense of the workers.[1]

Another writer 'Observer' pointed out that a policeman had to live in a respectable area, be physically fit, and devote his whole time to the service. He had to keep out of debt and be honest. During half the year he had to work all night, a practice doctors declared to be against nature; and shift work ruined his health by making him eat meals at irregular hours, and patrol in all kinds of weather, all for a miserable average wage of 30s. a week.

> All we ask is to be paid a living wage, so that we can live decently, keep our heads above water, resist temptation to do wrong, and give our wives the comforts and pleasures of other women, for many wives help their husbands to make good policemen.[2]

Letters such as these in the *Police Review* reveal widespread discontent which was not just confined to Essex policemen. The extra duties of war put increased stress on the ageing, depleted work force in Essex, and the long-awaited weekly rest day was one of the first casualties. Officers' problems were also increased by inflation. One letter writer reported buying five hundredweight of coal which had increased within a few weeks from 6s.3d. to 9s. 2d. The pay rise which had been granted was simply not enough. Young men were being advised not to join the Essex force as it was one of the worst paid in the country; even farm labourers received between three and five shillings a week more than Essex constables. 'We are living in 1915, not 1840, and fossils should move with the times, or give way to up-to-date men', wrote 'Oyez.'[3]

During the year from 1914 May 1915 only 59 members of the force from the 376 constables and 62 sergeants had been allowed to take annual leave, and many of the others were becoming stale and disillusioned. 'One of the Blues' complained to the *Police Review* that:

> everything is very dear in Essex and men with families have great trouble to pay their way and keep respectable. All round we see advances in pay ... it is time the standing joint committee should know great discontent exists in this force ... There is very little comfort in the police force, and if a man cannot have a decent home the job is not worth having. There was a time when the Essex Police was one of the best forces but now we cannot recommend it.[4]

It is easy to identify the sort of discontent which was to lead to the police strikes of 1918-19.

In April 1915 Captain John Alfred Unett became Chief Constable, as the Home Office ordered Captain Showers to retire because he was over 65. Staying just long enough to ease the new Chief Constable into the force, Raglan Somerset, deputy chief constable for 34 years, also retired on 1 September 1915. Captain Showers was reluctant to go; he issued an emotional farewell notice to all ranks in the force, referring movingly to the very long hours of work and arduous duties that all members of the force were having to perform.[5]

Colchester borough force gained from Captain Showers' enforced retirement. When war was declared Captain Hugh Charles Stockwell, Chief Constable of the borough force since 1913, wanted to rejoin his old regiment. The watch committee appointed Showers as acting Chief Constable. By the time the newly-promoted Colonel Stockwell resumed command in March 1919, the borough force had an establishment of one chief constable, one chief inspector, five inspectors, seven sergeants and 43 constables.[6] Captain Showers continued to live in Colchester after finally retiring in 1919; he died in 1925.

Soon after becoming Essex Chief Constable Captain Unett made a number of reforms. He reorganised the system of administration by introducing force orders and pocket books; he also restructured the special constabulary. Captain Unett also introduced procedures for dealing with speeding motor cars. One rudimentary method of organising a speed trap involved three constables with stopwatches over a quarter mile of road: the involved calculations needed by the officers at either end make it unlikely that many prosecutions resulted.

The needs of war made major organisational reform necessary. Each petty sessional district set up local emergency committees which were supervised overall by the Lord Lieutenant. The restructured special constabulary was given total responsibility for war duties under the supervision of a chief special constable in each petty sessional district. His rank gave him precedence over the regular force, where war duties were concerned. Regular police superintendents continued to control ordinary police divisions, and to deal with everything not connected with the war.[7]

By the autumn of 1914 approximately 6,000 volunteer special constables had been enrolled in Essex; initially they were organised by Captain Matthew Ffinch from his home at Hoe Mill near Maldon. The special constables in each parish elected their own leader who was responsible for organising their duties. These included patrolling roads, enforcing lighting regulations, and inspecting vulnerable points like telegraph posts. There were, however, no women special constables in 1914. When the question of appointing special constables was being discussed at a meeting of the standing joint committee, a member from Little Waltham commented that there was in his village: 'a very muscular lady—not an offensive term—who thought she might be of service in detecting spies'.

The councillor asked the Chief Constable's opinion about enrolling women as special constables. Captain Showers strongly objected, and to much laughter observed that he didn't want any more ladies—he had as many as he could manage. Approval was, however, given to any special constable who chose to take a lady out for a walk in the evening![8]

Not all the special constabulary leaders—usually called sergeant and corporal—were either keen or effective. George Heller at Stanway soon had enough and wanted to resign. Captain Ffinch refused to accept the resignation and wrote:

> I wish him to understand that three hours a week might by done by any man who has a spark of manliness in him when others are giving their lives for our safety, and it is his bounden duty to assist by doing the small task allotted to him ...[9]

With Essex being considered such a vulnerable county, all residents had to be alert to the possibility of spies. Special constables carried warrant cards and truncheons when on duty, and had to be observant enough to notice and question suspicious passers by, or the unusual conduct of local residents. Men with cars, cycles or horses were invited to use them for police duty, and they could be accompanied on patrol by their own dogs.[10]

The members of the standing joint committee were all in favour of help for their overworked regular officers, but it was the position of Captain Ffinch which caused both local and national controversy. Uproar was created when he was made a superintendent, and promoted to assistant chief constable for the duration of the war. Local feeling against the decision prompted letters to *Police Review*, which responded with a scathing editorial:

> We have always contended for giving the plums in the police service to those who have earned them ... and we think that military officers of high rank would have just cause for complaint if police officers, however meritorious, were transferred to high rank in the army, to the displacement of men whose military training and service had fitted them for promotion and entitled them to reward for their devotion. Is it not equally unjust to appoint soldiers to the higher posts in the police service? ... We do entirely disapprove of this military invasion of the police. Just, now, it would seem that the exceptional virtues and capacity of all trained military officers ought to be at the disposal of Lord Kitchener; but apart from this temporary emergency the system of placing soldiers in police posts when they are no longer wanted in the army is a bad one...

Two weeks later *Police Review* was obliged to apologise for not checking its facts, when Captain Ffinch was found to be a man in his fifties who was unfit for further military service after an accident.[11]

Drill was considered an important part of the special constabulary training, but not everyone thought so. To one special constable who objected, Captain Ffinch wrote:

> Drill is part of a constable's duty—all regular police have to learn it ... if only the men could be taught to understand that their efficiency and mutual self-help and confidence rely on being able to keep together, and this can only be done by drill, I think their reluctance would vanish.[12]

What did the remaining members of the regular force think about the appointment of specials in such numbers? There are hints of problems, as the Chief Constable had to remind Captain Ffinch that specials were not to report cases of irregularity to the regular police, but were to deal with complaints themselves:

> If through want of knowledge they make a mess of a case I shall simply look upon the matter as a case of instruction. I am convinced that the regular police will be ever willing to advise specials and not look down on them. I should be very sorry if the special constables got that idea into their heads. I believe in the system of giving responsibility and judging by the results.[13]

As the war progressed, the Admiralty arranged with the police to telephone to them any reports of aircraft sightings within 60 miles of London. Possible sightings were made of airships over Chelmsford on 3 and 4 January 1915, and between February and April that year bombs were dropped at Maldon and Colchester. On the night of 1 April 1916 five airships tried to reach London, one of them dropping a bomb about 200 yards from headquarters at Springfield on its return.

Later in 1916, on the night of 23/24 September, at least two Zeppelins bombing London visited Essex between 10.40 p.m. and 1.15 a.m: both crashed. Captain Unett recorded that one was brought down in flames at Burstead near Billericay:

> We watched it gradually sink through a cloud and then fall to pieces in blazing masses. It was a terrible and awful sight. Hardly had it become dark again before the telephone rang to inform me that another zeppelin had come to ground at Wigborough. I ordered the car to be ready at daybreak.

There were no survivors from the Burstead Zeppelin, and souvenir hunters flooded into the area causing major crowd control problems. The Chief Constable strongly objected to military regulations which allowed soldiers to take and sell scraps of metal to sightseers. A court of enquiry had to be convened when it was alleged that the bodies of the crew had been robbed: an iron cross, quantities of buttons and papers were missing. A 16-year-old boy who picked up a chart from the airship refused to return it, and his employer had framed and hung it on his wall before police had a chance to take it back. None of the Zeppelin's crew of 22 survived; their bodies were buried in Great Burstead churchyard on 27 September 1916.

The second Zeppelin crashed near New Hall cottages at Little Wigborough, near Colchester, bringing special constables from their beds at about 1.20 a.m. Special Constable Edgar Nicholas was cycling to the scene when he met a company of men marching towards Peldon who asked how far it was to Colchester. In his written statement Special Constable Nicholas recorded his conversation with one who spoke broken English. The German sailor wondered whether Nicholas thought the war was nearly over. 'It's over for you anyway', he retorted. 'Goot, goot', came the reply.

As the strange procession reached Peldon Hall Farm it was joined by another special named Trayler, and Sergeant Ernest Edwards from Hatfield Broad Oak who was on leave in the area. Special Constable Nicholas suggested to the sergeant that they make for Peldon post office which had a telephone. When they reached the post office Sergeant Edwards and the German commander went in to find the local regular constable, Charles Smith, trying to telephone army intelligence and police headquarters. Sergeant Edwards told the surprised constable that the German crew was outside, and asked what he was going to do with them.

Pc Smith then seems to have taken control—a fact which was later recognised by his field promotion to sergeant and the award of the merit star. Politely refusing the German

7. The night of the Zeppelins has a special place in Essex history. This contemporary sketch represents
the crew of German sailors who survived the bringing-down of Zeppelin L33 at Little Wigborough, being
led towards Colchester by Special Constable Edgar Nicholas.

commander's request to use the telephone, Smith marshalled all the other special constables
into a circle round the Germans and marched them the mile-and-a-half to Mersea Strood where
their surrender was accepted by the military authorities.

After that night the Zeppelins became part of Essex folklore. In order to mark the
occasion for those involved, a collection was made in order to present them with silver
watches. Captain Unett diplomatically thought the Billericay specials ought to be included, but
the appeal for funds in that area was not so successful. Some of the inscribed watches are still
heirlooms in the families of those who received them. At the end of the war all serving special
constables were granted a medal, and their names were illuminated on framed cards hung in
every petty sessional court: some hang there still.[14]

Captain Unett was looking forward to the end of the war, for the reduction in regular
officers had provided the opportunity to reconsider how manpower was distributed within the
force. He also convened a committee to consider such matters as labour disputes, police
housing, forming a first police reserve and the use of cars rather than horses. Some of the same
subjects were later covered at national level by the Desborough committee's investigations.

At the end of 1918 it was decided to fill the position of deputy chief constable which
had been vacant since Raglan Somerset's retirement. The advertisement appeared in February
1919 and caused an outcry within the force: with an age limit of 40, none of the 11 Essex
superintendents was eligible to apply. Only two of the applicants were serving police officers,
and there was only one local candidate: Inspector Thomas Joyce, aged 35, who had served at
headquarters for 11 years.

Joyce was promoted to superintendent, and the Chief Constable was given committee
approval to make him his deputy. However, when a large number of other senior officers
threatened to resign, Superintendent George Page was appointed as deputy chief constable
instead. Written references have been found to Superintendent Thomas Joyce acting as assistant
chief constable, but it does not seem to have been a formal appointment. Joyce retired as a
superintendent from Clacton in 1931.[15]

8. Special Constable Edgar Nicholas, wearing the duty armlet and lapel badge which represented the special constabulary uniform in the First World War.

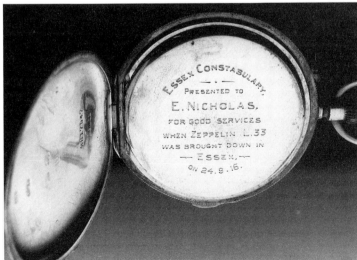

9. Public subscriptions provided pocket watches for the officers directly involved in the Zeppelin operation. This is the one presented to Edgar Nicholas.
[Photographed by courtesy of Mr. William Nicholas.]

One of the most devastating wars in English history had a permanent effect on all aspects of life. From the police point-of-view, chief constables had become accustomed to receiving directions from the Home Office; this led to regular conferences of chief constables, and to better liaison between forces. At a local level thousands of older men had served their communities by becoming special constables, and women constables had—for the first time in Essex—played a small role on the periphery of police work; this will be considered in detail in Chapter 14. But for the families of the 22 Essex and eight Southend policemen killed in action, nothing would ever be quite the same again.[16]

Notes and References
1. *Police Review*, 19 March 1915.
2. *ibid.*, 16 April 1915.
3. *ibid.*, 7 May 1915.
4. *ibid.*, 26 February 1915.
5. ERO T/P 181/17. Captain Showers appears to have been genuinely concerned with the welfare of his men. In February 1912 he was presented with a silver tea tray by the members of the force 'as a mark of high esteem and in recognition of the great interest he takes in their welfare'.
6. Colchester Watch Committee minutes.
7. Chief Special Constable for Witham Petty Sessional area was Dr. J. H. Salter of Tolleshunt D'Arcy, who later sponsored a competition cup for excellence in police duty and first aid. The Salter cup is still competed for by Essex special constables. His *Diary and Reminiscences* was edited and published by John Lane, Bodley Head, in 1933, the year after his death.
8. ERO T/P 181/17/19.
9. ERO D/Z 77.
10. ERO J/P 2/6 When police had to investigate complaints that signalling was taking place at Wrabness, it was found that the wind had made a cottage blind sway. There was such hysteria about spies that the postmistress at Little Dunmow for 23 years was reported for having 'socialistic tendencies'; police found no evidence of disloyalty.
11. *Police Review*, 4 and 18 June 1915.
12. ERO D/Z 77.
13. *ibid.*
14. *ibid.* Special Constable Nicholas's watch and Chief Special Constable Dr. Salter's arm band are on indefinite loan to the Essex Police Museum. Some of the illuminated rolls of special constables' names are also deposited there. In 1920 specials became eligible for the special constabulary long service medal, which was struck in bronze rather than the silver of the wartime medal [ERO C/MSj 4/4].
15. *Police Review*, 6 and 26 June 1919. A review of Superintendent Joyce's career when he retired, shows him to have been assistant to Captain Ffinch in administering the war-time special constabulary. He also seems to have been responsible for preparing the 65 illuminated rolls of special constables' names; the total cost was £48 8s. 6d. [C/MSj4/4]. Joyce was superintendent in charge of the Recruiting Department in 1919, and later in charge of Braintree and Clacton divisions. The jealousy of his colleagues was referred to by the chairman of Clacton bench when Joyce retired. 'I would not like to go so far as to say that the superintendent has endeared himself to everyone (laughter) for that would be adding an eighth to the existing seven wonders of the world...'
16. For the names of the officers killed in action in the First and Second World Wars, see *Roll of Honour*, published by Essex Police in 1992.

Chapter 12

Post-war Depression, 1919-1938

Police strikes 1918—Desborough Committee 1919—Post-war recruiting—Geddes' 'Axe'
and its effects—General Strike 1926— murder of Pc Gutteridge 1927—motor patrol
department—death of Captain Unett—Captain Peel becomes Chief Constable 1933—
wireless patrol cars—driving school begins 1937.

The end of the First World War did not bring stability: Britain was left with industrial, economic and social problems. Policemen had their own troubles as well; the difficulties of war-time policing had been made even worse by almost subsistence pay levels and poor working conditions in most forces. A trade union of police and prison officers in London demanded an improvement in wages but, when their demands were ignored in August 1918, many Metropolitan police officers went on strike. Despite a pay increase there was a second strike in July 1919; although fewer London officers took part, some provincial forces, particularly the Liverpool Constabulary, were badly affected.

There is little evidence that either of the strikes affected Essex police directly. Force orders printed a memo from the Home Secretary which threatened dismissal for any officer failing to report for duty, but the Chief Constable seems to have acted to remove some of the causes for discontent. Captain Unett wanted the men to be able to express their views on welfare matters without fear of recriminations, so in September 1918 all ranks were represented at the preliminary meeting of a new representative council. There were three superintendents and four inspectors, with one sergeant and two constables chosen by their colleagues from each division. Plans were made to have a committee in each division, with a regular general meeting being held at headquarters. The first general committee meeting met in January 1919 when various matters were discussed, including the promotion system, a new style of great coat, a memorial fund, pensions, and allowances. Also on the agenda was a suggestion that everyone in the force should wear uniform caps, with helmets being worn only on special occasions.

One effect of the second police strike was a national enquiry into police conditions. Lord Desborough's committee reported promptly, making a number of recommendations which included substantial pay rises. Many of the other proposals were soon incorporated into the Police Act of 1919 which perceived policing for the first time as an integrated service. Standard pay and conditions throughout the country were recommended—rather than the old system of each force making its own regulations. There was to be a police council, with consultation between the Home Secretary, the police authorities, and representatives from all ranks. Consultation between ranks lower than superintendent was provided for by the setting-up of the Police Federation. Police officers were forbidden to join a trade union, but members of the federation were allowed to bring to official notice 'all matters affecting their welfare and efficiency'.[1]

Police regulations and conditions of service were standardised by the Police Act of 1919, and officers were entitled to receive rent free accommodation or an allowance in lieu. Many counties—including Essex—did not like losing their freedom to decide police wages and conditions, and there were moves by some police authorities to go against the Desborough recommendations.

In Essex, police pay had been related to the wages of agricultural labourers, and unskilled workers like road men. The County Architect undertook an investigation into the housing of police and road men: the two occupations were considered together because both needed to live in rural areas where housing was in particularly short supply.[2] Accommodation for policemen had long been a problem. As the war was drawing to an end Captain Unett issued a force order laying out his proposals for moving men around. After a course at headquarters, recruits would be sworn-in and posted to a divisional station where they might expect to stay for at least four years: senior constables and sergeants' postings would be at least six years in any place, those of inspectors from five to seven years, and superintendents from six to eight years. After such periods all ranks could expect to move, but normally only between October and March. Any man who wanted to marry was advised to find a house first, and then ask to work at a station nearby: nothing could be guaranteed because of the shortage of houses. Policemen returning from war service—and new recruits—were often left to find lodgings wherever they could, sometimes at a considerable distance from their wives and families.

A shortage of post-war housing had been predicted by Captain Unett almost as soon as he became Chief Constable in 1915, and the standing joint committee had authorised him to buy any suitable houses which came on the market. Nevertheless, in 1920, 241 sergeants and constables were still obliged to rent their own houses, while only 15 lived in houses hired for them by the county.[3]

Fred Joslin (born in 1896) was one of 21 men who joined the force as soon as recruiting was resumed in June 1919. He had experienced all the horrors of war, including fighting at Gallipoli where he was wounded, his family being told he had died. After leaving the army Fred Joslin thought it seemed better to join the police rather than try to settle back into the life of a farm worker. He was posted to Romford, a divisional station from 1916, and lived in single men's quarters at the station where there was a resident housekeeper who cooked meals for the young men. At the end of his probation Fred Joslin applied for permission to marry and considered himself lucky to be posted to Hadleigh, where he and his new wife were able to rent half a house as their first home.[4]

A second officer, Harry Salmon (born in 1895), had also intended to join the Essex Constabulary after army service. He was on the way to Colchester railway station from his father's shop in Magdalen Street, when he decided to call at the headquarters of the borough police in the town hall. A chief inspector named Simpson told him there were many vacancies in the town, and suggested he see the acting Chief Constable, Captain Showers—'a homely sort of man'. Harry Salmon joined the borough force two days later.[5]

At the end of the war a government of national unity looked at various ways of getting Britain out of its post-war economic problems. In 1922 a committee was set up under Sir Eric Geddes to investigate ways of controlling public expenditure; the recommendations soon earned the committee the title of 'Geddes' Axe'. Expenditure was drastically cut on education, police, unemployment benefit, the civil service and the military. Electing a Labour government in 1924 made no difference: the cuts continued, and many of Desborough's more expensive proposals for the police were shelved.

The newly-established Police Federation objected strongly but without much effect. Some counties considered abolishing the pay rises given under Desborough as their contributions to economy, but the Home Office wanted much more: police manpower had to be reduced. No Essex officer was actually dismissed, as Captain Unett had decided that the force needed a minimum of 485 men to function effectively at the height of the summer season. No further recruiting was allowed, and the 25 recruits then under training were retained as reserves who could be moved around wherever they were needed.

The economies continued into 1925—just one example being that the small number of recruits then allowed were paid at civilian rates until they were sworn-in, because it saved £1 a week on each officer. Civilianisation was another recommended economy; clerks and civilian chauffeurs were appointed, except at headquarters where the chauffeur's job was still done by a policeman. Rent allowances were reduced for everyone.[6]

Shortages in manpower during the twenties led to numerous complaints about the lack of police attention, particularly from the developing areas of Upminster, South Weald and Romford. Special constables were appointed for large events, because there were not enough policemen. At Romford complaints arose from a demonstration which could too easily have provoked violence. About 2,000 unemployed men from Barking and Ilford marched towards

10. Mounted officers of the Colchester Borough Police under the direction of Sergeant Wynn, assembled outside Colchester Castle c.1910. The force did not maintain a permanent mounted section, but for ceremonial occasions borrowed horses from the army or hired them. The inspecting officer is believed to be Mr. S. R. Midgley, Chief Constable.

Romford on 17 October 1922. They intended to try to persuade the Poor Law Guardians to increase their poor relief from 9s. a week, or to provide work. At the boundary with the Metropolitan Police district, they joined a group of Romford men who were escorted by three Essex officers.

Earlier peaceful demonstrations had taken place without the need for police intervention, so Inspector Frank Hyde had made no contingency plans and his men were overpowered. The Guardians refused to speak to the deputation, so the men imprisoned them in their offices. Captain Unett himself motored to Romford, persuaded the Guardians to receive the deputation of unemployed men, and the crowds dispersed. It was later decided to allow unemployed men in Romford and Ilford to claim poor relief at the higher rates given by the Metropolitan workhouse unions.[7]

The force bought its own car in 1916, and by 1922 cars were increasingly used, although horses and carts still had their place: those at Witham police station, for example, were not sold until May 1923. Occasional prosecutions for motoring offences were reported in local newspapers, e.g. in the *Essex Chronicle* for 15 September 1922 when a law student was summoned for driving at an excessive speed at Witham. Pc Reader gave evidence that the offender had driven at 30m.p.h., and when signalled to stop had carried on for another 30 yards. The defendant insisted he was only going at 12 m.p.h., and had asked people on the path to confirm his speed. Not liking their replies, he told them they were fools and as ignorant as country coppers. The magistrates found the driver guilty and fined him £2.

The general strike in May 1926 was a symptom of the discontent which still existed throughout the country. Miners went on strike rather than accept reductions in pay, and the Trades Union Congress organised strikes by other key workers in sympathy with them. Trains ceased running, there was no postal service, and pickets appeared in the Grays docks to stop lorries entering Thames Haven and Purfleet. Government mails were delivered to headquarters every day by road from London, and motor cyclists distributed them throughout the rest of the county. From 3-10 May the Grays area was reinforced by an inspector, four sergeants and 46 constables. When some workers decided to return to work they needed police protection, and three more sergeants and another 42 constables were sent to Grays to patrol roads, and escort wagons in and out of the docks. With the force still short of manpower, special constables replaced the regular officers who were sent to Grays; others found themselves compulsorily employed on policing the pickets.[8]

Basic training for police recruits at that time consisted of lectures on police duty and scripture during the day, plus practical work with an experienced constable in the evenings. When Cliff Hymas joined the force in March 1926 he found some of his practical work involved being sent to Grays to help police the strikers. The recruits travelled in a canvas covered lorry, and were billeted in a hotel near the docks. Convoys leaving the docks had to be escorted, but the dockers disliked the special constables who usually performed such duties, and considered them to be blacklegs. One group of recruits acting as convoy escorts was bombarded by dockers, who thought they were throwing things at the special constables. When they found it was not the case, they went the next day to apologise to the recruits.[9]

As the numbers of motor cars gradually increased, criminals as well as police officers began to make more use of them. The brutal murder of an Essex constable in September 1927 shocked both the force and many people in the country. The general facts of George Gutteridge's death are well-known, because of the horrific nature of the murder, and because of the way in which ballistic evidence was used to identify the weapon which killed him. The case has been the subject of many books and articles, and many radio and television programmes.

In the early hours of 27 September 1927 Pc Gutteridge, aged 38, left the house rented for him at 2 Towneley Cottages, Stapleford Abbotts, where he lived with his wife Rose and children Muriel, 11, and Alfred four. He was scheduled for foot patrol, which involved making a conference point at about 3.30 a.m. with Sidney Taylor, the constable on the adjoining beat.

Much later on it was discovered that Pc Gutteridge had stopped a Morris Cowley car, TW 6120, on the remote road between Stapleford Abbotts and Abridge, and had been shot in the head. Horrifying as that was, it was the additional shots through each of his eyes which caused the unusually strong revulsion that was felt by many members of the public. The car, which had been stolen from Dr. Edmund Lovell's house at Billericay, was later found abandoned in London. Because of the complexity of the case, and the London involvement, the Chief Constable called in the Metropolitan Police to take charge of investigations.

Chief Inspector James Berrett was the Metropolitan detective appointed to work closely with Essex officers. After enquiries lasting several months, Frederick Guy Browne and William Henry Kennedy were eventually traced, tried and convicted of murder—both were hanged. In Captain Unett's letter of thanks to the Metropolitan Police he referred to the thoroughness and foresight of all the officers concerned, commenting that the circumstances and enquiries relating to Pc Gutteridge's murder would provide 'a measure of instruction in detective work which will bear good fruit for many years to come'.[10]

What happened to Pc Gutteridge's family? Muriel was born while her father was stationed at Grays; she remembered her family being better off than some of the families of her friends. She had toys, proper shoes, pretty dresses and a piano; her father also had a motor cycle and side car which was used for family outings. A policeman's family was looked up to, and the children were expected to be well-behaved. After her husband's murder Mrs. Rose Gutteridge was given a widow's pension of £78 4s. 3d. a year—one third of what her husband would have earned in a year. Allowances of £15 12s. 10d. a year were also granted for each of the children, and money was also donated by colleagues and members of the public. The force found it difficult to re-house the family, and Mrs. Gutteridge resisted suggestions that the children might be better off in the police orphanage. Eventually a new policeman was appointed for the village. Because of the housing shortages Pc Robert Merchant and his wife Frances had to move into Towneley Cottages with Mrs. Gutteridge and her children; life was difficult for both families. Mrs. Gutteridge's brother-in-law, Pc Frank Meadows, found two rooms for them near his own station at Braintree, and the Gutteridge family lived there for about a year before getting a council flat in Dagenham.[11]

Massive publicity was given to the whole case, but the inquest on Pc Gutteridge revealed some wide-ranging communications problems. The policeman's body had been found at the roadside by William Alec Ward, a mail van driver, who had driven to Stapleford Tawney post office to telephone for an ambulance. Romford police station refused to accept the call as Pc Gutteridge was not stationed there; they asked Ward to ring the police at Ongar. When the operator demanded payment of five pennies (about 2p) for the emergency call, the postmistress had to intervene in the ensuing argument: much time had therefore been wasted.[12]

The *Essex Weekly News* began a local campaign for better telephone facilities in rural areas; such moves were also being encouraged by the National Federation of Women's Institutes. The *Weekly News* reporter interviewed Captain Unett, who said that 39 police stations had telephones, including most of the sergeants' stations; but that all the telephones in the world would not have prevented Pc Gutteridge from being murdered. Many rural police houses were not owned by the county, and the Chief Constable did not think it practicable to install a telephone in every one; he could see the need for a public telephone in every village, but not necessarily at the police house.

The *Essex Weekly News* campaign to increase the numbers of telephones in rural areas encouraged the AA and the RAC to provide police with keys to their call boxes, then being installed on increasingly busy roads, like the A12 and A13. The Road Traffic Act of 1930 created new offences and introduced a 30 m.p.h. speed limit. In October 1930 force orders advertised for 12 constables to constitute a motor car and motor cycle patrol section. The men were to supervise road traffic and detect crime. Because motor cycles were still regarded as unreliable machines, applicants had to be single, and undertake not to marry for two years; they also had to be expert drivers or motor cyclists. The Chief Constable was asked to be very careful over who was selected for motor patrol duties; they needed to be diplomatic individuals who would inevitably come into contact with people of all classes.

The motor cycle patrol officers were available for duties anywhere in the county, and its members took turns at being on call at night. Ernest Keeble patrolled the A13 in much the same uniform as he wore to walk the beat.[13] Cliff Hymas was turned down on his first application because he was married, but was later to become a long-standing member of the section. At first officers received allowances for the use of their own machines, but by 1931 it was costing the force around £30 a week in mileage expenses for what had become known as 'courtesy patrols'. The Home Office was willing to meet some of the expenses, but only where a force owned its own machines. Captain Unett was therefore authorised to buy 10 solo Triumph motor cycles for patrol work, and two Ford and Humber open-topped tourer cars, one for Romford and the other for Grays.[14]

In 1931 and 1932 the British economy was still under strain, and a National Coalition government ordered more cuts in the pay of public servants. Essex could not afford to recruit any men, but those forces which did were only allowed to pay 55s. a week; the probationary period was also extended to two years. Superintendents and above had their pay reduced by 10 per cent in two stages; every one else had two wage deductions. The first cut in September 1931 stopped five shillings a week from a constable's average pay of between £3 14s. and £4 4s.; sergeants lost 6s. 3d. from their weekly wage of between £5 2s. 6d. and £5 10s.[15] Further deductions were made the following year.

Stress on the Chief Constable must have been considerable, and Captain Unett suffered from increasing illness which caused his death in office on 6 December 1932. During his long illness Captain Unett became aware that his savings had depreciated, and that he did not have enough service for a police pension. He wrote a touching letter to the standing joint committee asking them to remember all the welfare work his wife had done within the force—Mrs. Unett was awarded a gratuity.

The new Chief Constable, Captain Francis Jonathan Peel, was the first in the force to have walked the beat as a constable. The 35-year-old Chief Constable had a service background like all his predecessors, but joined the Liverpool City Police in 1920, quickly moving up through the ranks before becoming Chief Constable of Bath in 1931.

By the time Captain Peel had taken stock of his new command some of the financial restrictions had eased. Ever since the force began, one of the divisional superintendents had also acted as deputy chief constable; it was a position rather than a rank. Sometimes a deputy had also been described as an assistant chief constable, as in the case of George Page in 1919, but Captain Peel wanted his deputy to hold the permanent rank of assistant chief constable and have no divisional responsibilities. His request was granted, and Superintendent John Crockford left the Romford division in 1933 to become the first holder in the force of the permanent rank of assistant chief constable.[16]

A new Road Traffic Act passed in 1934 gave police the responsibility for enforcing speed limits in built-up areas. Because the pre-1930 legislation had not been enforced adequately, the Home Office wanted the Act strictly enforced from the start, so more man-power was needed. Because of all the financial restrictions, there were not enough policemen or vehicles in Essex to do the job properly. The Home Office therefore sanctioned the appoint-ment of one extra inspector, three sergeants and 34 constables, and were so keen to increase the number of police vehicles that for some time officers with their own cars were again offered an allowance to use them on patrol. The Chief Constable's Report for 1935 refers to the increasing amount of work in connection with road traffic; about three per cent of manpower was then involved in motor patrols.

11. John Crockford, appointed as the first permanent assistant chief constable in Essex in 1935; he retired in 1953.

Better roads out of London, and the growth of sprawling suburbs, made it easy for London-based criminals in cars to commit crimes in Essex. In May 1932 motor patrols were placed under the control of George (known as Harry) Totterdell, first holder of the rank of detective superintendent in the force. Motor vehicles and crime investigation were treated equally, and the 'speed cops' had daily patrols which allowed them to visit every police station and police house, delivering dispatches relating to crimes that had occurred during the preceding 12 hours. Totterdell organised frequent checks of vehicles on main roads; theatregoers or businessmen soon passed through these road blocks, but those who chose not to account for their actions were followed by members of the mobile section. In one week alone 23 identified criminals were arrested in possession of stolen cars or house-breaking implements.[17]

Following the report of a Home Office committee of enquiry into detective work, much higher priority was given to training detectives, and the use of scientific apparatus and communications. National training schemes were set up, and were funded as common police services: half being paid by the Home Office, and the remainder by forces which contributed in proportion to the size of their establishments.

Dick Coe joined the force in February 1935 and spent the early part of his service at Grays. He had served a five-year motor engineering apprenticeship, so relished the chance to work on motor car duties after passing a strict driving test. Motor cycles were now being used on patrol less frequently, as they had been involved in too many accidents. The first two Essex wireless cars were taken into use in May 1936, and Dick Coe found himself posted

HE'S A BACHELOR.—Only unmarried policemen are eligible as recruits for the motor-cycle patrol formed by the Essex Constabulary to enforce the new traffic laws. Moreover, the men are required to remain single for two years. Here is one of them questioning a motorist. They are provided with high-speed machines.

12.   Ernest Keeble (ex Pc 276) was one of the earliest members of the motor cycle section formed in 1930. With a colleague he patrolled the A13 between the Metropolitan Police boundary at Beam Bridge and the end of the Stanford-le-Hope bypass. This photograph was taken at Dovers Court, Rainham on 2 December 1930.

to Brentwood to cover the work of an established traffic officer being trained as a wireless operator by the Metropolitan Police.

The Metropolitan radio network at Scotland Yard covered part of Essex. Urgent messages—such as stolen vehicles—could be telephoned to the Yard from whence they were transmitted by morse code to the nearest radio car: acknowledgements could only be made by telephone. The first two Essex radio cars patrolled the divisions where signals could be received; the rest of the county had patrol cars without wireless. Two-way radio was not possible in Essex until after the Second World War.[18]

A government priority in the late 1930s was to increase the regulation of road traffic, and Essex, Lancashire, Cheshire, and London were four forces chosen by the Home Office to take part in an experimental scheme for providing additional motor patrols; they were later nicknamed 'courtesy cops'. The purpose of the scheme was persuasion rather than prosecution; policemen were to be trained to drive in such a way that they set an example to other road users, and encouraged higher standards of road behaviour.

To achieve such objectives specialist training was needed. In May 1937 two Essex officers were sent to the Metropolitan Police driving school to be trained as advanced driving instructors under Lord Cottenham, a former racing driver. Having qualified, they had to teach their skills to colleagues at the force driving school, then based at the old police station in Guithavon Street, Witham. One of the first instructors, Inspector Eric Postons, received the merit badge in June 1938 for his 'exceptional ability and initiative in organising the advanced wing of the driving school'.

The Home Office financed the advanced driving scheme which was launched nationally on 1 April 1938. Eight different types of car were provided, plus two for teaching skidding. Plans were being made for a new driving school building, but they were destined to be delayed. The whole scheme was closed down at the start of Second World War.

Notes and References

1. Stead, *The Police of Britain*, published 1985, p.76.
2. ERO Q/APp 14. Between 1919-1923 26 and 28 Coronation Avenue and 100 and 102 Victoria Street Braintree, 39 Arbour Lane Chelmsford, 69-73 Kings Road Halstead, 2 Raymead Villas West Mersea, 2 Hall Cottages Wickford, and 1 cottage at Copford were purchased. In 1920 12 houses were built at Cromwell Road in Grays. When the County Architect surveyed the 12 divisions in the force there were 27 sets of married quarters for inspectors and above; 36 for married sergeants and constables, and 78 for single constables. The force was then 146 below its authorised establishment of 466.
3. *ibid*.
4. Taped interview with Fred Joslin in 1991. He died in November 1992.
5. Taped interview with Harry Salmon, carried out by the 'Colchester Recalled' project.
6. ERO C/MSj 4.
7. *Essex Chronicle,* 2 October 1922.
8. *Essex Chronicle*, 13 May 1926.
9. Taped interview with Cliff Hymas in April 1991.
10. *When I was at Scotland Yard*: autobiography of Chief Inspector James Berrett, p. 25.
11. Taped interview with Muriel Alexander, née Gutteridge, May 1991; and force personnel records. John Alexander, the boy who eventually became her husband, lived next door to the Gutteridge family in Towneley Cottages. Pc Robert Merchant who took over the Stapleford Abbotts beat had a somewhat chequered career. In November 1929 he saw four men changing the wheel on a car in London Road, Grays, and realised that the car had been stolen in London two days earlier. In attempting to arrest the driver he was violently assaulted. Two of the four were arrested by Merchant, who was awarded the KPM in 1930.
12. Government licences to construct telephone lines had been issued originally to small local companies, but by 1890 most had been absorbed into the National Telephone Company. Post Office policy did not encourage the concept of telephones as part of a public service until well into the 1930s. The 999 emergency system was introduced in London in 1937 after a serious fire in Wimpole Street resulted in calls jamming the switchboard of the local exchange: there was no way at that stage of distinguishing which calls were urgent. The first telephone kiosks were built after 1924, mostly in profitable town areas; few were built in country districts until after 1935. An emergency button was provided for those not having a dialling facility (British Telecom Museum and *Person to Person* by Peter Young, published 1991 by Granta).
13. Letter to the author dated 8 July 1992.
14. ERO C/MSj 4.
15. *ibid*.
16. *ibid*. Appointments as assistant chief constable had previously been made on an occasional basis, e.g. George Page between 1919 and 1921. The permanent position of assistant chief constable was not then considered necessary until John Crockford was appointed in 1933.
17. Chief Constable's printed report for 1935.
18. Taped interview with Dick Coe in August 1991.

Chapter 13

Another War and its Effects, 1939-1969

Second World War—bombs at HQ—new training methods—Colchester borough amalgamated 1947—better communications—1953 floods—new towns—mobile columns—1964 Police Act—John Nightingale becomes Chief Constable—Romford transferred to the Met. Police 1965—university education—Regional Crime Squads 1965—Southend borough amalgamated with Essex 1969.

Conflicts throughout Europe during the 1930s suggested the likelihood of another war, and after devastating incidents in the Spanish Civil War the Home Office began running courses on air raid precautions in April 1936. Most forces sent a man to be trained as instructor: and he in turn trained his colleagues. It took two years for Inspector George Hodges to train everyone in the Essex Constabulary; after war was declared on 3 September 1939, a crash course of refresher training was carried out, with an emphasis on fire fighting and dealing with explosives.

Policemen were soon conscripted for military service, and within three months of war being declared Essex had lost more than 100 of its police officers. War duties and manpower were too important to be left to the discretion of individual chief constables, and the Home Office took direct responsibility for ensuring that every force had sufficient staff. Several different types of auxiliary were recruited, ranging from full-time war reserves and special constables, to women and boys. Each force was also required to enrol and supervise air raid wardens and local defence volunteers. The title of the latter group was later changed to the Home Guard:—it is better known to later generations as 'Dad's Army'.[1]

Ronald Shayshutt—then a 16-year-old living in Grays—joined the Police Messenger Auxiliary Service. These auxiliaries were boys willing to use their own bicycles for carrying messages if the telephone service failed. Each boy had a lapel badge inscribed PMAS and, although they received first aid and anti-gas training, their main rôle soon became that of fire watchers.[2]

In 1941 a school was opened at police headquarters to train auxiliaries from Essex and neighbouring counties in police work, civil defence and first aid. One of the women auxiliaries, Florence Smith, was an experienced first aider who was later given the job of teaching the subject. With the assistance of a skeleton named Enoch, and a friendly butcher who supplied sausage skins and bones, her practical sessions were especially realistic. It was something of a novelty to have a woman instructor, and to make sure that the men were behaving themselves the officer-in-charge listened at the door while her lessons were taking place.[3]

70

Civilian clerks and telephone operators were appointed at headquarters and divisional stations to help co-ordinate the police response to air raids. As the only woman auxiliary at Epping, Joan Hurley often had to cycle to the police station in complete darkness because of the blackout regulations; her principal duty was to take most of the telephone calls during an air raid. As bombing in Essex grew more frequent, Captain Peel started a daily police bulletin which listed the latest reports of bombing incidents throughout the county.[4]

The docks around Grays and Tilbury were particularly vulnerable, and two sergeants and a squad of constables from Nottingham were drafted in to help patrol them. Ernest Keeble, then chauffeur to Superintendent Ernest Marriage, remembered the Nottingham men being billeted in the old police station at Tilbury; former sergeant Ralph Jones, then stationed at Tilbury, remembers their farewell dinner in the Oddfellows Hall at Grays.[5] Police headquarters also seemed a likely place to be attacked by German paratroopers, and a permanent armed guard of one sergeant and two acting sergeants was supplemented by traffic officers. As a traffic man, Dick Coe took his turn at the 24-hour guard duties. When things were quiet, one man patrolled the front of the buildings and the other stayed at the back. Numbers were doubled for a bombing alert; and in addition someone had to go onto the roof to identify aircraft.

The year 1940 saw a good deal of bombing throughout the county. Just before midnight on 30 April a German Heinkel bomber crashed into a house at the junction of Skelmersdale Road and Victoria Road in Clacton. Magnetic mines the plane was carrying were released, and the crew was killed by the explosion which followed several minutes later. There were at least 106 other recorded casualties, and two deaths amongst people living in the area. About 67 houses were destroyed, and 170 more were damaged. Inspector Sidney Smy was later commended for the able manner in which he controlled police involvement in the whole incident.[6]

Chelmsford was bombed on many occasions, at least two of the incidents directly affecting police headquarters. On 19 August 1940 the police house at 20 Gainsborough Crescent received a direct hit. The house was occupied by Sergeant Albert (Ted) Oakley, brother-in-law to the Detective Superintendent George Totterdell. Ted Oakley and his son Gordon escaped injury, but the blast killed his wife, their 10-year-old daughter, and his sister who had been visiting them.[7] The Chief Constable's house was also damaged in the attack, and further damage was caused when on 16 November 15 high explosive bombs fell in the Springfield area. Six of the bombs fell in the grounds of police headquarters, and two policemen were killed: Pc Alexander Scott who was the duty traffic man, and Pc Maurice Lee, an interpreter attached to CID.[8]

The strains of war made a pleasant social life even more important. Musical evenings and amateur dramatics flourished at headquarters, and in 1942 Sergeant Ken Watson was prime mover in forming the first official Essex police dance band—'The Peelers'. While the war lasted, routine administrative work was cut to the minimum; partly because there were more urgent jobs to do, but also because of the paper shortage; the backs of older documents were often used to make carbon copies of letters and reports. It was not considered appropriate to mark the centenary of the force in February 1940: that had to wait for another 50 years!

Road safety was an urgent priority. Despite lack of petrol there were still many road accidents, and the effects of the blackout must have made matters worse; large numbers of people were still being killed and injured on roads.[9] It was not until 1946 that a road safety department was formed at headquarters, and police officers were encouraged to visit schools and youth organisations, as they had done more informally before the war.

The Home Office anticipated a large number of recruits to police forces when the war ended, and many plans were made for their training. There were recruiting campaigns amongst servicemen, and Essex organised a postal course on law and procedure for men returning from military service. Ronald Shayshutt was in India with the army when he saw a circular which referred to a commission of chief constables being in Rangoon, to interview suitable candidates for the English police. Having been a boy messenger in Grays he had decided on the police as a career, preferably in the Essex force. After making the long journey to Rangoon to be interviewed, he was accepted and, returning to England in 1946, was posted to Romford.[10]

It was no longer considered adequate to train recruits on the job. Now all police recruits were to be sent on a 13 week course to one of the residential training centres set up in each region. Eynsham Hall near Oxford was the training centre for Essex recruits, and instructors were drawn from forces all over the region: among the first was Inspector Stanley Barnicoat from Colchester Borough Police.[11]

The introduction of English methods of policing in the forces of former enemy countries was also part of Home Office planning, in consultation with other government agencies. Towards the end of the war, volunteers from English police forces were asked to work in Germany and Malaya. Some inspectors from Essex went to Germany with army ranks as members of the Control Commission. They included Ralph Hagger, Leonard Murray, Roland Barnard, Sidney Smy, and Bill Warricker; Ralph Hagger and Sidney Smy were both promoted to the rank of major.

Before the war began some small police forces in seaside areas were compulsorily amalgamated. Their chief constables were told that this was only temporary but, when the experiment was found to be successful, the post-war Labour government decided to make these amalgamations permanent, and to implement others.[12] The resulting Police Act of 1946 compelled borough forces in towns with less than 100,000 people to amalgamate with neighbouring county forces.

Colchester came into that category and, when Joseph Baker joined the Colchester borough police in August 1946, he was one of its last recruits. There was a waiting list for training at Eynsham Hall, so he spent his time reading *Moriarty's Police Law* and being introduced to the technicalities of working a beat. In practice that meant spending a lot of time on point duty at the top of North Hill. A few days after returning from Eynsham Hall, there was a ceremonial parade to mark the ending of Colchester's independence as a borough force. On 1 April 1947, Lieutenant Colonel Hugh Stockwell retired as Chief Constable, and Colchester became part of the Essex Constabulary. Superintendent Harold Phillibrown took charge of the new division and, while there was a certain amount of resentment from older borough officers, the new superintendent's diplomacy ensured that everyone worked together to make the amalgamation a success.[13]

Police pay and conditions had not kept pace with those of other occupations, so in 1948 the government set up a committee chaired by Lord Oaksey to investigate. It reported in two stages the following year, but its numerous recommendations on recruiting and pay scales do not seem to have made any impact on problems in Essex where the force was almost 200 below its authorised establishment of 989 men, and only had 13 of the permitted 23 women.

In the aftermath of war, burglary rates soared. A programme of crime prevention advice was introduced, and improvements were made in communications. In 1948 the force wireless scheme began, with a main transmitter at headquarters, opened in September; a

13.   The end of the Second World War saw an increase in the number of burglaries. Night-time checks of vehicles became more common, and this photograph was believed to have been taken near Sun Corner, Billericay, in about 1947. The sergeant on the left is Kenneth Alston.

second came into use at Great Bromley in December. The central Information Room was set up to receive and distribute messages, and the new communications department provided technical and administrative backup. Twenty-six police cars were fitted with two-way wireless, and a new patrol scheme began. Each territorial division was patrolled every night by an area car driven by a specially trained driver. As a welcome change from foot or cycle patrol, each rural beat officer took it in turns to act as observer when the car was in his part of the division; the occasional mobile duties were anticipated with pleasure.[14]

The year 1953 is remembered not only for the coronation of Queen Elizabeth II and the conquest of Mount Everest, but also for the major flood disaster on the night of 31 January which made more than 21,000 people homeless, and killed 119. The disaster was caused by freak weather conditions which led to massive high tides; sea walls along the whole Essex coast were breached, and substantial parts of the county were flooded.

The emergency began just before 10 p.m. on Saturday 31 January 1953 when the Harwich harbour master called at the police station to say that an exceptionally high tide was expected, and he thought there would be some flooding. Within 15 minutes the tide was starting to cover Harwich quay. Officers at Harwich telephoned Clacton and headquarters to warn other police stations that might be affected, which included Southend, Canvey Island and Grays.[15]

In the headquarters of the borough force the alarm on Southend pier rang at 11.37 p.m. This indicated that the tide had already reached 21 feet above high water, and the BBC was asked to broadcast a flood warning on the midnight news. By 3 a.m. parts of Grays were flooded, and two-thirds of Canvey Island was under water.

Further up the coast the Clacton superintendent, Arthur Simpson, and the newly-promoted Chief Inspector Kenneth Alston were trying to get to Harwich to see what was happening. Their car ran into a five-feet-high bank of water across the road, and both men and their driver got soaked while trying to push the car free. When they returned to Clacton, Superintendent Simpson decided to stay there, to supervise what was obviously going to be a major operation. Kenneth Alston went back to his old station, where he was able to use his local knowledge to help Inspector Norman Wood, his successor there. They found Harwich under water from the quay to the police station, and with hundreds of people needing to be rescued and cared for.[16]

At first each community was only aware of its own problems. It was some time before the whole picture became clear: flooding extended along the whole Essex coast from Harwich to West Ham. On night duty the Information Room staff was normally scaled down, and at that time, between 2 a.m. and 4 a.m, consisted only of Sergeant Edward Greenland with two constables, reduced further to the sergeant and one constable between 4 a.m. and 6 a.m. Between them they had to handle the teleprinter, telephone switchboard and radio which could only send out one message at a time. As the emergency developed, an extra teleprinter and extra telephone lines were installed.[17]

14.   At the height of the floods in 1953, police officers found themselves obliged to perform unusual duties. These two were rowing around the flooded roads of Jaywick helping to rescue stranded householders.

For an emergency on such a scale, the county force needed far more policemen than were then available. Under the mutual aid scheme, Hertfordshire sent officers to help at Clacton, while the Metropolitan Police provided a sergeant and nine constables for every shift at Tilbury until 10 March. Men of the Metropolitan Police Special Branch at Parkeston Quay were involved in taking details of the homeless. Within an hour of Southend borough police being asked for help, an inspector and seven constables were at work helping to evacuate Canvey Island. The Southend force provided a sergeant and 12 constables for policing Canvey every day for the next month, and those officers did not forget the intense cold and wind, and the shock of seeing so much water in a residential area.[18]

Such a major incident involved a lot of police time and effort beyond the normal call of duty. Several policemen were commended for their good work in the Coronation Honours list, including Inspector Norman Wood at Harwich, and Sergeant William Howes at Canvey; for his rescue work Special Constable Joseph Batchelor received the British Empire Medal. When the full extent of modest 20-year-old Constable Donald Harmer's bravery became known, it was recognised by the award of the British Empire Medal for Brave Conduct.

On the night of 31 January 1953 Pc Donald Harmer (later a chief inspector) had already spent two hours on foot patrol in Clacton, trying to secure shop blinds that were being blown down by the force of the wind. He was then told to accompany Inspector Stanley Barnicoat and Pc Joe Burgess in a patrol car to Jaywick, a holiday area about two miles from Clacton; riding in a police car was something of a novelty in those days, and Pc Harmer had never been right into Jaywick before: 'Jaywick was mostly wooden bungalows on stilts, and it didn't take long before the rows of buildings started to get up and walk about. There were houses everywhere ... and it was pitch black without any sort of street lighting'. As the crew was taking the Jaywick postman and his wife to safety the car 'suddenly reared up into the air, and when it came down the windows were covered by water'. Managing to escape, the officers took shelter in a local cafe, which rapidly became a refuge for around 300 soaked and weary homeless people. Soon the three policemen needed more help, and Donald Harmer found himself volunteering to give the station at Clacton a situation report. With all roads flooded, the only way he could do so was to get onto the sea wall. Battling against the freezing cold, gale force winds and waves the managed to cling onto the brick work of the sea wall and crawl towards the first martello tower at Clacton, not appreciating that there was more than a mile between that and the second one, which had a telephone kiosk nearby. Reporting the situation to Clacton police station he was then told to go back to the inspector. 'I was only 20', he recalled, 'and if you were given a job to do you just did it. When I got back to Jaywick they said "fancy coming all this way back". I thought that was what I was supposed to do!'

After being dried off, Donald Harmer rejoined the rescue attempts and recovery of bodies that was going on in Jaywick but, when released from duty many hours later, collapsed in the street when he tried to walk back to his lodgings in Clacton. A member of the public rang Clacton police to say that one of their drunken officers needed help![19]

As a postscript to the floods, the official report of Superintendent Arthur Simpson included a touch of black humour. He described how Sergeant Wilfred Savill had recovered a dead body at Jaywick. On the table in the man's house was the book he had been reading—*The Cruel Sea*.[20]

Although some of the flood victims were homeless for months, most were eventually rehoused: police officers were not always so lucky. Some police houses had been built, and one or two new stations, but there were still officers who had to find lodgings near their places of work while their wives and families lived elsewhere, sometimes many miles away.

In 1955 there was a national reduction in police working hours from 48 to 44 a week. In theory it meant officers then had three rest days each fortnight, but because the force was still drastically under strength the extra rest day had to be worked and paid for as overtime. This practice continued for more than 20 years.

Even more policemen were needed after the government decided in the late 1940s to draw residents away from overcrowded London by building new towns. Basildon new town absorbed seven historic parishes, to become home to around 250,000 people. Harlow was centred on a small medieval market town, with neighbourhood clusters based on existing rural parishes. Both new towns needed police stations and officers to man them: the latter were still in short supply throughout the 1950s.

Despite the shortages in manpower, most serious crime in Essex was eventually solved, although one unsolved murder from 1958 still arouses journalistic interest.[21] Mary Kriek was a 19-year-old Dutch girl, working at a farm at Eight Ash Green near Colchester. After a weekend in London with a friend, Mary was last seen getting off a bus near her place of work at 10.45 p.m. on 5 January 1958: the next morning her dead body was found 12 miles away at Boxted. The murderer has never been found.

Another sort of crime also aroused considerable media interest. Criminals travelling in stolen cars were believed to be using explosives to open safes in a series of burglaries all over Essex. One Sunday in 1958 it was decided to put all available police manpower onto main roads to make checks on every car and its occupants. The media publicised the road checks, and Detective Superintendent Jack Barkway was believed to have been the first serving officer to appear live on television in a programme which discussed the ethics of the whole operation.[22]

The threat of nuclear conflict was a new hazard after the Second World War. All sorts of plans were in operation for civil defence, and each force had to provide training for its officers. One national scheme was concerned with organising a 'mobile column' of police officers in special vehicles which could be deployed wherever they were needed. For two weeks in April 1960, policemen and vehicles took part in an exercise at Fingringhoe army camp. Officers from Essex, Hertfordshire, Norfolk and Suffolk lived under military conditions, and learned how to cook in field kitchens and set up mobile communications. They travelled around East Anglia taking part in civil defence exercises under Sir Jonathan Peel, the regional police commander designate. Day-to-day responsibility was carried out by Superintendent Kenneth Alston.[23]

Another group, the Campaign for Nuclear Disarmament, was also concerned about the threat of nuclear war. In 1961 the CND held a large demonstration at the United States air force base at Wethersfield. Because Essex Constabulary was still under strength, it had to call in officers from the Metropolitan Police, and the Hertfordshire and Southend forces. Seventy people were arrested and taken to the secondary school in Braintree which became a temporary police station and court house.[24]

Where should ultimate control of the provincial police lie? That was one of the questions considered by a Royal Commission under Sir Henry Willink which began in January 1960. Did the future lie with a national police force under the Home Office, or with the regional amalgamation of forces? The Police Federation at that time wanted central control, or at least regional amalgamations. While it could see no objection to a national force, the Commission was in favour of keeping local forces, although it re-defined their functions and responsibilities. The resulting Police Act of 1964 abolished standing joint committees. They were replaced by a county council police committee, which was to be responsible for maintaining an 'adequate and efficient police force', and ensuring that it was properly housed and equipped.[25]

By the time the Act was fully implemented, Sir Jonathan Peel had retired. The new Chief Constable was John Nightingale, who had joined the Metropolitan Police in 1935. Before becoming assistant chief constable of Essex in 1958, John Nightingale had served on the directing staff of the national police college, which was then situated at Ryton-on-Dunsmore in Warwickshire. He had also served as Commandant of Eynsham Hall police training centre.

In addition to the changes introduced by the 1964 Police Act, the Essex force was also affected by the London Government Act of 1963 which created the Greater London Council. Before the Essex Constabulary was founded, the parish of Romford had approached the Metropolitan Police Commissioner asking for his men to set up a station in the town. When the Metropolitan Police borders were extended in 1840 they stopped short of Romford, which became a station in the Brentwood division of Essex Constabulary. In 1963 the wheel turned full circle. It was not practicable to have a London borough policed by a county force, so the whole Romford police division -including Hornchurch, Collier Row and Rainham—was transferred to the Metropolitan Police on 1 April 1965.[26]

Kenneth Alston was then the chief superintendent in charge of the 229 officers working in Romford division. He remembered a good deal of preliminary work being carried out before the Metropolitan Police took over. A ballot was held, and 139 officers chose to stay where they were by transferring to the Metropolitan Police: the remainder wanted to remain in the Essex Constabulary. The two forces agreed to stagger the transfer of personnel over six months, rather than trying to relocate 90 Essex officers all at once. A new police station then being built in Main Road Romford was transferred directly to the Metropolitan Police, which also took over existing stations at Hornchurch, Collier Row, Plough Corner, Emerson Park, Rainham, Harold Hill, and Upminster. How did the transfer of Romford to the Metropolitan Police affect police officers, and civilian support staff? Officers with children at school had the Commissioner's assurance that they would not be moved unless they chose, or unless they were promoted or seriously disciplined. Civilian staff had the same assurances about removal, and their pension rights were transferred to the civil service scheme. One of the few serious grumbles came from a part-time cleaner at Rainham police station who objected to the increased bureaucracy. She resigned after realising that permission for a change of duty had to be obtained from her supervisor on the other side of London rather than the local sergeant.[27]

Recruiting continued to be a problem right through the 1960s, although the extra officers from Romford did help the manpower situation. The Chief Constable's annual report for 1963 commented that it was unusual to find a police recruit with formal educational qualifications. Two years later he reported that: 'the education and quality of recruits is still such as to raise a real doubt as to whether it will be possible in future to fill the higher posts in the service with men of the right calibre'.[28]

Re-designing the cadet system was one way of getting better qualified recruits: university education was another. After a government report recommended the extension of higher education to wider sections of the population, a number of new universities were set up. Essex University was created on 18 May 1961, and in October 1964 the first students were admitted to the buildings at Wivenhoe Park, about two miles out of Colchester.[29]

As the only university graduate in the force at that time, Chief Constable John Nightingale was keen to raise the educational standards of his officers, and show support for the new university. In March 1965 he wrote to the university vice-chancellor with details of his plans for a residential cadet training school for boys between 16 and 18; he thought they could be potential senior officers of the future after courses of university study. After discussions, Essex University was asked if it would take suitable police officers as full-time students, to read for degrees in police-related subjects.

The police committee agreed to provide three years' paid leave for two such officers each year, and in October 1967 Inspectors Peter Joslin and William Gray started their studies for the BA honours degree in social sciences. Peter Joslin is currently Chief Constable of Warwickshire, and Bill Gray the retired deputy chief constable of Bedfordshire. The scheme continues to this day.[30]

Militancy in universities of the 1960s sometimes led to change, but without militancy the force was changing under John Nightingale's command. The need for regional crime squads and sharing the experience of detectives had often been discussed at conferences of chief constables. The number five region, of which Essex was part, appointed its first regional co-ordinator of crime squads in February 1965; he was based at Welwyn Garden City, while the detectives worked from offices in the forces of the region.[31] Basildon, Colchester and Harlow housed the original Essex crime squad offices. The experienced detectives who formed the squad were all trained to use firearms, and were instructed to cultivate professional informants amongst criminals, and maintain a good liaison with detectives in their own forces. They were expected to carry out surveillance on criminals believed to be planning serious crime, and were also available to assist with investigations into murders and serious crime throughout the region. One of the earliest Essex incidents involving the crime squad was in August 1965, when the escaped Great Train robber Ronald Biggs was thought to have been hiding in a house at Little Chesterford. Within 30 minutes of receiving the call, 11 members of the squad were travelling towards the scene: Biggs, however, had gone elsewhere!

In 1967 Detective Sergeant Jack Bridge was seconded from Southend to the regional crime squad at Brentwood, where he stayed for the next 12 years. He showed an aptitude for undercover observations and, together with colleagues such as Detective Constable Les Shaw, found himself working all over the country on some sensitive enquiries, including a long-standing association with a 'supergrass' named Charlie Lowe.[32]

Because of the continuing shortage of police officers in many forces, schemes were devised in various parts of the country to make the best use of available manpower. Senior police officers in the new town of Harlow gave some of their constables individual responsibility for defined areas of the town, known as unit beats. Extra men and cars were provided, and another officer at the station was designated as collator; it was his job to record information collected on local criminals and their activities. The unit beat system with its panda cars— small cars painted with a stripe—was adopted in a modified form in other Essex towns, including Grays, Clacton, Chelmsford, Basildon, Colchester and Brentwood.

Panda cars were introduced to help make police officers more mobile over wider areas. At the same time thought was already being given as to whether helicopters had a place in police work. In 1964 experiments were carried out using a helicopter to patrol the M6 motorway. Two years later the Home Office approved an experimental scheme to test the use of military helicopters in police work. A course in Hampshire was organised for police observers, and as Essex was one of the forces which sent officers to be trained, the force was allowed use of the helicopter for two weeks in March 1967.

The trained observers were all chief inspectors or inspectors and included John Poston, George Manning, Eric Fretton, Donald Harmer and Harry Smith. At the end of the whole experiment a detailed report was compiled by officers from all the police forces which had taken part. It revealed that there had been some problems with communication; it was also

15.   One of the military helicopters, photographed on the sports field at police headquarters, with *(left to right)*: John Postan, Donald Harmer, George Manning and Harry Rand.

pointed out that the roofs of police cars needed marking to make them identifiable from the air. In general, however, helicopters were considered to have potential use in police work.[33] By the time Essex hired its own helicopter in July 1990, each car had its individual radio call sign painted on the roof.

Southend had become a county borough in 1914, and had maintained its own force from then until the 1960s. During those years the town had grown into one of the largest seaside resorts in the country. There were seven miles of bathing beaches, 25 acres of amusement parks, nearly 200 licensed premises and more than 100 establishments with public music singing and dancing licences. While the Essex Constabulary was continually short of manpower, Southend had no recruitment problems. The borough force was able to deal efficiently with the drugs, gambling and youthful exuberances which often occurred in the summer season.

The 1964 Police Act allowed the Home Secretary to order compulsory amalgamations of forces, even when they were considered perfectly efficient. Voluntary amalgamations were also allowed by the Act, and the Home Secretary proposed such an amalgamation between Essex and Southend in 1966. Southend's watch committee made strenuous objections, and on 26 September 1967 a public enquiry opened at County Hall in Chelmsford under Mr. Edgar Stewart Fay, Q.C. Apart from anticipating a large increase in the cost of policing, the county had no objection to the proposed amalgamation.

The enquiry took four days, during which many Southend people described the efficiency of the borough police officers. The Southend watch committee was concerned that, if the amalgamation went ahead, its men and women would be moved out to solve the shortage of officers in Essex. When it was pointed out that police regulations did not allow borough officers to be forced to move, the watch committee tried a different objection: it claimed the county force had no experience of policing a popular seaside resort. Sir John McKay, Her Majesty's Inspector of Constabulary, gave evidence which proved that the county force had plenty of experience: there had been 'mods and rockers' disturbances at Clacton, Frinton and Walton in 1964. Sir John himself was in favour of the proposed amalgamation, as he thought that small forces lacked flexibility, adequate resources and a good promotion structure. There was also difficulty in the impartial enforcement of discipline because of undesirable local pressures.

The government inspector's report was published on 3 January 1968. It acknowledged that the Southend force was efficient, but suggested that amalgamation with the county force would produce even greater efficiency. Officers would have better promotion prospects, improved communications, and access to more specialised services. A combined police authority was set up to oversee the proposed new force, with 18 representatives from Essex and six from Southend. John Nightingale was appointed as Chief Constable of the new force, which was to be called the Essex and Southend-on-Sea Joint Constabulary. It came into being on 1 April 1969.[34] Amalgamating the two forces was not easy, as each was jealous of its own politics and identity; great sensitivity was needed to bring them together. Working parties

16.   On 1 April 1914, 73 of the police officers then serving in the Southend area chose to transfer to the newly-created Southend-on-Sea Borough Constabulary. Wearing the distinctive white helmets, their successors paraded through the town's streets in March 1969 to signify the end of their independence: Essex and Southend were again policed by the same constabulary.

were set up to anticipate problems, and to deal with those that inevitably arose. Personalities in the two forces were introduced to one another through an in-force newspaper, *The Law*, which made its first appearance on amalgamation day. In time most variations between the two forces have been gradually eliminated, although Southend still retains a strong sense of its own identity.

Notes and References

1. Critchley, *op. cit.,* p.224.
2. Taped interview with Ronald Shayshutt in July 1990. The Police Messenger Service was disbanded in June 1945. For an experimental 24 hour period in August 1940 all use of telephones at headquarters was prohibited, in order to test alternative methods of communication.
3. Taped interview with Florence Smith in July 1990.
4. ERO T/A 679.
5. Written information provided in letters to the author in 1992.
6. Records at police headquarters.
7. Details in Totterdell's autobiography *Country Copper*, published by Harrap in 1956.
8. Of the 291 members of the force who served in the war, 24 were in the navy, 4 in the marines, 165 in the army and 98 in the RAF. Twenty four Essex policemen were killed in action, plus 1 from Colchester and 6 from Southend. Three were injured too badly to return to work. Five policemen were seriously injured in air raids, and 9 were slightly injured [Details from the Chief Constable's report after the war].
9. A fatal road accident on Chelmsford's stone bridge at 10.40 a.m. on Monday 30 March 1942 provided the first known occasion when a police radio car was used to appeal for witnesses. The politely delivered words gave the time and circumstances of the accident, and then asked anyone who witnessed it or knew anything about it to report to the police car or the local police station. Unfortunately Sergeant Maurice Pink later had to tell the inquest that no witnesses had been found (Information from Stan Jarvis).
10. Taped interview *op. cit.*
11. Each force paid a proportion of the cost according to how many personnel it had. Training schools became part of the common police services fund, established in 1939 to pay for resources shared by a number of forces.
12. These included Guildford and Reigate with Surrey, the Isle of Wight and Winchester with Hampshire, and nine borough forces with Kent (Critchley, *op. cit.*, p.241).
13. Taped interview with Joseph Baker, September 1991.
14. By 1951 there were mobile receivers and transmitters in 47 cars and a police launch. By 1952, 999 emergency calls could be made in most parts of the country. Originally they went to the nearest manned police station, but moves to have them directed to a central point meant that on 1 January 1953 Information Room started receiving 999 calls from all over Essex.
15. Hilda Grieve, *The Great Tide*, p.87. This book is a very detailed history of the 1953 floods in Essex.
16. Taped interview with ex-Assistant Chief Constable Kenneth Alston, 1992. He died in June 1993.
17. ERO C/DC 11/Fd—Hilda Grieve's original files for *The Great Tide*.
18. ERO Tape SAO313.
19. Donald Harmer died in January 1993. Just before his death, journalists from the radio station Breeze AM interviewed him for a programme commemorating the 40th anniversary of the 1953 floods. His recorded recollections are therefore quoted by permission of the interviewer, Ray Clark, and the producer, Anton Jarvis.
20. Report submitted by Superintendent Arthur Simpson, dated 26 February 1953.
21. See, for example, *The Essex Triangle* by David Thurlow, published by Robert Hale, 1990.
22. Chief Constable's published reports.
23. Report submitted by Superintendent Alston [at headquarters].
24. Chief Constable's published reports.
25. Emsley, *op.cit.* pp. 163-5.
26. 'Romford Police—Anniversary of Change' by Bernard Brown in *Police History Society Journal* no.7 (1992).
27. Taped interview with Kenneth Alston, 1992.

28. By this time the police college had moved from Ryton-on-Dunsmore to its present home at Bramshill House in Hampshire. Officers passing specified courses at the college were eligible to apply to certain universities to read for a degree. It was known as the Bramshill Scholarship scheme, and the Chief Constable wanted Essex University to be part of it. The Home Office wanted Bramshill Scholarships to be separate from arrangements made with local universities.

29. See *A University in the Making*, the Reith Lectures for 1963 by Albert E. Sloman, published by the BBC in 1964.

30. Applicants must have the capacity to reach the rank of superintendent, and sufficient academic ability to complete a degree course. They must also be a credit to the police service, and be reasonably likely to remain in the force.

31. The regional crime squad was actually operating before the co-ordinator was appointed, being supervised by Chief Constable John Nightingale from October 1964. There were eight branch offices initially, in five District regional crime squads, with an inspector in charge of four men in each office. In addition, Essex sent detectives to work in crime squads at Barkingside and Gravesend. By 1967 the regional crime squad establishment in Essex was one chief inspector, four inspectors, seven sergeants, eight constables (including two women) [Chief Constable's report for 1968].

32. Taped interview with Jack Bridge, May 1991.

33. Unpublished research by Bryn Elliott used with his authority. The Essex Police first hired its helicopter in July 1990.

34. ERO Printed report of enquiry into the amalgamation.

Chapter 14

Women of the Force

*First woman superintendent 1970—policemen's wives 1891-1916—female patrols in the
First World War—campaigns for women police 1926-40—women auxiliaries Second
World War—regular policewomen 1946 onwards—equality*

Combining the two forces meant there were more policewomen, and for the first time a
woman superintendent was appointed. Helen Welburn moved from the Cheshire Constabulary
in March 1970, having enjoyed a varied police career in areas that were not then usually open
to women. She found that Essex policewomen were used to working mainly in plain clothes
while they consulted with social workers of all sorts, and investigated cases involving women
and children. Southend policewomen also had a social work rôle, but were more used to
patrolling in uniform amongst the bright lights of a seaside town.

    Why were the experiences of the two groups so different, at a time when the country
had just lived through the 'swinging sixties', and equal pay and opportunities for women were
already being discussed? It was mainly because of the different ways in which society—and
senior male police officers—perceived the rôle of women. Earlier generations of senior Essex
officers had maintained that policewomen were unnecessary—long after they had been employed in some forces. Many felt that a policeman's wife could carry out any duty which
needed a feminine approach; the work of Jane Clarke, wife of the Newport superintendent in
the 1850s, appears in an earlier chapter. Other police wives involved themselves even more
actively. The *Essex Weekly News* for November 1891 reported a burglary at Fyfield. Mrs.
Sarah Kemp, wife of Pc James Kemp and a mother of five, had seen two suspicious men in
the area at night, and 'being a true policeman's wife, ever on the alert to assist her husband
in the execution of his duty', had sent him in pursuit after them.

    In June 1896 Mrs. Mary Ann Barham—mother of six children—went to the aid of her
husband, Pc Charles Barham, when he was attacked at Great Oakley. The constable called for
assistance from two men in the crowd. They refused to help him, and joined in with jeering
and shouting 'give it to him, he's a pretty policeman' which Mrs. Barham heard as she was
going to bed. Hurriedly dressing, she shouted, 'If there is no man here, I must take the part
of a man', and went off to get a horse and trap for her husband to take the prisoner to Mistley.
She then helped her husband tie up the prisoner's legs: which made the man threaten them
both. The local paper called Mrs. Barham a plucky woman, and the magistrates sentenced the
offender to six months' hard labour.[1]

    Until well after the Second World War a policeman intending to marry had to submit
details of his fianceé and seek the Chief Constable's approval. Rural policemen's wives in

particular played an important support rôle to their husbands for many years, but in some of the larger police stations there was need for a more formal presence to chaperone women in custody, and matrons were often appointed.[2] In 1916 force orders instructed that all female prisoners were to be cared for by a police matron, who would accompany them, if required, to the workhouse, hospital or prison.

The First World War gave women their first real chance to be involved in preventative police work. When the criminal law amendment committee of 1914 investigated the potential rôle of women within the police, *Police Review* of 5 June wrote a light-hearted review of the committee's deliberations. The article asked whether policewomen would prevent the wicked from pursuing their ways, 'alone, in pairs, in flocks, or coupled with a male so that the brace embodied the perfect police entity of wisdom, perception and experience!'

When the committee recommended police forces to employ properly qualified women to take statements in intimate cases, and to search and supervise female prisoners, the general reaction was negative. A Home Office circular asked each chief constable to consider ways of employing a woman in his force; in Essex the Chief Constable chose to ignore the suggestion. At Colchester the borough police were more enlightened. Two women constables were appointed in July 1918; paid £2 15s. a week, they received five shillings a month plain clothes allowance and one shilling a week for boots.[3]

From the early days of the war two groups of women had been working in parallel, although neither had any police powers. The Women Police Service intended its members to be trained and regarded as a group of professional women working full-time with the police. The second group were volunteers, organised by the National Council of Women Workers for the duration of the war. There were local branches at Romford, under a Mrs. Cantill, and at Brentwood, under a Miss Newton. Each volunteer gave up a few hours each week to patrol near army camps and railway stations, advising girls on the dangers of associating with soldiers.

Apparently the volunteers did a good job, and in December 1917 Romford justices asked for women police patrols in their town. At that time the Chief Constable chose to take no action but, six months later, in June 1918, he was authorised to employ and pay two women to act as police patrols at Romford for six months. The women patrols were paid five shillings a day, with 1s. 3d. a month deducted for insurance, and a monthly boot allowance of 3s. 8d. They were not permanent members of the force, and had no police powers: and, although no record has been found of their names, they seem to have been sponsored by the National Council of Women, which provided their greatcoats and asked the Chief Constable to reimburse the cost. The women patrols' relationship with the regular force must have been amicable, for they appear on a photograph of Romford police in 1918. Their contracts were extended for periods of six months at a time, but when the Chief Constable was asked to provide them with 'summer coat frocks' for the coming year he decided to terminate their appointment from 31 October 1919.[4]

In 1926 the Federation of Essex Women's Institutes began a campaign for policewomen in Essex. The Chief Constable, Captain Unett, agreed that the two women patrols at Brentwood and Romford had prevented improper behaviour, but with the dispersal of army camps he considered that normal standards of morality had been restored, and there was no further need for women to be involved. He was bombarded with letters from members of women's organisations who had been urged to make their individual views heard. By 1930 Captain Unett was being visited by deputations of women. They were all told the same thing: Essex had no need for policewomen.

No progress was made after Captain Peel's appointment as Chief Constable in 1933. The campaign continued until the Second World War when a question was asked in the House of Commons about his negative attitude, and the Chief Constable of Colchester was asked to tell the Essex police authority how he employed his women officers.[5]

The shortage of policemen in 1941 provided the final incentive. Twenty-one full-time, paid members of the Women's Auxiliary Police Corps were appointed as clerks and telephonists at headquarters and at some stations. Previously acquired skills such as shorthand and typing were tested before appointment, and then the women were given some training in basic police duties, first aid, self defence and air raid precautions. They had no power of arrest because they were not police officers. The first uniforms were navy blue wrap-round overalls with WAPC embroidered on one breast; later a made-to-measure jacket and skirt was provided for each woman.

Three of the first women auxiliaries at headquarters were all called Smith, but were not related. Diana Smith joined in December 1941, having actually been born at headquarters where her father was the administration superintendent. Florence Smith joined in August 1942, and spent a lot of her time teaching first aid. Evelyn Joyce Smith (better known by her married name of Joyce Jones), joined in February 1943. Some of the other auxiliaries, such as Nancy Challis and Bernice Coe, were married to serving officers.[6] Southend borough force, was also reluctant to appoint policewomen after voluntary patrols were disbanded. There were no policewomen in the borough force until 1941, when full-time auxiliaries were appointed. Southend received authority to appoint six policewomen in 1944, but the first one only lasted a month: it was some years before there were any more. The borough force employed a permanent matron to care for women and girls held in custody at a police station or in court.[7]

Some sections of the public did not think that office-bound women auxiliaries were an adequate alternative to employing operational policewomen. Captain Peel eventually agreed that suitable auxiliaries could be appointed for outside duties, but they had to be supervised by serving policewomen. Several experienced women police from other forces were interviewed, but none was found acceptable. The Chief Constable was obliged to accept a woman sergeant on secondment from the Metropolitan Police. In November 1944 she transferred to Essex as Woman Inspector Dorothy Jordan, changing her name to Hodges in 1951 when she married Superintendent George Hodges.

Dorothy Jordan did not have an easy job; no one else wanted to work in a force which was so reluctant to employ policewomen. She herself had problems in finding suitable lodgings, so was able to appreciate some of the difficulties experienced by her policewomen. Landladies often expected companions rather than lodgers, and male officers did not seem to understand that policewomen wanted lodgings with bathrooms and privacy. As policemen started to return from war service some of the more antagonistic attitudes eased: they were used to working with women on more or less equal terms.[8]

On 11 January 1946 the *Essex Chronicle* carried an advertisement for women to join the Essex Constabulary as constables with full powers, but specialising in work with women, girls and children. They had to be between 22 and 35, and single or widowed; marriage meant compulsory resignation. Eighteen policewomen were authorised, but it was a long time before that number was reached. Only two of the women auxiliaries chose to apply for the regular force when the Women's Auxiliary Police Corps was disbanded.

Joan Hurley was the only former auxiliary to last beyond her initial training and become a regular policewoman. A course in Birmingham prepared her for the new rôle, but not for what awaited her on the first day at her new station. Required to accompany two detectives to the scene of a child murder, she was given the unpleasant task of unpacking the parcel containing the baby's body.[9] Joan Hurley was soon joined by Olive Butler, who served in the Land Army during the war, and eventually reached the rank of superintendent.

Woman Sergeant Dorothy Watson was already an experienced policewoman when she joined the Colchester Borough Police in 1925. She had joined the Women Police Service in 1916 as a 19-year-old, and been attached to the Ministry of Munitions throughout the First World War. After six years in the Hove borough police she applied to work in Colchester, which was much nearer to her home town of Bishops Stortford. Policewomen who married had to leave the force, but in August 1937 she secretly married a constable in the borough force named David Miller Kirk. Only when her husband was killed in action in June 1944 did Dorothy Watson officially admit what she had done. Because she had broken the rules, her application for a widow's pension caused great consternation. The matter was referred to the Home Secretary but, when he learned that the Colchester watch committee was not taking any action against her, Sergeant Kirk was granted her own full pension rights and allowed to receive her late husband's pension.[10]

With the amalgamation of the Colchester Borough and Essex constabularies in 1947, Woman Sergeant Kirk had to supervise the policewomen at Braintree as well as Colchester. Joan Hurley was the first full-time policewoman in Braintree, which provided a busy and varied work load for a woman officer, because it was close to the large United States air base at Wethersfield. There was also a prisoner-of-war camp at High Garrett, where she found herself impersonating a German woman who had communicated illegally with one of the inmates. In reply to the man's torrent of German she gave the full extent of her vocabulary, 'Ja'. With that he was arrested by the military authorities and tried by court martial—very unfairly she thought—for conversing with a British subject.[11]

A national police post-war committee recommended that policewomen should undertake the full range of police duties, and a woman who initiated an investigation should be entrusted with the same opportunities as a man in completing it, and presenting the case to a court. Women were to be made to feel an integral part of the service, and not merely a section with restricted and specialised duties.[12]

For this philosophy to be effective there needed to be more women police. By 1953 there were still only 26 in the force, and 20 women special constables who were regarded as reserves to help out with office work. Although the women were trained on equal terms with men—and could then marry without having to resign—they were still regarded as specialists in cases involving women and children, although Iris Gay (later Kemp) was the first woman to qualify as an area car patrol driver at Chelmsford in December 1951.

Vera Bayliss joined the force in 1953 and worked in Romford for several years, often in plain clothes because of the surveillance and decoy work that women specialised in. Vera Bayliss and her colleague Muriel Roberts earned a much-publicised commendation for chasing a purse snatcher through Romford market, and frog-marching him up South Street to the police station. Decoy work to catch sexual offenders was an important part of a policewoman's duties, because the power of arrest for indecent exposure then depended on the offender being 'found committing'.[13]

Two years before Woman Chief Inspector Hodges retired in 1963, the first 16-year-old girl cadets were appointed in the force. The first three—selected from numerous applicants—were Gillian Fisher, Janet Holmes and Zelma Kegley.[14] When the residential cadet school was opened in 1969, girl cadets still had to live at home and work at their nearest police station.

17. Four of the Essex policewomen *c*.1953. From left to right: Sergeant Olive Butler (who retired as superintendent); Inspector Dorothy Hodges (née Jordan, who retired as a chief inspector); Sergeant Peggy Sandford (who transferred to Surrey as a chief inspector in 1967 and retired as a superintendent); and WPc Iris Kemp (who now lives in Australia).

Only after 1973 could they live in the cadet school, and follow the same courses of training as the boys.

By the time Helen Welburn became superintendent of policewomen in 1970, the establishment had risen to 81, although only 60 policewomen were actually serving. For several years prior to 1970, women police representatives had met at headquarters to discuss common problems and policy. Chairing her first meeting at the end of March 1970, Superintendent Welburn was able to tell delegates that approval had been given for suitable policewomen to train as advanced drivers, and work full-time on traffic patrol. WPc Jane Pepper (later Reece) earned a first class police driving permit, and soon afterwards was the first woman posted to the traffic division on equal terms. In October 1970 Maureen Wildin (later Clark) became a detective constable on equal terms at Southend. Superintendent Welburn also hoped more women would soon be working in CID, and other specialist branches such as juvenile liaison.[15] Shortly afterwards, Vera Bayliss became the first woman detective sergeant in the force, and most divisional stations had at least one woman detective constable stationed there.

The women police department had its own promotion structure and sense of identity. It was recognised as a specialist department in the same way as CID: there were conferences of women police, and separate social and sporting activities were enjoyed by members of the department. In 1973 a 10-mile sponsored walk of policewomen raised enough money to pay for the first garden party for police pensioners and widows. While the garden parties continue, the sponsored walks have not!

The Sex Discrimination Act of 1975 made an immediate impact on the police service. Because there could now be no distinction in recruitment or deployment on the grounds of gender, attempts were made by the Federation to have the police made exempt, because it thought that: 'the very nature of the duties of a police constable is contrary to all that is finest and best in women'.[16]

Three years before the Act took effect, the Metropolitan Police disbanded its separate policewomen's department, and women were completely integrated with the men. Superintendent Welburn, and her deputy Chief Inspector Olive Butler, had already started to prepare the ground for such a move in Essex. While it was lawful to have one, a separate policewomen's department remained, but women officers were also attached to the patrolling shifts at each divisional station. They alternated for several months at a time between traditional specialist duties, and the full range of ordinary patrol work. When sex discrimination became unlawful in December 1975, the policewomen's department disappeared overnight, and in theory all police work was then open to everyone. Some of the duties formerly performed by women were later taken over by a new branch, called community services, which employed both men and women officers.

Robert Bunyard, who was then the Chief Constable, did not want women involved in public order incidents or training. However, many women officers wanted the experience of such police work and other duties which were just as controversial. After an increase in general firearms operations, it was decided to train selected policewomen in the use of firearms. The first training course for women in April 1977 expected its students to reach the same standards as the men but, because of media interest and the number of photographic sessions, the course had to be extended by three days. The students and their instructor, Sergeant (later Inspector) Ivor Montgomery, received a great deal of publicity throughout the whole country.[17]

18.   This photograph of all available policewomen in the county was taken in May 1973 after one of the regular conferences at headquarters, shortly after the white-topped hats had been issued. Women Superintendent Helen Welburn is in the centre of the front row, flanked by Chief Inspector Olive Butler (left) and Inspector Mary Easton. The officers in plain clothes are either members of the CID or the Community Services Branch.

"First thing I'm going to "do" if I pass is a bank"

19.   The fact that policewomen were being taught to use firearms occasioned a great deal of media interest. This Giles cartoon appeared in the *Sunday Express* on 1 May 1977.
[Reproduced by permission of Expresss Newspapers.]

In the years since the Equal Pay and Sex Discrimination Acts, many more women have joined the Essex Police. They have gradually won the right to carry out the full range of police duties: it is no longer a novelty to have women detectives, traffic drivers, trainers, or members of the force support unit. Nonetheless, Joanna Sell's appointment in July 1984 as the first woman in the mounted section still attracted the press, as did Valerie Smith's posting in 1977 to the diving section, and Lesley Rosenwould's appointment as a dog handler in 1991. Women officers now make up around 11 per cent of the force, and the many who continue to serve in almost all departments do so because they are *qualified* for their rôle.

Notes and References

1. ERO T/P181/8/25.
2. In 1927, to make the matrons more obvious in court, each one was issued with a hat. The matrons were: Mrs. Self (Braintree); Mrs. Fisher (Brentwood); Mrs. Bartlett and Mrs. Lewin (Chelmsford); Mrs. Monk (Epping); Mrs. Housden (Grays); Mrs. Parker (Romford); and Mrs. Crickmore (Saffron Walden).
3. The 1924 Bridgeman committee on policewomen reported that there were only 110 in the whole country—six in county forces, and 27 in city and borough forces.
4. Printed Minutes of the standing joint committee.
5. *ibid.*
6. Joyce Smith (later Jones) became secretary to Captain (later Sir Jonathan) Peel, and Mr. (later Sir John) Nightingale. She retired in 1978. Florence Smith transferred to Pitsea as an auxiliary, and then joined the civilian staff when the auxiliaries were disbanded; she retired in 1974. Diana Smith remained on the civilian staff at headquarters, retiring in 1986.
7 *Southend Police Golden Jubilee* booklet by Doxsey and Williams. The situation was little better in some other forces in the region. In October 1943 a survey on numbers of policewomen showed the Metropolitan Police leading the field, having employed women since 1918. Borough forces were better than most counties, with Colchester, Cambridge and Ipswich all having had policewomen since at least 1920. Bedfordshire, Cambridgeshire, Hampshire, Suffolk and Surrey had none, while Hertford county had three, two of whom had been appointed in 1928.
8. Dorothy Hodges died in August 1986. She was interviewed by the author in 1972.
9. Taped interview with Joan Hurley in 1991.
10. Dorothy Gladys Watson, spinster aged 34, and David Miller Kirk, bachelor aged 29, were married at Christ Church in Paddington on 21 August 1937, from what appears to have been his parents' address. His occupation on the marriage certificate is given as police officer, while her profession is blank. David Kirk was a Colchester borough constable from 1934. In December 1939 he joined the Royal Artillery as lieutenant; he was a temporary major when he was killed in France on 16 June 1944 [Records at St Catherine's House]. Dorothy Kirk's force personnel record gives her date of birth as 5 March 1897. This suggests that in addition to not declaring her occupation when she married, she also lied about her age. She retired in 1952, and died in 1977.
11. Taped interview, 1991.
12. *Police Review*, 10 February 1950.
13. Section 4, Vagrancy Act 1824.
14. Gillian Fisher was a policeman's daughter, and later married Superintendent Peter Fairhead. Janet Holmes is now the wife of Chief Superintendent Robin Blackmore of Colchester.
15. Police officers in juvenile liaison scheme supervised the behaviour of children who committed offences like shoplifting, rather than taking them to court or issuing official cautions. The scheme operated with a full-time woman juvenile liaison officer in Southend from 1964, and Brentwood from August 1966. Its part-time implementation in large town centres like Basildon gave officers too large a case load, and eventually led to the posts becoming full time.
16. Quoted on p.8 of *Policewomen and Equality* by Sandra Jones, published by Macmillan in 1986.
17. The first women to qualify were: WPcs Julia Foster (now Inspector Julia Jeapes), Lesley Czuba (now Butcher), Elizabeth Jenkin, Sandra Hilton, Maureen Hales (now Inspector), Catherine Donaldson (now Kennedy), Barbara Washbrook and Jennifer Robdrup. Julia Jeapes subsequently became the first woman firearms instructor in charge of the armed officers at Stansted Airport.

Chapter 15

Discipline

Ex Police inspector in debt 1842—criminal allegations against constables—disciplinary offences before 1919—start of Police Federation and effects on discipline—Chief Constable in county court 1910—Southend Chief Constable imprisoned 1966—Police Complaints Board 1976.

The previous chapter was devoted to the influences that led to women police officers being appointed, and their current rôle within the force. This chapter will consider a selection of officers' transgressions against the discipline regulations from 1840 to the 1970s.

Since the force began in 1840, a policeman in debt has always been liable to disciplinary action. In July 1842 John Rough, 'formerly a police inspector, and late of South Ockendon and Orsett', was declared an insolvent debtor. Evidence was heard that he owed debts of £35 after his wife failed to pay their grocery bills, although he had given her the money. Married women had no rights so, as Rough was liable for her debts, he lost his job when he was sent to debtors' prison.[1]

There are a number of examples of early police officers who committed criminal offences. Charles Drake joined the force on 30 November 1848 and was stationed at Dunmow. About two weeks after he arrived, the first of a series of fires occurred. Drake was thought to be responsible, and the case went to court although most of the evidence against him was circumstantial. Pc Amos Coote told the court how his colleague had commented that policemen had a wonderful chance to set fire to anything if they had a mind to, and several members of the public reported seeing Pc Drake near other fires, and hearing him say how much he liked to see a good blaze; he had also been seen with rags in his possession. On the judge's instruction Pc Drake was acquitted, but he was dismissed from the force in May 1849.[2]

In 1868 Pc Thomas Valentine was suspected of committing an offence then called 'having carnal knowledge', when it was alleged that he had fathered an illegitimate child. At the time the evidence was inconclusive enough to justify his dismissal, but he soon compounded suspicions by taking a girl of 'weak intellect' away from her home to frighten her into obedience; the opportunity was then taken to require his resignation.[3]

For much of the 19th century parish constables and county policemen worked in parallel—not always peacefully. It was some years before the responsibilities of the two groups were settled conclusively, and disputes about rights were not uncommon. On 23 April 1843 the *Chelmsford Chronicle* reported a case where Inspector Charles Marnie of Thaxted, Pc James Sanderson of Lindsell and Pc George Downes of Great Easton had been summoned for highway robbery. At 1 a. m. on the previous Sunday morning the three officers had met at a conference point on the Great Easton to Thaxted road, when they saw a travelling pastry cook named Moses Johnson coming towards them with his basket of goods. Pc Sanderson asked what was in the basket and Johnson had replied, 'I shan't tell you; I'll suffer to be taken back to Thaxted cage first'. Realising the man was drunk, Inspector Marnie recognised him as living in Duton Hill, Great Easton, and suggested that Pc Downes should carry the basket of goods while Johnson was taken home to his wife. This was done, and the inspector went on to Dunmow to report the incident to Superintendent Thomas Redin who instructed the magistrate's clerk to draw a summons against Johnson for being drunk in public. Two days later the inspector and the two constables each received a summons from the Thaxted parish constable, alleging that they had unlawfully stopped Moses Johnson and taken his basket of goods. All three officers were required to attend next day at Thaxted vicarage, residence of the magistrate, Reverend Thomas Jee.

By that time Captain McHardy had been informed, and he also attended with James Parker, force solicitor, Superintendent Redin, and Superintendent John Hoy from Bardfield. It was then that the legal arguments started in earnest. The force solicitor pointed out that the officers were wrongly named on the summonses, which should have been warrants because the allegations concerned a supposed felony. He also maintained that the three had done nothing wrong; they had acted in accordance with the home secretary's instructions:

> If after sunset and before sunrising the constable should see anyone carrying a bundle or goods which he suspects are stolen, he should stop and examine the person and detain him; but here he should also judge from circumstances such as appearance and manner his account of himself before he actually takes him into custody.

Captain McHardy saw the credibility of his new force at stake, and asked for the case alleging that his officers had committed assault and robbery to be heard in open court at Dunmow on 1 May 1843. In front of the full bench in a packed court the Reverend Mr. Jee insisted that he was a supporter of the police, but still thought they had no right to take Johnson's basket, as: 'After acting as a magistrate for upwards of 30 years and having conducted a variety of difficult cases ... I think I may be allowed to act without interference...'. The whole incident provoked discussion at the petty sessions, as the rights of county constables against parish constables were discussed by the full bench of magistrates. The Reverend Mr. Jee walked out of the court in contempt as his fellow magistrates discussed what powers the police and parish constables had to stop individuals. The chairman summed up the matter: 'I have always conceived it to be a point of common law that a parish constable, or any constable, would be justified in stopping a person under such circumstances, at such an unreasonable hour, and if it were not so it would overturn all the useful part of the police'.

Allegations against the three policemen were dismissed. The next case to be heard was the charge against Moses Johnson for being drunk in public. He was found guilty and fined 16s. 6d., including costs, but given two weeks to pay as 'he appeared lame and it was said that his wife was in a delicate state'.[4]

In May 1851 there was another court case—lasting four hours—which shows that the conflicts continued between county and parish constables as they tested their procedural rights. Captain McHardy was present at Chelmsford court when Pc 163 George William Oakley charged Henry Harris, blacksmith and parish constable of Danbury, with drunkenness. Harris pleaded guilty and was fined five shillings plus expenses, the chairman of the bench remarking that: 'it was highly discreditable on the part of the one set for the maintenance of order and peace, that he should, on his own confession, have been guilty of drunkenness'.

Harris then made a counter charge against Pc Oakley alleging that on the night in question he too had been drunk, and had threatened the parish constable that if he did not go home, 'I'll handcuff you and put you in the cage'. Pc Oakley was then said to have pushed Harris along the road, while striking him several times with his staff. A scuffle had followed after Harris maintained that his power as a parish constable was superior to that of the police, and had sought assistance to arrest Pc Oakley; witnesses testified that Pc Oakley had been perfectly sober. As there was no police station in Danbury, the parish constable had been detained overnight in the policeman's house before being taken to Springfield police station the following morning. Harris told the court that he had been intimidated by the presence of a pistol in Pc Oakley's house, but had been afraid to complain when they went to police headquarters in case he was locked up. Evidence was given that police constables were only provided with a truncheon and handcuffs, with no authority to use pistols.

Harris's solicitor started to enquire into the instructions for using handcuffs when Captain McHardy interrupted, pointing out that the case was a charge of assault and not an enquiry into police instructions. He then agreed to give evidence as to his instructions for the use of handcuffs on male prisoners being moved from place to place. Adherence to the order was imperative, the Chief Constable insisted: its violation had cost an Essex constable his life 'the other day', [Pc Bamborough was murdered in 1850]; the use of truncheons could not be defined, continued Captain McHardy, but on no occasion was unnecessary violence to be used. After hearing all the evidence the justices retired, decided that Pc Oakley had acted correctly, and acquitted him of all charges.[5]

Police officers have never been above the law they are paid to enforce, and in the 1840s and 1850s procedures were still evolving to deal with policemen who committed offences which were not triable in a criminal court: what would now often be regarded as breaches of police regulations. Drinking on duty is still taken seriously, but is now sometimes treated as a welfare matter, except where the driving of a vehicle is involved. In the early days of the force, policemen were forbidden to enter a public house when on duty unless they were on police business. Working-class people drank ale more frequently than tea or coffee, and a pint of ale was one way of refreshing a tired policeman who might have to walk anything up to 20 miles in one night's patrol. However, if he was caught in a public house then it usually meant dismissal.

In 1859 Pc John Maguire from West Bergholt was dismissed after going into a public house four miles from home to buy refreshments. Investigation of the incident opened up a complicated story involving allegations against him of assault, and he lost his job. When Maguire failed to find other work, he and his family became destitute, and had to enter the Lexden and Winstree workhouse.

The *Essex County Standard* printed a long letter from the former policeman, in which he detailed his circumstances,[6] and asked for justice because the force would not give him a reference. The newspaper ran a campaign on Maguire's behalf, and printed supporting letters. A subscription fund was started so that Maguire could support his family outside the work-house, and all the letters relating to his cause were reprinted as a pamphlet in order to raise funds. The force was criticised severely for refusing to give Maguire a reference after his dismissal for such a relatively minor breach of discipline.[7]

There could be no recourse to higher authority about the harsh conditions of the police service, or the treatment administered by senior officers. Even a man's religious views could subject him to criticism or dismissal. James Marchbanks joined the force in April 1851, and two years later was dismissed for what force records described as being 'connected with Mormons'. The introduction of the Church of Latter Day Saints into England in 1837 aroused a good deal of suspicion, because its members were allowed to practise polygamy.

Pc Marchbanks was baptised into the Mormon church on 21 September 1851 at Ingatestone, and thus served most of his police service as a Mormon. One wonders if he managed to keep his religion to himself until he suddenly caused his own dismissal by doing something controversial: like taking a second wife?[8]

Men who dared to criticise the police usually did so in letters which appeared under pen names in journals like the *Police Review* and local newspapers. After the Maguire case there were other letters of complaint in the *Essex County Standard*. Some smacked of sour grapes, such as where a writer signing himself 'An Ex-Policeman' called for an investigation into the so-called model force which had denied him promotion.[9]

In April 1856 the *Essex Standard* printed a letter signed 'A Looker-On': the details are such that it must have been written by a member of the force. The letter claimed that officers who had travelled to Wivenhoe Park to police a royal visit had been allowed no time for rest or refreshment, or even an allowance with which to buy food. They had been obliged to work for 10 hours without anything to eat or drink, and one man had even been reproved by his superintendent for eating a biscuit in public. Men who had travelled by train were able to claim their fares, but the majority had been been obliged to walk to Wivenhoe before their long duty had even started. The letter writer called the Essex Officers 'Captain McHardy's white slaves!'[10]

Welfare considerations played no part in a later royal visit to Wivenhoe. 'A Looker-On' wrote again. He complained that Essex men had been sent straight from night duty without time to eat or sleep. Colchester borough police were much better treated. When the owner of Wivenhoe Park offered them all a good meal at the end of the visit, the Essex policemen had not been allowed to accept it.[11]

Complaints were made that the Chief Constable had reduced the pensions of some men who had committed minor disciplinary offences; this actually happened, as surviving records confirm. Before the advent of the Police Federation and recognised negotiating procedures, however, such complaints had little chance of being satisfied. Standardised classification of both disciplinary offences and punishment also dates from the Police Act of 1919. Before then, a county chief constable decided what behaviour he was going to punish, and the penalty to impose; in borough forces such decisions were sometimes made by the watch committee.

In the 1870s three Grays officers, sent to London to carry out enquiries, were late back because they missed the train. Each was fined a half day's pay, which varied from 1s. 11d. to 1s. 7d. because they were all different grades of constable. A sergeant was reduced in rank for being drunk and disorderly, and for concocting a lie with one of his constables to try to save himself. The constable concerned was fined 4s. 6d., and moved at his own expense from Margaret Roothing to Brentwood. Another man was obliged to resign after catching a particularly virulent form of venereal disease which, it was said, would damage his future efficiency.[12]

A member of the Colchester borough force, Pc Frederick Peak, was dismissed for entering a public house with a soldier. His defence that he had taken the soldier there, rather than just giving him the necessary directions, was not accepted; the watch committee took a far more serious view of his actions.[13]

In 1885 Pc John Stuffin of Canewdon admitted stealing 10 fowls. The owner of the fowls refused to take proceedings against the policeman, much to the annoyance of the Chief Constable who wanted the matter to be dealt with in court because 'a scoundrel in his position, placed for the protection of property, richly deserves the severest punishment'. Stuffin was fined a week's pay and dismissed.

In general force orders for October 1885 an inspector and a constable were both severely reprimanded for having 'a considerable want of ordinary sharpness and intelligence' after they failed to check the story of a man who rode into Ongar on a horse which only had a halter. When the horse was found to have been stolen, it cost the force £1 17s. 9d. to circulate its details; and the inspector was charged two-thirds of the bill.

As police conditions gradually improved, further sanctions could be imposed for discipline offences. Between 1902 and 1909 a sample set of discipline records shows punishments being imposed of fines, severe reprimands, forfeit of annual leave and rest days, and being moved to another station. The offences committed were neglect of duty, using objectionable language in the police station, being drunk on duty, being asleep on duty, and failing to keep items of uniform in good repair.

In 1910 a severe reprimand and a caution were imposed on two officers who were absent from a beat and late for court. A man who paraded an hour late for duty was dismissed, but

20. A cheeky policeman, photographed as part of a series taken by Fred Spalding, well-known Chelmsford photographer. The sergeant is Joseph Hurrell, who joined in 1874, was promoted sergeant on 1 October 1891, and retired in December 1901. The photograph is believed to have been taken at Danbury where Sergeant Hurrell was stationed. The pretty girl is his daughter so he was not disciplined.
[Spalding Collection photograph, by courtesy of the Essex Record Office.]

one assumes he had some previous transgressions which were taken into account. Sergeant Frederick Lancum was reduced to the rank of constable, for improperly advising a landlord to open his public house during prohibited hours. Sergeant George Griggs—who borrowed money from a landlord—was severely reprimanded, cautioned and moved to another station. A man who was absent from a conference point had to forfeit six rest days, and when the same officer was found drinking on duty (presumably to drown his sorrows) he was reduced in pay for two months. However, when Sergeant Martin Mynott was reported for riding his bike on the footpath instead of being taken to court, the Chief Constable fined him five shillings and cautioned him. At the other extreme, Pc Herbert Whybrow was ordered to resign for marrying without the Chief Constable's consent, and telling lies about it.

The Chief Constable himself appeared in the county court in February 1910, having been sued over a dog which had been found without its collar by a constable at Benfleet, and taken to the Billericay dogs' home; no one had claimed the animal within seven days so it had been destroyed. Mr. Sargent of Ingatestone later claimed the dog was a valuable grey-hound which had previously been in police custody; he maintained the police should have recognised the dog and returned it to him. Mr. Sargent won his case; the standing joint committee paid him the value of the dog and his court costs.

The offences committed by policemen, and the way that the force dealt with them, reflects the attitudes of society as well as the views of the Chief Constable. In 1912 one of the star detectives of the force—Superintendent Alfred Marden—was disciplined for offences going back to 1903; unfortunately the surviving records do not give the background to the disciplinary enquiry. Marden was involved in the investigation of some important cases, ranging from the murder of Inspector Simmons to the murder of Miss Holland at Moat Farm. Charges against him included the unorthodox questioning of prisoners, being untruthful, using bad language, and being disrespectful towards the Chief Constable and principal officers of the standing joint committee. Marden was reduced in rank from superintendent to inspector, and resigned shortly afterwards. In December 1920 he was fined £5 at Grays Magistrates' Court for asserting that he was still a police officer. When he persisted in doing so, he was threatened with a further reduction in his pension.

In the period before the First World War discipline offences seem to have been evenly divided between laziness and anti-social behaviour. Pc Arthur Cross was fined five shillings for issuing and countersigning a blank declaration form for the movement of swine. Pc Caleb Young had his pay reduced for three months for refusing to clean up police quarters and using improper language, as did Pc Henry Thorogood for hay making when he should have been on duty, and for making false statements about the incident. Pc Ernest Drain was fined 10 shillings for allowing himself to be photographed with some soldiers at a yeomanry camp, and Pc Arthur Popple was reprimanded for smoking at an election.[14]

The Police Act of 1919 created—amongst other things—the Police Federation and a national discipline code, and attempts were made to adopt a more consistent approach to disciplinary matters.[15] Not until 1927 were police officers granted the right to appeal against punishments to the Home Secretary. In the years between 1910 and 1920 around 20 men each year were formally reported for disciplinary offences. After the national standard discipline code was introduced, the number of reports rose from 20 to 75 in 1921, before dropping to 41 the following year. The initial increase seems to have occurred because it was then necessary to record all complaints—whether or not they were taken any further. Proper evidence—rather than suspicion—also had to be provided to prove all allegations.

In 1921 a member of the public complained that Pc Edwin Cole had gone into the public bar of the *Ram and Hogget* public house at Bradfield and made some discreditable comments in public about Christianity. He was supposed to have said, 'I don't believe in the church or the people who go there, kneeling down and eating their prayer books. They are all dammed hypocrites, and I would go into church and tell them so to their faces'.

The comments could not be proved so, although the complaint had to be recorded, no further action was taken. In 1923 Pc Herbert Chapman was directed to stand at the Rectory Lane crossing in Witham while the Prince of Wales went past on a train. When the constable failed to get there in time, he was fined £1 for neglect of duty.[16]

There is plenty of evidence of private vendettas being pursued against individual officers, usually by their sergeants. George Totterdell was reported by his sergeant in 1913 for twice failing to attend a conference point on the bridge over Westcliff railway station. The sergeant had watched Pc Totterdell standing on the platform while two trains had come and gone. Because he then went into the porter's room rather than onto the bridge, the sergeant reported him. Pc Totterdell was severely cautioned. In 1945—when Totterdell was detective superintendent—he reported himself to the administration superintendent for damaging a police car. A large black dog had run across Springfield Road, immediately in front of the police car that Superintendent Totterdell was driving. Despite braking hard Totterdell had hit the dog, although it had run off 'yelling its head off and holding up one of its hind legs'. The incident may have been the original model for the force legend about a 'county dog' that causes accidents to police cars!

Southend borough policemen also committed a variety of offences against the discipline regulations and even the Chief Constable was not exempt from complaint. In 1924 Sergeant James Stent made several accusations against his Chief Constable, Henry Maurice Kerslake: they included neglect of duty and being guilty of tyrannical conduct. Sergeant Stent had been a delegate to the short-lived Police Union, which preceded the Police Federation. The sergeant alleged his Chief Constable had threatened to dismiss him because of his union involvement—hence the allegation of tyrannical conduct. In the subsequent enquiry Chief Constable Kerslake was exonerated: Sergeant Stent had already resigned.[17]

In 1937 a sergeant learned of the marriage of one of his constables at a local church. As the ceremony had taken place without permission from the force, the constable was questioned. He admitted marrying without permission: his wife was pregnant, and he had totally forgotten the necessity of asking the Chief Constable as well as the intended bride! The constable was reprimanded, and not allowed to claim married men's allowances till long after the child was born.

In 1936 another Southend constable was fined £1 and ordered to refund his rent allowance when he was found to have been letting rooms in his house: 21 visitors were said to have stayed there. The constable did not dispute the charge, but said the rooms had only been let when nearby lodgings were full: there had been no cards or advertisements, so the force had not been compromised. The inspector's allegation of 21 visitors at once had been a 'grossly exaggerated libel'.

Highly trained traffic officers in the county and borough forces were often allowed to give driving instruction to members of the public. Driving schools in Southend found such a practice very annoying, and one complained about a particular policeman who had been canvassing their pupils, saying he could teach them better at a cheaper rate. 'It's got to stop', wrote the complainant. 'It's upsetting our living'.

By the 1950s penalties for lesser offences like oversleeping on early turn ranged from making up the time later, to cautions and fines. Each man reported for oversleeping apparently tried to think of a new excuse. One checked his alarm and found the button hadn't been properly set; he blamed it on the quick change from late shift to early turn. Another had woken at 4. 50 a.m. and made his wife and himself a cup of tea. Sitting on the side of the bed to drink it, he suddenly found the clock said 5 50 a.m. and he should have been at work. He concluded that he must have gone back to sleep with his eyes open.[18]

The 1964 Police Act made many important changes to the structure and organisation of forces. Internal disciplinary matters were to be dealt with separately from complaints about police behaviour from members of the public. Proper records had to be kept when anyone complained about an officer's behaviour, and thorough enquiries were to be made. The results of such 'complaints investigations' had to be reported to the Director of Public Prosecutions, unless it was clear that no criminal offence had been committed. Apart from the Metropolitan Police, Essex was one of the first forces to establish a complaints department employing a full-time superintendent.

The increasing affluence and developing consumer society of the 1960s meant that officers had more contact with all levels of society, some of whom had a greater inclination to question the traditional authority and powers of the police. Members of several forces suffered from allegations of corruption and false arrest, and a number of officers were sent to prison. Chief constables of borough forces were not exempt from investigation, and at least two received prison sentences; one of them was William Alexander McConnach, Chief Constable of the Southend-on-Sea Borough Constabulary.

In 1964 the Southend borough treasurer became concerned about the amount of money his chief was charging to a special account for CID expenses, and suspicions were reported to Her Majesty's Chief Inspector of Constabulary. In the subsequent interview the Chief Constable declined to produce detailed information, but denied that he had been using public money to fund his own drinking and entertainment. An investigation was carried out by the then Chief Constable of Carlisle, Frank Williamson. Evidence was given which showed how McConnach had revitalised the sporting and social life of the borough force: morale was high. Each of the recreation rooms had liquor licences, and many prominent people in Southend had been encouraged to become honorary members; visiting sports clubs also received generous hospitality. McConnach's senior officers were generally loyal to him, but enough evidence was found to charge him with fraud and false pretences. In 1966 William McConnach was tried at the Central Criminal Court, and sent to prison for two years.[19]

Police officers are ordinary citizens, and although they have never been exempt from having to comply with the law, there will always be times when an occasional officer commits a criminal offence or contravenes the discipline code—just as they did in the past. The Police Complaints Board was established in 1976, after public opinion felt the need for an independent body to assess the evidence against officers who did commit offences. The board has now been replaced by the Police Complaints Authority, which liaises closely with the deputy chief constable in each police force—for he has an overall responsibility for discipline. Police officers have always been accountable to the communities they serve, but disciplinary procedures have now moved a long way from the time when each chief constable investigated all complaints, and then administered his own punishments.

Notes and References

1. *Chelmsford Chronicle*, 5 July 1842. At present it cannot be proved whether this is the same John Rough who was the Billericay inspector when Pc Robert Bamborough was murdered in 1850. Bamborough's Inspector Rough joined the force in 1841 when he was 45—he had previously been a soldier—and was posted to Billericay in 1844, resigning from there in December 1850 after Bamborough's death. Force records do not show him having a break in service, which would have been the case if he had gone to prison in 1842 as the newspaper account (and the original bankruptcy court records) suggest. John Rough, aged 54—a Chelsea pensioner—and his wife Anne, aged 64, appear in the 1851 census as living in Billericay High Street: that seems to be Bamborough's inspector. There is only the one John Rough in Essex police records, and no surviving record of him being stationed at Ockendon or Orsett.
2. *Chelmsford Chronicle*, 25 June 1849.
3. ERO J/P 2/1.
4. *Chelmsford Chronicle*, 25 June 1843.
5. *Essex County Standard*, 9 May 1851.
6. *ibid.*, 11 February 1859.
7. *ibid.*, 8 March 1859.
8. Letter to author dated 3 April 1992 from Mormon Historical Department, Salt Lake City, USA.
9. *Essex County Standard*, 18 March 1859.
10. *ibid.*, 2 May 1856.
11. *ibid.*, 5 September 1856.
12. Essex Police Museum discipline books.
13. ERO Colchester Watch Committee minutes.
14. All the previous examples are taken from discipline books and personnel files in the Essex Police Museum.
15. In March 1917 a force order gave a list of 34 offences which members of the force could commit under the general headings of misconduct or neglect. They included insubordination, disobeying a verbal or written command, neglecting to carry out regulations, tyrannical or oppressive conduct to an inferior in rank, using abusive or insulting language, receiving or soliciting a gratuity or testimonial without the Chief Constable's consent, being late for duty, leaving home without permission when on sick leave, losing or damaging clothing, being dirty or untidy, neglect of duty, borrowing or lending money, drinking on duty, communicating with the press or an unauthorised person, using unnecessary violence, and making an anonymous complaint to the Chief Constable. They were later rescinded when a standard discipline code appeared, although some of the offences are similar.
16. Essex Police Museum, discipline records.
17. *ibid.*
18. *ibid.*
19. ERO D/BC 1/7/5/21-23. William McConnach was born in 1910 in Aberdeen. He joined Plymouth City Police in 1931 and became its deputy chief constable in 1949. He was appointed Chief Constable of Southend in 1953, and undertook a major restructuring of the force, leading to the opening in 1961 of its new headquarters in Victoria Avenue. He died in March 1989.

Chapter 16

A Chronicle of Recent Times

Weeley pop festival 1971—public order training methods—the Barn murder—technological developments—Operation Lager—1981 riots—Stansted hijacking 1982—murder of Pc Bishop—miners' strike 1984—celebrating 150th anniversary of force in 1990

The last two chapters concentrated on specific topics in Essex police history—the developing rôle of women and discipline. This, the final chapter, covers the period from 1969—after the Essex and Southend-on-Sea constabularies amalgamated—until 1990, when the renamed Essex Police celebrated its 150th anniversary.[1] Because the period covered in this chapter is so recent in historical terms, it can make no claim to being a comprehensive record of events.

Essex and Southend came together again at the end of the 'swinging sixties', a decade which generated a whole variety of new social conditions. Dealing with the effects of strikes and public disorder had always been part of the police rôle, but the developing youth culture and its involvement in pop music and drugs gave police officers extra responsibilities when the era of the teddy boys was followed by those of 'mods and rockers' and 'skinheads'. One invasion of Southend by 'skinheads' received national media coverage when police officers—led by Sergeant Bill Gosling[2]—devised a simple method of immobilising them: their boot-laces and braces were confiscated.

Earlier massive pop music festivals had been held at Reading and on the Isle of Wight, and in January 1971 Clacton Round Table planned a similar event at Weeley over the August Bank Holiday weekend that year. Despite many local objections the organisers were granted a music and dancing licence for an estimated 10,000 people. As it turned out, something like 10 times that number actually attended. Consultations with Hampshire and Thames Valley police suggested that drugs were likely to be a problem at such a festival, and the force sent representatives to Reading in Spring 1971 to observe methods of searching and charging prisoners for drugs offences. On the August bank holiday weekend all leave was cancelled, and officers deployed at the Weeley festival were warned to be good humoured, helpful and tolerant. It soon became clear that the organisers had failed to meet their obligations. Parking arrangements and access to the site were inadequate, too few stewards had been employed, and conditions for selling alcohol were breached. Fights took place between groups of 'hells angels', and more than 112 arrests were made. The Weeley festival cost the force more than £40,000 in police overtime and catering bills.

In the 1970s different strategies for dealing with public disorder had to be considered at a national level. Discontent led, in 1972, to miners striking over a pay claim, with consequent disruption and power cuts. Other groups of workers also expressed their discontent with pay and conditions by holding strikes. People were no longer willing to disperse on demand and policemen called to deal with the effects of some of these strikes were not adequately trained in public order techniques; much thought was given to such problems at national level. In the Essex force a working party recommended the introduction of riot shields, goggles and reinforced helmets, as well as training in the different techniques required for their effective use.

Two cases in the early 1970s attracted a lot of attention from the media. On 30 July 1971 five-month-old Denise Weller was stolen from her pram outside a Harlow shop and, despite tremendous public co-operation, three days of intensive police searches and house-to-house enquiries failed to trace her. Details of the baby and her unusual birth mark were circulated to medical officers and social services throughout the country, and almost a month later baby Denise was found in Hull after a woman tried to make a false registration of her birth. Twenty-one years later two of the honoured guests at Denise Weller's birthday party were WPc Rosemary Palmer—the first officer at the scene of the abduction—and ex-Detective Chief Superintendent Len White who had headed the CID enquiries. Both officers had retained close contact with Denise and her family over the intervening years, Len White being Denise's godfather.

In the early hours of 5 November 1972 several 999 calls led to police and ambulance men being called to the Barn Restaurant at Braintree, where three members of the Patience family—the proprietors—had been robbed and shot by two men. Beverley Patience was seriously wounded in the attack, but her mother died from injuries a few days later. The death of Mrs. Muriel Patience led to a long series of enquiries and crown court trials which subjected the force to some severe public criticism. Information given to Scotland Yard suggested the involvement of a man named George Ince. Ince was also suspected of having been involved in the county's biggest ever robbery six months previously, when a lorry carrying nearly £400,000 of silver bullion had been hijacked near Mountnessing. The way in which Beverley Patience was shown a series of photographs formed the basis for some of the criticism the force received, for she later picked out George Ince at an identification parade.

George Ince consistently denied being involved in the attack on the Patience family, but in May 1973 he was tried at Chelmsford crown court, where the jury failed to reach a verdict. A retrial before a different judge resulted in his acquittal. Several weeks later detectives received information which led to a man named John Brook, who was working in a hotel in the Lake District. A search of his room revealed a pistol and ammunition, and ballistic tests proved that the gun had killed Mrs. Patience. Detailed enquiries traced Brook's accomplice, Nicholas de Clare Johnson, and the two were eventually tried and convicted in January 1974. There had been cases all over the country where identification evidence had caused problems in court, and the Barn Murder case helped to provide an even greater impetus for a national inquiry into identification methods. The enquiry was undertaken by Lord Chief Justice Devlin, and resulted in strict guidelines being introduced.

One of the benefits of having closer liaison between police and Home Office research departments led to the increasing use of technology to aid police work. The continuing problem of speeding motor vehicles resulted in the development of VASCAR (Visual Average Speed Computer and Recorder) which allowed police officers to calculate the speed of a vehicle, where it was known how long it had taken to cover a set distance. Police Constables Don Barrell and David Jennings were trained to use this equipment, and in 1971 they became force instructors, and consultants to other forces which bought the same equipment.

After some years of research and development, the first phase of the police national computer became operational on 1 August 1974. It had previously taken weeks to check whether or not a suspected car had been stolen, but with details of all abandoned and stolen vehicles entered into the computer the answer could be supplied instantly. On the first day the new computer went live, it assisted in the recovery of seven stolen vehicles in Essex alone.

The 1970s brought some financial problems for police forces in general, when less money was allocated by central government and more had to be found from local rates. Essex suffered economies which included the abandonment of cadet recruiting; the completion of the new headquarters building was also delayed, and it was not opened until February 1979. Police officers were now very discontented with the way they were being treated, and a national ballot to assess feelings about a police strike showed 65 per cent of Essex officers in favour. Such discontent helped to encourage another enquiry into police pay and conditions chaired by Mr. Justice Edmund Davies. His report recommended greatly improved pay scales, which were implemented in two phases, starting in 1978.

In 1978 Sir John Nightingale retired, and his deputy Robert Bunyard—formerly assistant chief constable of Leicestershire—became Chief Constable. He instigated preliminary work into establishing a new branch of the force to undertake the more caring rôles formerly undertaken by policewomen. The new community services branch was set up by the then Superintendent Geoffrey Markham, and Chief Inspectors Ralph Crawshaw and Lorna Baker. The branch dealt principally with children at risk, and schools liaison work, and was promptly nicknamed 'Mothercare' by the rest of the force!

Drugs enquiries were now playing an increasing part in police work; one enquiry spanned the decades of the seventies and eighties. 'Operation Lager' began with information that a house in Rainsford Lane, Chelmsford was being used for distributing drugs. In May 1978 the first of more than 150 arrests was made, and an international investigation began into the links between smuggling cannabis, heroin, cocaine, amphetamines and weapons. How 'Operation Lager' got its name was the subject of much press speculation, but it actually resulted from a series of surveillance photographs that were produced in the early stages of the enquiry. The shot of one particular woman in the mass of photographs could not be identified—until someone remembered that the woman's photograph had appeared on a calendar advertising lager; presumably the photographer had tested the focus of his camera on the calendar before starting work.

No one had anticipated just how long 'Operation Lager' would last. Detective Chief Inspector Barry Tarbun, head of the operation, thought it might be cleared up over one weekend! Instead the operation and its subsidiary enquiries ran for almost a decade before everything was complete and the cases came to court. The close-knit team of Barry Tarbun, John Garrard, Brian Spraggon, Larry Nevin, Colin Prest and Geoffrey Benton were supplemented over the years by more than 80 other officers involved in different stages of the operation. Links were followed up between American air bases in Britain and the Palestine Liberation Organisation. There were close links with Holland, and co-operation between Essex officers, and Dutch police and customs officers.

As a result of the 'Lager' investigations some new techniques were developed for scenes-of-crime work; it was unexpectedly discovered that fingerprints could be taken from such places as the inside of a lorry's diesel tank. The first series of 'Operation Lager' trials began at Chelmsford crown court, which was then in the Shire Hall. Because of the number of defendants and counsel, and the length of time the trials were expected to take, the interior of the Shire Hall ballroom was rebuilt as a court. At the conclusion of all the trials, Judge Francis Petre commended the original team and their exhibits officer Keith Gurney. All the officers were later awarded the first high commendation certificates issued in 1981 by the Chief Constable.

During the 1980s some of the most spectacular incidents in the forefront of force history are concerned with violence. Arming the police has always been a contentious issue, but changes in society have made it necessary for individual officers to be armed at certain times in order to carry out their duties effectively.

In March 1979 Paul Howe, a young man with an emotionally disturbed background, was believed to have committed a burglary in Swiss Avenue, Chelmsford, and stolen a substantial amount of cash. Officers who wanted to talk to him about the allegation were told that he was also suspected of having committed a second offence where a shotgun and ammunition had been stolen. When armed police went to the house to arrest Paul Howe he ran off, later forcing another young man at gun point to drive him along the A12 towards Harwich. Later the two were briefly besieged by police on a German boat in Harwich docks, but then escaped in a stolen police transit. That evening Paul Howe and his hostage went to the *Castle* public house in the village of Ramsey; they stayed there for the rest of the night. Telephone calls by police negotiators went unanswered; but Anglia Television's 'News at Ten' reporter was more successful when he carried out a telephone interview which was broadcast on the national TV news. It seemed clear that Paul Howe was determined to die in what he called a 'shoot-out' with the police. The following day the hostage managed to escape, and when Paul Howe later advanced on police officers with his semi-automatic shotgun ready to fire, he refused all their attempts to persuade him to give himself up. One shot was fired; and Paul Howe was taken unconscious to hospital where he died shortly afterwards. It was the first time an Essex firearms officer had been obliged to kill in self defence, and the effects on the officer and his colleagues at the scene were traumatic.

The year 1981 will be remembered for the riots which occurred in various parts of the country. Over the weekend of 10-12 April 1981, a series of disorders occurred in the south London suburb of Brixton, where police were attacked with stones, bricks, iron bars and petrol bombs—the first time such a weapon had been used on the British mainland. Many of the rioters were black youths protesting at what they considered to be oppressive policing and harassment. Over the next few months there were 'copycat' riots in Southall, Liverpool, Manchester and the West Midlands. The subsequent public enquiry led by Lord Scarman looked in detail at what had happened in Brixton. Scarman's report recommended that major changes were made affecting all British police forces. His proposals included radical changes to methods of police recruitment and training; much greater attention was to be given to community-awareness education for all officers. Essex Police training school adapted its courses accordingly.

Training procedures for dealing with major incidents was also carried out in the 1980s. For many years a public debate had waged on the need for a third London airport; Stansted was the main contender for such a rôle, but in 1982 no official decision had yet been taken. The existing small airport was regularly used to test emergency procedures, and at the beginning of 1982 such a training exercise was held to test emergency plans for the possible hi-jacking of an aircraft. A few weeks later such an incident actually occurred, when a Tanzanian Airways Boeing 737 landed at Stansted on the afternoon of Saturday 27 February. The 87 passengers and crew of four had been on an internal flight to Dar-es-Salaam when the aeroplane was hi-jacked by four men: their arrival at Stansted had been preceded by a nightmare journey via Nairobi, Jeddah and Athens.

21. Within 30 minutes of leaving Mwanza Airport in Tanzania for an internal flight to Dar-es-Salaam, this Boeing 737—'Kilimanjaro'—was hijacked and forced to fly half way across the world. This picture was taken on the ground at Stansted as the hostages were released into the freezing cold of a Sunday afternoon in February 1982.

Chief Superintendent Mike Humberston was the principal force negotiator. His task was to build up a relationship with the hi-jackers and try to persuade them to give themselves up; the other two officers in his team were Chief Inspectors Ralph Barrington and Gordon Waller. All through that night demands were made, and negotiations with the Tanzanian hi-jackers and embassy officials resulted in the gradual release of groups of hostages. The following afternoon the siege ended peacefully, all the remaining hostages were released, and the hi-jackers gave themselves up. With the aid of Swahili interpreters and translators, a large team of officers took statements from passengers and crew. The four hi-jackers and another man were later convicted of air piracy at the Old Bailey. Because of the success of the whole operation, Chief Constable Robert Bunyard and Chief Superintendent Mike Humberston were invited to give many lectures—including a series in Australia.

In August 1984 the force was deeply shocked when Pc Brian Bishop (commonly known as Bill) was murdered on duty. Brian Bishop was a firearms instructor keeping observation in Frinton where a robbery was expected to take place. When the robber suddenly returned to the scene he was challenged by armed officers. The robber opened fire, causing severe head injuries from which Bill Bishop he died five days later. Sergeant (later Inspector) Mervyn Fairweather was also shot in the same incident but went on to make a good recovery. In February 1986 the Police Memorial Trust erected a monument to Brian Bishop at the scene of the attack in Central Avenue, Frinton.

New methods of riot control training were introduced after 1 March 1984, when the announcement of the closure of several pits in South Yorkshire heralded the beginning of a miners' strike, the repercussions of which affected the whole country. A national reporting centre in London was set in motion to co-ordinate calls for manpower from chief constables in mining areas; media attention suggested it was the start of central control by a national police force. Essex policemen were mainly deployed in Nottinghamshire, Derbyshire and Leicestershire where they found themselves billeted in old army camps, and working long hours while following strange shift patterns.

There are, of course, no coal mines in Essex, but one effect of the strike in Essex was the picketing of five small private ports at Rowhedge, Brightlingsea, Wivenhoe, Mistley and Colchester Hythe which were being used to import coal from Germany and Poland. An operational headquarters was set up at Wivenhoe Town football ground, and police officers were accused of trying to break the miners' strike as they endeavoured to keep the unregistered ports and their small communities free from more than the legal numbers of pickets.

Some of the procedures which had been so criticised during the miners' strike were revised by the Police and Criminal Evidence Act of 1984 which was given a practice-run in the force at the end of 1985. Under the new Act strict new guidelines were established for

22. Generations of police officers have been part of a scene such as this as they helped to ensure the safety of members of the public. There have been many Royal visits to Essex over the lifetime of the force, each one giving police officers responsibility for the safety of the Royal personage as well as the many people who throng the streets on such occasions.

dealing with prisoners, and suspects were given more legally enforceable rights. The Act's most immediate effect was to cause a loss of 40 officers from outside duties to fill the newly-created posts of custody officer.

About two years before the 150th anniversary of the force, a committee was set up to discuss plans for marking the occasion. With representatives from every department and division it soon became very unwieldy, and was temporarily put into abeyance. In 1987 Robert Bunyard left the force to become Commandant of the Police Staff College at Bramshill, and John Burrow was appointed as his successor. The anniversary committee was reconstituted under the chairmanship of assistant chief constable James Conlan, and detailed plans were made for celebrations—although some proposals had to be severely curtailed because of expense. Although the force as a whole expressed some interest in celebrating the anniversary, problems with time and the deployment of manpower meant that the main co-ordinating rôle fell to retired officers and their wives, notably Frederick Feather and Frank Shepherd.

The celebrations were planned to start in April 1990 with an international police march along a specially created footpath around Danbury and Chelmsford; the footpath was dedicated to Admiral McHardy, the first Chief Constable. Many police stations arranged special open days during 1990, and there were other commemorative events appropriate to particular districts. Concerts were given all over the county by the force band, and many different sorts of exhibitions were held. Colchester military tattoo in August 1990 included a large police input, with the usual displays from police dogs and horses being supplemented by a pageant depicting colourful events in force history. To round off the celebrations a service was held in Chelmsford Cathedral on 23 September 1990. The music of the cathedral's choir and organ was supplemented by that provided by the Essex Police band and the new force choir, and the whole service was a fitting conclusion to the celebrations marking 150 years of policing in Essex.

All police men and women—whatever their rank—hold the office of constable; they are primarily ordinary citizens who have accepted additional powers and responsibilities towards their equals. This fact serves to emphasise the local accountability which is an essential part of every English police force. Knowledge of how the past shapes the present can help us to understand how present events may affect the future. Whatever form Essex police takes in future, its county origins will ensure that it continues to be part of the community it serves. The police service in Essex must understand enough of its own origins to comprehend the pressures upon it, and to honour the men and women who made it what it is. By looking to our past, we who are 'sworn to serve' can therefore equip ourselves to face the uncertainties of the future with confidence.

Notes and References

1. The name of the force was changed to Essex Police on 1 April 1974. At the same time a new force emblem took effect: three floating seaxes in parallel rather than in diminishing order.
2. Sergeant Gosling was well-known throughout Southend as 'Uncle Bill'.

Appendix I

Note on Sources

The notes at the end of each chapter provide detailed references to printed books and original documents quoted in the text. However, for the benefit of anyone wishing to read about the subject of policing in greater depth, I have found the following printed works to be particularly useful:

Critchley, T. A., *A History of Police in England and Wales*, Constable, 1978.

Emsley, Clive, *The English Police: A Political and Social History*, Harvester Wheatsheaf/St. Martin's Press, 1991

Emsley, Clive, *Policing and its Context 1750-1870*, Macmillan, 1983.

Foster, David, *The Rural Constabulary Act 1839: A National Legislation and the Problems of Enforcement*, Standing Conference for Local History, 1982.

Radzinowicz, L, *A History of English Criminal Law and its Administration from 1750: Volume 3, Cross Currents in the Movement for the Reform of the Police;* and *Volume 4, Grappling for Control,* Stevens and Sons, 1956 and 1968.

Steedman, Caroline, *Policing the Victorian Community*, Routledge and Kegan Paul, 1984.

Storch, Robert, D., 'Policing Southern Rural England before the Police' in *Policing and Prosecution in Britain 1750-1850,* ed. Hay and Ward, Oxford, 1989.

Appendix II

RULES MADE BY THE MARQUIS OF NORMANBY, SECRETARY OF STATE, FOR ESTABLISHING POLICE FORCES UNDER THE 1839 COUNTY POLICE ACT (2 & 3 VIC. CAP 93)

TO: THE JUSTICES OF THE PEACE FOR THE COUNTY OF ESSEX

Gentlemen, — The recent act for the appointment and establishment of county constables having enacted, with a view to uniformity of system, that rules are to be made by one of her Majesty's principal Secretaries of State for the government of constables so appointed, I have the honour to transmit to you the enclosed copy of rules, made by me, for the government of constables appointed under that act for the county of Essex.

As the first step towards the establishment of a Constabulary Force will be the appointment of a chief constable (who is to be appointed by the justices at quarter sessions, subject to the approval of the Secretary of State), I request your attention to that part of the rules relating to qualifications of chief constables.

I have given directions for a short summary to be drawn up, respecting the duties and powers of constables, which may be useful for their instruction and guidance after they have been appointed, and I will transmit a copy of this summary to the magistrates as soon as it is completed.

I have only to add that, if the magistrates are desirous of receiving from me further information upon the subject, I shall be most ready to afford to them all the information in my power.

I have the honour to be, Gentlemen,

Your obedient servant

NORMANBY

QUALIFICATIONS FOR SUPERINTENDENT AND CONSTABLES

To be under 40 years of age; to stand five feet seven inches without shoes; to read and write, and keep accounts; to be free from any bodily complaint, of strong constitution, and generally intelligent.

No person shall be appointed a superintendent or constable who shall be a gamekeeper, wood-ranger, sheriff's bailiff, or parish clerk, or who shall be a hired servant in the employment of any person, or who shall keep or have any interest in any house for the sale of beer, wine, or spiritous liquors by retail; and if any person who shall be appointed a superintendent or constable shall, at any time after such his appointment, become a gamekeeper, wood-ranger, bailiff, sheriff's bailiff, or parish clerk, or shall act in any of the said capacities, or shall sell, or have any interest in the sale of any beer, wine or spiritous liquors by retail, such person shall thereupon become and be incapable of acting as such superintendent or constable, and shall forfeit his appointment of superintendent or constable, and also all salary payable to him as a superintendent or constable.

A certificate of character is to be signed by one or more respectable persons who have had personal knowledge of the candidate during the last five years at least, either singly or collectively.

CHIEF CONSTABLE

QUALIFICATIONS OF CHIEF CONSTABLE—1. His age must not exceed 45. 2. He must be certified by a Medical Practitioner to be in good health and of sound constitution, and fitted to perform the duties of office. 3. He must not have been a bankrupt, nor have taken the benefit of the Insolvent Act. 4. He must be recommended to the Secretary of State by the magistrates in whom the appointment is vested, as a person of general good character and conduct. If he has been previously employed in any branch of the public service, civil or military, he must produce testimonials from the proper authorities in such service as to general conduct whilst so employed.

SUPERINTENDENT

QUALIFICATIONS OF A SUPERINTENDENT—He must be qualified. In case of a vacancy in the office of superintendent it should be filled up by the most deserving constable.

CONSTABLES

QUALIFICATIONS OF CONSTABLES—No person shall be eligible who does not produce a testimonial, duly filled up, and who is not possessed of the qualifications stated. The chief constable is to keep a daily account which is to be laid before the justices of the county at each quarter sessions of the peace, or any adjournment thereof, showing the actual state of the constabulary for the period since the last preceding quarter sessions of the peace for the county. And once in every three-months, as soon as may be practicable after the termination of the quarter sessions of the peace in each county, the chief constable shall transmit a return in writing to one of Her Majesty's principal Secretaries of State that such daily account has been laid before the justices for the county in quarter sessions assembled; together with a copy of any note or minute, which may have been made by any of the said justices upon the same, expressing their opinion with regard to the effective state of the constabulary during the three months.

PAY

The pay of the chief constable is to be not less than £250 or more than £500 a year. Of a superintendent not less than £75 or more than £150 a year. Of a constable not less than 15/- or more than £1-1-0 a week. The above rates are intended to be exclusive of any allowance under the 18th section of the Act. The constable is to be supplied in addition with the following articles of

CLOTHING

First year, one greatcoat, cape to ditto, badge to ditto, coat, badge to ditto, two pair of trousers, one pair of boots, one pair of shoes, hat, stock. Second year, coat, badge to ditto, one pair of trousers, one pair of boots, one pair of shoes, hat. The supply for the third year will be the same as for the first year, and for the fourth the same as the second; and so on for successive periods.

ACCOUTREMENTS

A constable's staff is to be supplied to each constable, and a small cutlass may be supplied to any constable who is so situated that, in the opinion of two justices of the county, it is necessary for his personal protection in the performance of his duty. The cutlass is to be worn at night only, or at times when rioting or serious public disturbance has actually taken place or is apprehended, or upon any sudden emergency when orders have been given by the chief constable that one or more of the constables should be armed; and the chief constable shall on each occasion of giving any such order report the same, and the reason for such order, to any two justices of the peace for the county as soon afterwards as is practicable, who shall immediately transmit the said report to the Secretary of State.

GOVERNMENT

The chief constable is from time to time to frame such orders as he shall deem expedient relative to the particular service of the superintendent and the constables, their distribution, and the places of their residence, and all such orders as he may deem expedient for preventing neglect or abuse, and for rendering such civil force efficient in the discharge of all its duties: and he will keep in mind that the prevention of crime is to be made the great object of all the exertions of the constable. The chief constable must lay before the justices of the county assembled in the next quarter sessions, or any adjournment thereof, a statement of all orders issued by him; and a copy of the same is to be transmitted by him to one of Her Majesty's principal Secretaries of State, as soon after the Issuing thereof as may be practicable.

COMPLAINTS

In case of a complaint against the chief constable, the party complaining should give immediate notice to a justice of the peace, who will proceed thereon according to law if the offence be cognisable by him; and if the subject of complaint do not constitute any offence legally cognisable by him, the said justice will lay a statement thereof before the justices of the county at the next quarter sessions of the peace, or any adjournment thereof, and the justices will enquire into the same, and report the result of such enquiry and their opinion thereon, as speedily as possible to one of Her Majesty's principal Secretaries of State.

Immediate attention is to be paid to any complaint of misconduct against the superintendent, or any constable appointed under the said act. If the charge be for neglect or violation of duty in his office as constable, it shall be laid before two justices with the least delay possible, for their proceeding thereon under the 12th section of the said act; and in case of any other offence committed by such constable notice thereof shall be immediately given to a justice of the peace, who will proceed thereon according to law.

GENERAL INSTRUCTIONS

Parties in custody are to be taken before a magistrate as soon as possible, and the nature of the offence, with other particulars, entered in a charge sheet. The charge sheet is to be laid before the magistrate by whom the charge is to be heard, and when all the cases entered therein have been disposed of by the magistrate, the charge sheet is to be sent to the chief constable, or kept safely by one of the superintendents or constables, as he shall direct; and all such charge sheets are to be returned by the chief constable once in every three months to the clerk of the peace for the county, who is to keep them in his custody until he shall have received the directions of the justices of the peace for the county, assembled at any quarter sessions, as to the final disposal thereof.

If a charge against a party be not taken by the constable, an entry is to be made up by him, and the particulars filled up under each head, and transmitted to the chief constable, who will lay before the justices of the peace for the county, assembled at the next quarter sessions of the peace, an abstract stating the entire number of persons charged with offences as appears thereby, the nature of the charges and the results, with any other particulars that may tend to show the state of crime in the county.

The chief constable will also make an immediate report to two justices of the peace of any serious disturbance of the public peace that has taken place or is apprehended, and of any crimes of an aggravated nature committed, and for which the parties charged or suspected have not been apprehended and he will immediately transmit duplicates of such information to the Secretary of State for the Home Department, so as to ensure the earliest communication to the proper authorities of any matter affecting the public peace, in order that further arrangements, if required, may be made without delay.

Appendix III

Chief Officers

Authority to hold the rank of chief constable of a county dates from the County Police Act of 1839. The same Act required a chief constable to chose one of his superintendents as his deputy, for which £50 extra each year was payable. From then until after an assistant chief constable was regularly appointed, deputy chief constable was a role normally undertaken by the most senior of the assistant chief constables in a force. Deputy chief constable became a rank, rather than a role, under the Police and Criminal Evidence Act of 1984.

The first reference to a rank of assistant chief constable seems to be the appointment of Captain Matthew Ffinch during the First World War. His appointment put him in charge of the special constabulary. After his resignation on 1 April 1919 Captain Ffinch was not replaced immediately. However, from 1 October 1920 the position seems to have been filled on an intermittent basis. The first permanent post of assistant chief constable was created in 1935, and has been filled continuously ever since. A second post was added to the establishment in 1957, and a third in 1969, after the amalgamation with Southend Borough Constabulary.

By tradition chief constables had a military or naval career background. The 1919 Police Act incorporated recommendations of the Desborough Committee that police authorities should only appoint chief constables who had previous police experience, and that they should be made to retire on reaching 65. Both requirements were regularly ignored. Of the 15 chief constables appointed between 1919-1939 three came from the Royal Irish Police; four from the Indian Police; three from police ranks; and five from elsewhere. (David Wall: *The Selection of Chief Constables in England and Wales 1835-1985*) York University M.Phil. thesis, 1989.

There have been eight Chief Constables of Essex since 1840, and the following 'Who's Who' gives brief details of their lives. Sources for the information are mainly force records and publications, local newspapers, and publications such as *Who's Who* and *Who was Who* for various years.

1. JOHN BUNCH BONNEMAISON McHARDY
11 February 1840-31 October 1881

Born Nassau, Bahamas on 3 December 1801. Married Horatia Pasco 11 October 1830. Served in Royal Navy and Coast Guard, being promoted commander on 20 March 1835. Placed on reserved half pay list with rank of captain. Appointed first Chief Constable of Essex on 11 February 1840. Promoted rear admiral on 24 February 1858 and admiral 1 April 1870. Retired as chief constable on 31 October 1881, died 19 December 1882. Survived by five sons and two daughters. Buried in family tomb at Holy Trinity Church, Springfield, with the children who pre-deceased him. Widow Horatia died 3 October 1883.

2. WILLIAM HENRY POYNTZ
1 November 1881- 2 July 1887

Born Dublin 23 October 1838. First commissioned into Royal Marine Light Infantry 26 October 1853. Served in Hong Kong, China, Japan and Woolwich. Freemason from 1862. Married February 1870 to Henrietta Sainton. Chief Constable of Nottingham, 1871-1881. One son Edward Stephen Poyntz, born 1883. Published autobiography *Per Mare Per Terram* just before death in 1892.

3. EDWARD McLEAN SHOWERS
3 July 1888-30 April 1915

Born 1846 in Moulmein, India. Commissioned in 95th Derbyshire Regiment. 1872 studied law and police duties. Superintendent in Devon police 1884. Chief Constable of Exeter. First wife May Ayling died 1892. Married 1894 to Georgina, Countess D'Epineuil, sister of Raglan Somerset, deputy chief constable. One of first officers to be awarded King's Police Medal, 1909. Ordered to retire 1915 because of age, but appointed acting chief constable Colchester Borough Constabulary 1915-1919 while Captain Stockwell (borough chief constable) rejoined his regiment. Died 13 December 1925.

4. JOHN ALFRED UNETT
8 May 1915-6 December 1932

Born 3 October 1868. Educated United Services College, Westwood Ho. Served in Third Hussars from 1889; promoted captain 1898. Married Daisy Slater March 1905. Attached to City of London Police, then superintendent and chief clerk in Hertfordshire, 1909-1912. Chief Constable of Preston borough, 1912-1915. Prominent Freemason. Churchwarden of Springfield parish church. Died in post on 6 December 1932.

5. FRANCIS JONATHAN PEEL
1 May 1933-9 December 1962

Born 10 December 1897 Rock Ferry, Cheshire. After war service in Royal Field Artillery, graduated from Cambridge University. Joined Liverpool City Police as constable in 1920. Promoted through ranks becoming chief inspector 1928. Joined Bath City as ACC and then Chief Constable in 1931. Married Daphne Packenham in 1932. One daughter, one son Edmund Anthony Peel, born 1933. Knighted 1959. Died 6 December 1979.

6. JOHN CYPRIAN NIGHTINGALE
10 October 1962-30 June 1978

Born 16 September 1913. Graduated University College, London with B.A. in Classics. Joined Metropolitan Police as constable 1935. Selected for Lord Trenchard's accelerated promotion scheme at Hendon. Moved through ranks, with a break for war service in Royal Navy. Married in 1947 to Patricia Maclaren. January 1950 joined directing staff national police college, then at Ryton-on-Dunsmore. Commandant of Eynsham Hall police training centre from January 1953-February 1956. ACC Essex 1 January 1958. Knighted 1975.

7. ROBERT SIDNEY BUNYARD
1 July 1978-31 December 1987

Born 20 May 1930. Formerly a teacher. Married 1948 to Ruth Martin. Joined Metropolitan Police 1952. Transferred to Leicestershire as ACC 1972. Transferred to Essex as DCC 15 December 1977. Resigned 1987 to become Commandant of Police Staff College, Bramshill, with rank of HMI. Knighted in 1991. Author of: *Organization and Command* (1978) and *Police Management Handbook* (1979).

8. JOHN HALCROW BURROW
1 February 1988- Present

Born 21 July 1935 in Ulverston, Cumbria. Lieutenant 3rd Kenya Battalion King's African Rifles, 1953-55. Married Ruth Taylor 1958. Joined Metropolitan Police 1958. Bramshill scholarship to University College, London, gaining LL.B. (Hons.) in 1967. Appointed ACC of Merseyside 1 August 1977, and DCC on 1 February 1983. Took up appointment as Essex Chief Constable on 1 February 1988. National President of Association of Chief Police Officers, 1992-93.

The following list gives brief details in date order, and note form, of the superintendents who acted as deputy chief constable, and those who were appointed as assistant chief constable.

RICHARD STEER, superintendent and DCC
1841-30 April 1846

Born 1815 in Dartford, Kent. Formerly engineer. Joined force 10 April 1840 as constable. Resigned February 1841, but rejoined five months later. Promoted inspector December 1841. Promoted superintendent. Acted as DCC until April 1846. Resigned through ill-health.

EDWARD HARDY, superintendent and DCC
3 August 1849-18 June 1850

Lieutenant in Royal Navy from 1843. Joined force as superintendent in August 1849. Acted as DCC until leaving to join hydrographical office at Admiralty. Eventually promoted naval commander. Dead by 1874.

JOSEPH GACE, superintendent and DCC
6 November 1850-23 October 1851

Born Louth, Lincolnshire, in 1824. Royal Naval half pay lieutenant. Younger brother of Emily Fanny Gace, who was drowned with Captain McHardy's daughter Mary. Joined force as superintendent. In 1851 census living at Old Court with wife Jemima and daughter Emily Fanny, aged nine months—probably named after his dead sister.

JAMES YOUNG, superintendent and DCC
1 January 1853-28 February 1855

Joined force as 24 year old superintendent. Acted as DCC for two years before resigning to join Land Transport Corps. May have become Chief Constable of Ayrshire later.

WILLIAM HENRY LUARD PATTISSON, superintendent and DCC
1 December 1867-30 April 1874

Born 20 July 1837 at Witham. Joined force as inspector on 1 July 1859 after being withdrawn from St John's College, Cambridge when father went bankrupt. Initially stationed at Epping. Married January 1874 to Emily Celestine Hill. Resigned in April 1874 to become manager of Writtle Brewery. Died, aged 58, on 16 July 1895, following stomach operation.

WALLACE BRUCE McHARDY, superintendent and DCC
23 March 1874-30 November 1875

Born 19 February 1844 at Springfield, 5th son of Captain McHardy. Royal Navy to commander before joining Essex Constabulary in 1874. Acted as deputy to his father before becoming Chief Constable of Lanarkshire in 1875. Died in post in 1896.

WILLIAM BRIDGES, superintendent and DCC
1 January 1876-3 June 1883

Born Wexford, previously a farmer. On 9 January 1843 joined force aged 22. Promoted superintendent 1 October 1850. DCC from 1876 until his retirement.

RAGLAN MOLYNEAUX BOSCOWEN SOMERSET, superintendent and DCC
1 July 1883-31 August 1915

Born Stroud, Gloucester, son of Colonel H.C. Somerset and grandson of Lord William Somerset. Served as superintendent of Bingham division in Nottinghamshire Constabulary from 1 October 1878. Transferred to Essex 1 April 1882, becoming Chelmsford superintendent. Appointed DCC on 1 July 1883. Died unmarried 7 January 1923. Buried Holy Trinity Church, Springfield. Widowed sister Georgina, Countess D'Epineuil, married Captain Showers 1894.

GEORGE WILLIAM PAGE, DCC & ACC
4 June 1919-31 December 1921

Born 1 December 1867 Rayleigh. Formerly blacksmith. Joined force 14 September 1888. Promoted superintendent 8 August 1914; DCC 4 June 1919; ACC 1 October 1920. By November 1921 duties of an ACC had decreased, and when Page retired on 31 December 1921 no further appointment made for more than a decade.

WILLIAM THOMAS JOHN HOWLETT, superintendent and DCC
1 January 1922-30 April 1926

Born 16 May 1866 Little Maplestead. Joined force on 20 December 1886. Promoted superintendent 1 May 1916 at Romford. DCC on 1 January 1922 (no ACC being considered necessary). Died 12 June 1926, shortly after retiring.

ALFRED JAMES OFFORD, superintendent and DCC
1 May 1926-13 May 1933

Born Bury St Edmunds, Suffolk. Formerly grocer's assistant. Joined force aged 22, 2 April 1900. Initially posted to Dunmow, but soon moved to HQ as assistant clerk. Good example of popular view that promotion lay in clerical work rather than 'in the field'. Promoted through ranks in administration. DCC from 1 May 1926. Awarded M.B.E. for administrative work in the First World War.

JOHN CROCKFORD, first permanent ACC, and DCC
19 July 1933-2 January 1952

Born St Cross, Suffolk 2 January 1888. Formerly farm labourer. Joined force on 5 June 1911. Served for 11 years at Brentwood. One of earliest members of Detective and Enquiry Department (original name for CID). Detective inspector on 1 April 1927. Worked closely with Metropolitan officers investigating murder of Pc Gutteridge. Promoted to superintendent at Grays 8 May 1930. DCC in 1933 and first permanent ACC from

1935. Younger brother (by seven years) of George Crockford, Chief Constable of Southend Borough Constabulary, 1935-1939.

A written history which moves towards the present faces particular problems in knowing where to stop. Therefore out of respect for the personal privacy and security of mid-20th century chief officers—many of whom are still alive—the following entries only include bare details of their professional lives.

GEORGE PERCY SUTTON, ACC
3 January 1953-19 March 1959

Joined 11 August 1919 and posted to Romford. 1921 joined Detective and Enquiry Department; detective sergeant 1929. Promoted superintendent in charge of Traffic 1937. Military forces liaison officer during the Second World War. As divisional commander of Romford—then largest division—first holder of new rank of chief superintendent. Promoted ACC on 3 January 1953. Died 1982.

HAROLD SHELLEY PHILLIBROWN, ACC
1959-15 June 1965

Joined 19 January 1920. Son of Superintendent George Phillibrown. Promoted sergeant 1929. Chief superintendent at Brentwood 1953, having served in seven divisions of force. Appointed ACC in 1959, and retired as senior ACC and thereby deputy chief constable. Died 1988.

ARTHUR BURNS, DCC
16 June 1965-30 April 1968

Joined Derby Borough Police on 28 September 1939, and served in Cyprus police before becoming DCC of Norwich Borough. Essex ACC on 1 February 1963. DCC from 1965. Became Chief Constable of Suffolk on 1 April 1968.

CHARLES HOWARD WALLER, ACC
1 May 1968-30 July 1971

Joined Essex Constabulary 1934, spending much of his service in CID. Detective Chief Superintendent 1967. ACC 1 May 1968. Died 1991.

KENNETH FRANK ALSTON, DCC
1 April 1968-30 September 1971

Joined Essex Constabulary 1 June 1934 serving throughout county, including Harwich and Clacton. Divisional commander of Romford at time of Metropolitan Police takeover 1966. DCC on 1 April 1968 until his retirement. Died June 1993.

JOHN DUKE, DCC
1 August 1972-31 August 1977

City of London Police 10 April 1947-31 August 1969. Transferred to Essex as ACC 1 September 1969. DCC on 1 August 1972. Chief Constable of Hampshire from 1 September 1977. Died 1989.

WILLIAM PETHERICK, ACC OPERATIONS
1 October 1971-31 March 1981

Joined Essex 1938 and served throughout county, including Basildon and chief superintendent of Grays. ACC Operations from 1 October 1971.

HARRY ADAM TAYLOR, ACC ADMINISTRATION
1 August 1971-31 May 1983

Previous service in Durham to chief superintendent where he gained an M.Sc. degree. ACC Administration from 1 August 1971. Died 1986.

CHARLES HENRY KELLY, ACC PERSONNEL
1 August 1972-15 August 1976

Previous service in Isle of Man and West Riding. Transferred to Essex on 1 September 1969 as chief superintendent Basildon. Promoted ACC Personnel 1 August 1972. DCC of Staffordshire from 15 August 1976. Currently Chief Constable of Staffordshire.

MATTHEW DICK COMRIE, ACC OPERATIONS
20 September 1976-30 May 1988

Metropolitan Police from 21 August 1951. Transferred to Essex as ACC 20 September 1976. Retired May 1988.

BARRY PRICE, DCC
10 July 1978-28 February 1980

Served Metropolitan Police and Northumbria Constabulary. Transferred to Essex as DCC. Chief Constable of Cumbria from 1 March 1980.

RONALD STONE, DCC
1 March 1980-30 October 1986

Devon and Cornwall Police to rank of chief superintendent. ACC of Cambridgeshire before transferring to Essex as DCC 1 March 1980. Retired 1986, having been first holder of rank (rather than position) of DCC.

JOHN CHALLIS, Temporary ACC
1 July 1982-31 August 1983

All previous service in Essex. Appointed acting ACC in 1982 until his retirement.

GEOFFREY ROY MARKHAM, ACC
1 September 1983-Present

Joined Essex Constabulary in 1958, serving in many divisions and departments of force. While an inspector seconded to Essex University gaining first class B.A. (Hons.) degree. ACC Personnel from 1.9.1983. Currently ACC Operations.

ROGER RICHARDSON, Temporary ACC
1 January 1984-7 January 1985

Originally cadet. Joined force 25.2.1954. Experienced CID officer. Several secondments to Regional Crime Squad. Promoted detective chief superintendent January 1981, and acting ACC Operations from 1 January 1984 to retirement.

PETER JOHN SIMPSON, DCC
30 October 1986-27 October 1993

Son of former Essex Chief Superintendent Arthur Simpson. Previous service in Hertfordshire to chief superintendent. Essex ACC Personnel from 11 May 1981. Promoted to rank of DCC from 30 October 1986.

FRANK GEOFFREY SHEPHERD, Temporary ACC
1986

All previous service in Essex. Promoted chief superintendent 16 May 1977. Acting ACC from 1986. Retired as chief superintendent 26 June 1987.

JAMES DICKINSON, DCC (seconded)
1 March 1992-Present

Southend-on-Sea Borough Constabulary to 1969. Service in Essex to detective chief superintendent. Promoted ACC 1987. December 1989 seconded to office of Her Majesty's Chief Inspector of Constabulary. Currently deputy commandant of Police Staff College, Bramshill.

JAMES ALOYSIUS CONLAN, ACC
20 June 1988-Present

Metropolitan Police from 1959. Transferred to Essex as ACC Administration on 1 July 1988. Currently serving as ACC Personnel.

TERENCE RANDS, ACC
4 January 1989-Present

Southend-on-Sea Borough Constabulary and Essex to chief superintendent. Temporary ACC Personnel on 4 January 1989, later made substantive. Currently serving as ACC Administration.

Chief Officers of Borough Forces

Southend-on-Sea Borough Constabulary
amalgamated with Essex on 1 April 1969

Henry Kerslake	1914-1935
George Crockford	1935-1939
Arthur Hunt	1939-1953
William McConnach	1953-1965
(Acting) Henry Devlin	1965-1969

Colchester Borough Constabulary
amalgamated with Essex on 1 April 1947

J.A. Neville	1836-1837
W. Rand (called watch sergeant)	1837-1847
A. Kent	1841-1843
J. Dunn (called superintendent)	1854-1857 (force remodelled in May 1856)
W. Turrell (called superintendent)	1857-1858
O. Downes (head constable)	1858-1873
G. Mercer (head constable)	1873-1883
R.O. Coombes (chief constable)	1883-1892
S.R. Midgely (chief constable)	1902-1912
H.C. Stockwell (chief constable)	1912-1915
E.M. Showers (acting chief constable)	1915-1919
H.C. Stockwell (chief constable)	1919-1947

Harwich Borough Constabulary
amalgamated with Essex on 1 February 1857

Initially the force was part time. William Burton was appointed as chief constable by the watch committee between 1836-1838.

Thomas Wilding	1838
[gaps in records]	

George Coleman (superintendent) appointed in January 1848 when the borough force was made full-time and modelled on the Ipswich Borough Constabulary. On 1 February 1857 Harwich was amalgamated with the Essex Constabulary, and Inspector Robert Banks was put in charge of two sergeants and four constables stationed there.

Maldon Borough Constabulary
amalgamated with Essex on 1 April 1889

Records are scanty for the earlier period when the force was only part-time, but the borough was only policed by two constables who had equal status. Frederick Chilvers (formerly of Essex Constabulary) was appointed borough constable in 1853. The HMI report for 1860 commented that one of the constables was 73! The force was not declared efficient until 1872.

[gap in records]
William King (head constable)	1872-1878
George Wombwell (head constable)	1878-1888
Charles Halsey (head constable)	1888-1889

Saffron Walden Borough Constabulary
amalgamated with Essex on 1 November 1857

Early records are scanty, and chief officers are not clearly defined. William Campling was the head constable between at least 1848 and November 1849 when he was murdered. Records of chief officers for the remainder of the force's existence are erratic, even after it was reconstituted in 1855 with printed regulations.

James Goss	between March-July 1852
Benjamin Judd (sergeant and chief constable)	July 1852-June 1856
Oliver Kirby	August 1856
Richard Harvey (ex-Cambridgeshire County Constabulary)	September 1856-October 1857

Appendix IV

This section is a summary of selected references to changes in style and content of Essex police uniforms, extracted from quarter sessions accounts (ERO Q/FAc), general police orders, force orders and memos, and entries in local newspapers (mainly the *Chelmsford Chronicle*). Entries are in date order and note form. There are separate headings for special constables and policewomen.

1840
First issue of uniform supplied by Charles Hebbert & Co. of Pall Mall East, London; based on uniform of Metropolitan Police.
Superintendents: frock coat with braid on collar and cuffs; silk skirt to coat; silver buttons; silk stock; dress trousers.
Constables: blue dress coat with embroidered collar; dress trousers; 'undress' trousers; waterproofed greatcoat with embroidered badge; pair of boots and pair of shoes; cape; hat; rattle; stock and clasp. Uniform buttons inscribed 'Essex Constabulary'. Crown and numerals on collar.

1844
New hats issued 'to admit air and keep policemen's heads cool'.

1855
Frock coats of different patterns according to rank substituted for dress coats:
Constables: single breasted blue cloth coat with eight buttons and two on hips; county arms on coat; embroidered collar bearing crown and number.
Sergeants (rank introduced 1854): same, but crown only on shoulder (sergeants not numbered until 1907).
Inspectors: same style, except double breasted, eight buttons each row and half inch black braid around collar.
Superintendents: same as inspectors, plus half inch silver lace around top of cuffs.

1865
Leather leggings and capes to be issued every third year.

1875
Quarter sessions approve helmets instead of hats; supplied by Christy & Co. (those for superintendents and inspectors weighed 7¼ ounces and cost 13 shillings each). Uniforms to 'strictly follow patterns of Metropolitan Police', except for retaining 'present neat silver embroidered crown on collar'. Uniform for all ranks made to measure. Sergeants' uniforms have black buttons. Frock coats still being issued.

1876
All members of force surveyed to ascertain views on future style and weight of uniform. Large proportion in favour of helmet and serge tunic; therefore wearing of caps to be discontinued.

1877
Day belts ordered from Hebbert's.

1881
All uniforms to have black buttons. Sergeants' coats to have stripe in darker colour; chains on capes. Staffs to be scraped clean and varnished (i.e. no ornamental truncheons).

1882
Superintendents allowed to buy loose patrol jacket and morocco leather sling belt at own expense. Belts issued to inspectors: worn over tunic and underneath patrol jacket. Belt buckles and plates to be bronzed. Standard style of gloves: all officers to buy from HQ with cost deducted from pay. Capes to be folded flat when carried. New summer uniform Norfolk jacket (made of serge), serge trousers and cap.

1883
New pattern stiff caps for superintendents and inspectors: superintendents to wear crown badge below cap band, inspectors above. Black leather chin straps to be carried in pocket for use when required. Superintendents and inspectors must wear helmets for court or 'in command of detachments'. Letters SX discontinued on shoulder straps of constables and sergeants; crown badge remained. Sergeants to wear letter S on shoulder where constables wear crown.

1885

Plain leather belts introduced; to be polished with blacking. Advice given for waterproofing night duty capes: 'dissolve half pound of sugar of lead and half pound of alum in bucket of soft water; let settle; pour off clear water; soak cape for 24 hours then drip dry'.

1887

Men holding rank of acting sergeant to wear constable's tunic with chevrons only (no crowns) on arms, and numerals on collar. Men passing St John's ambulance exams allowed to wear badge on left sleeve of tunic, just above cuff.

1888

New patterns approved for superintendents' helmets and greatcoats; also new style cap and badge.

1889

Whistles introduced instead of rattles. Cost £16 4s. to equip whole force.

1918

Ex-soldiers allowed to wear chevrons earned by war service overseas on uniform or plain clothes; positioned on right forearm four inches above bottom edge of sleeve.

1920

Changes in styles and method of issue of uniform: that issued to recruits to be fitted under supervision of drill instructor and approved by Chief Constable. Officers in charge of police stations to approve fitting of other officers' uniform. Inspectors to have new style cloth jackets with braided shoulder straps, and brown leather gloves. Sergeants and constables to have loose fitting coats with turn down collars (in style of City of London Police), thin summer jackets, cork covered helmets, knitted gloves. Uniformity of approach adopted for wearing of badges and distinctions: one chevron for 17 years' efficient service, two chevrons for 22 years' good conduct and efficiency. Merit badges, ambulance badge, army service chevrons and wound stripes could be worn on uniform jacket sleeves.

1949

Oaksey committee recommends issue of open necked tunics and ties in all forces, and abolition of insignia such as merit and first aid badges (left to discretion of individual chief constables). Helmets now general uniform wear for most forces. Stitching on peaks of inspectors' caps no longer hand embroidered. Close necked tunics remained in use for night duty until late 1950s.

1974

National recommendation for police hats to bear navy and white diced cap bands. Issued in Essex on 1 April 1974 with change of force title to 'Essex Police'.

1981

Open neck uniform shirts issued.

1982

NATO jumpers ('woolly pullies') issued on experimental basis in Halstead, Benfleet and Thurrock sub-divisions. Issued to all men and women officers, 1984.

1987

Staff uniform issued to civilian members of force coming into regular contact with public, e.g. at front counters of police stations.

Policewomen's Uniform

1940

Women police auxiliaries issued with navy blue wrap round overall with WAPC embroidered on one breast. Later provided with made-to-measure jackets and skirts, shirts with detached collars, ties, and flat caps.

1959-60

Patroller style caps introduced.

1970

New style jackets without belts; whistle worn in hip pocket with chain clipped to second button. Light weight skirts and open neck blouses. Black leather shoulder bags issued.

April 1973

White topped 'air hostess' style hats issued, initially worn between 1 April and 30 September each year.

September 1976

Trousers issued if requested. Special regulations imposed as to when they could be worn. 1978 Trouser suits issued to all women officers. Not to be worn for court or other specified occasions. Bowler-style protective hats approved for wear (not till 1979 for female cadets).

February 1989
Black and white checked cravats taken into use instead of ties.

Special Constabulary
Formalised in October 1915 with following badges of rank, each worn on an armlet over civilian clothes while on duty: Chief Special Constable (in each petty sessions area): silver crown between two silver stars, mounted on two inch circle of blue cloth. Armlet worn on left wrist. Chief Superintendent: silver crown above silver star, mounted on two inch circle of red cloth. Armlet worn on right wrist.
Superintendent: silver crown mounted on two inch circle of green cloth. Armlet worn on right wrist.
Sergeant: letter S in brass on armlet. Worn above right elbow.
Corporal: letter C in brass on armlet. Worn above left elbow.
Full uniform issued to special constables from Second World War.

1 January 1978
Special constables issued with navy and white checked cap bands in line with regular officers; new rank structure and badges of rank introduced. To draw special constables into main stream policing, commandant was regular chief officer (firstly Matthew Comrie, ACC Personnel); followed by Geoffrey Markham from September 1983 till 30 October 1989 when ex-Chief Superintendent Thomas Rodgers became commandant.

ESSEX SPECIAL CONSTABULARY

RANK STRUCTURE

BADGE	RANK	DUTIES
	Commandant	Senior Officer in force
	Divisional Officer	Senior Officer in each Territorial Division
	Sub-Divisional Officer	Senior Officer in each Sub-Division
5016	Section Officer	Shift Supervisor
5017	Special Constable	—

31. Badges of rank of the special constabulary, 1990.

Commandant (in charge, county-wide): four bars on epaulettes.
Divisional commander: three bars.
Sub-divisional commander: two bars.
Section officer: one bar.

1993
Special constables now issued with helmets. Special constable shoulder flashes to be removed.

Appendix V

Facts About the Force

The following reference sections give 'potted histories' **in note form** on a selection of police-related topics. Entries are arranged alphabetically under five broad subject headings: **Policy and Administration; Departments and Sections; Trophies and Medals; Buildings; Social.** Main sources are force orders, home office circulars, minutes of the standing joint committee, and force publications such as *The Law*, and the now defunct *Truncheon* and *Essex Police Magazine*. The following abbreviations have been used:

ACC	(assistant chief constable)
DCC	(deputy chief constable)
SJC	(standing joint committee)
HQ	(police headquarters)
DTC	(district training centre)
HMI	(Her Majesty's Inspector of Constabulary)
CSB	(community services branch)

Policy and Administration

Age Limit (Minimum) for recruits
In 1840 all recruits to be 'under 40'. Minimum recruiting age reduced to 18½ from 1 July 1975.

Amalgamations: Other Forces with Essex
Saffron Walden Borough police: 1 November 1857; Harwich Borough: 1 February 1857; Maldon Borough: 1 April 1889; Colchester Borough: 1 April 1947; Southend-on-Sea Borough Constabulary: 1 April 1969. British Airports Authority Police at Stansted Airport: 1 March 1975.

Breathalysers
Introduced under Road Safety Act 1967. Electronic breath tester from 1981.

Civilianisation Policy
First four civilian ushers replaced policemen at quarter sessions in 1951; provided with gown and 21 shillings for each day worked. Three-year plan from 1967 to release more police officers by appointing 121 clerical and 25 manual workers. From March 1971 administration superintendent replaced by civilian chief administrative officer: first holder Mr. Ivor Abel.

Competitive Catering
Introduced 1 August 1990 under Local Government Act, 1988.

County Arms
Badge of Essex Police taken from Essex County Council coat-of-arms, which was granted by College of Arms on 15 July 1932. Heraldic device described as: Gules, three Seaxes fessewise in pale Argent, pomels and hilts Or, pointed to the sinister and cutting edges upwards. Centre point is three seaxes—obsolete weapons once used by Saxons. Prior to 1974 badge of former Essex Constabulary displayed seaxes in diminishing order. When Essex and Southend-on-Sea Joint Constabulary became Essex Police in 1974, new badge designed with three seaxes floating in parallel, rather than diminishing order.

Crown Courts
Under Crown Court Act 1971, quarter sessions and assize courts replaced by crown courts: effective from 1973.

Force Magazine
The Truncheon started 1925; last issue in July 1948 after break during Second World War. Eventually replaced by *Essex Police Magazine*, first issue dated November 1952; last in Summer 1989.

Force Newspaper
First issue of *The Law* on 1 April 1969.

Force Orders

'A' covers law and procedure; 'B' covers personnel matters; both introduced 1 January 1936. First force order 'C' introduced 17 November 1981 to summarise recent case law and new legislation.

Health

Even before National Health Service began in 1948, regulations required police authorities to provide free medical and dental treatment for every police officer. During 1932 economic stringencies, Essex Chief Constable tried to economise by insisting potential recruits provided dentist's certificate saying their teeth were sound; if taken on, recruits could not claim dental expenses until probationary period confirmed. Free medical treatment not introduced in Essex till 1938, although officers could seek financial help with medical bills resulting from job-related illness. Force medical scheme established 1980, and occupational health scheme on 1 January 1989.

Motorways

First nine miles of M11 opened in June 1975 between Birchanger and Harlow; extended 1980. First stretch of M25 in Essex opened on 13 December 1982 between Dartford Tunnel and A127. By 1990 Essex responsible for policing 34 miles of M11 and 23 miles of M25.

Mutual Aid between Forces

County and borough forces first allowed to consolidate and inter-change officers after 1840 Police Act. 1856 Police Act allowed county and borough officers to exercise powers in each other's areas; many occasions. Outside forces supported Essex on several occasions, e.g. 1889 dock strike; policing Grays and Tilbury in Second World War, and 1953 floods. Most recent large-scale mutual aid provided to Midlands forces during miners' strike of 1984.

Neighbourhood Watch

National crime prevention initiative, launched in Essex October 1984 after Home Office circular 8/84 advocated inter-agency co-operation and partnership approach.

Pay Parades

Originally officers paraded in person at each divisional station to receive wages; ceased 1949.

Pensions

Police Act 1840 allowed each county force to set up superannuation fund for providing pensions for recommended officers (not automatic). Financed by sale of cast-off uniform and fines for misconduct. 1856 Act allowed superannuation to be funded from police rates. Police Act 1890 allowed each authority to set pension scale for its own officers over 50 with more than 25 years' approved service after age of 21. Anyone serving 26 years or more entitled to two-thirds pension. An officer incapacitated on duty with at least 15 years' service could receive special pension if medically retired. Police Pensions Act 1921 introduced half pay pension after 25 years' service, two thirds after 30 years' service and improved widows' benefits.

Pillar Phones

No mention found of pillar phones in Essex Police area, but in 1939 Colchester borough force had 17 connected to central police station. Removed in 1955 after public telephone boxes became more common.

Pocket Books

First issued 1916 (previously officers had to supply their own). New style blue plastic cover with 100 page flip-up inset pads first issued October 1974.

Police and Criminal Evidence Act 1984

Partially implemented April 1985 with new procedures for complaints against police. All Essex officers given intensive training programme before new procedures for dealing with prisoners introduced on experimental basis in November 1985. PACE 'went live' on 1 January 1986. Act created new post of custody officer at police stations designated by Home Office to receive prisoners.

Probationary Period

Constables in 1840 on probation for two months. More formal probationary period from 1885 after progressive pay scales introduced: officers appointed as third class constables and subject to either six months or two years probation; progress monitored by superintendents. Advanced to second or first class when probationary period completed satisfactorily. Currently two year probationary period after appointment.

Prosecutions Authorities

Since 19th century police had power to prosecute all summary offences in magistrates' courts. County prosecuting solicitor established under Section 15, Local Government Act 1888, prosecuted cases on behalf of police. Director of Public Prosecutions first appointed under Prosecution of Offences Act 1879. With creation of independent Crown Prosecution Service on 1 October 1986 police lost power to prosecute; allows force to give official cautions to juvenile and elderly offenders.

Ranks

All police officers hold ancient office of constable whatever their police rank. First Essex policemen appointed from February 1840 were 100 constables and 15 superintendents. Rank of inspector introduced November 1840. Rank of sergeant introduced 1854, and described by HMI in 1857 as invaluable to 'well working of a force'. Borough forces of Southend and Colchester had chief inspectors, but rank not introduced into Essex until 1940—originally on temporary basis. In 1942 badges of rank were one star for temporary inspector; two stars after one year in rank; three stars for chief inspector. Oaksey Report 1949 allowed police authorities and Home Secretary to appoint 'such ranks as they think necessary'. Two posts of chief superintendent then introduced in Essex, one at HQ (first holder Frederick Smith); second in Romford because that division had more than 150 officers (first holder George Sutton). ACC became permanent rank in 1933 (first holder John Crockford). DCC became rank in October 1986, rather than rôle performed by senior ACC (first holder of DCC rank was Ronald Stone): retired October 1986). References often found from mid-19th century to 'chief clerk'; not rank, but position previously allocated to any policeman with appropriate qualifications, depending on circumstances and authorised establishment of force; usually a superintendent with sergeant as deputy. Admiral McHardy originally classified ranks in different grades; the others were phased out at various times, but superintendents grade I and II remained until the two were amalgamated on 1 September 1972 after a review of rank structures in force.

Rent Allowance

Houses to rent scarce from 1880s, so in November 1882 quarter sessions approved system of rent allowances for constables and sergeants; if rent exceeded certain amount they could apply for subsidy from SJC. Practice was standardised from 1 January 1901; sergeants and constables paying more than 3s. 1d. weekly rent could automatically claim rent aid. By 1928 anyone having to pay more than 10s. a week could claim rent aid for difference, e.g. at the time a house in Malvern Road, Romford, cost 15s. weekly to rent; one in Silver End, near Witham, cost 12s. 6d.

32. Plan of rank structure of regular force, 1990.

Resettlement Course

First run under Police Federation auspices in May 1974 for officers eligible to retire within two or three years; later taken over by commercial company acting on behalf of force training school. Officers on very first course had total of 939.7 years service!

Rest Days

One day off each week-subject to exigencies of duty-allowed by Police Forces (Weekly Rest Day) Act 1910; implemented in Essex on 1 July 1914. Officers were still not free to leave their stations without permission. From January 1918 officers could go out on rest day if not required to work, but two days' notice, details of their whereabouts, and the address if staying away, had to be given to their superintendents.

Standing Orders
Captain McHardy published first printed volume of force instructions in 1849. Almost every successive chief constable has authorised his own version, usually issued to each officer personally. Difficulties with updating, so in January 1982 Orders and Legislation department created to provide fully indexed and regularly updated volume for each each station and department.

Taped Interviews with Suspects
Trials carried out from 1 June 1986.

Training Recruits
Before the Second World War recruits usually trained in-force. Home Office regional training schools introduced after Second World War with 13 week course of instruction. From 1963 recruit training also included continuation course at DTC half way through probationary period, supplemented by 'day release' training within force, initially half day each week, but one day every fortnight from 1970. Classes held at designated study centres within force (sometimes divisional stations), with five full-time training sergeants travelling between them. Probationers had to pass monthly written exam set by force training school. In 1973 initial training restructured and reduced to 10 weeks. After run-down of cadet school released accommodation at HQ, probationer training courses made residential from October 1976. After Scarman Report, redesigned system of probationer training introduced on 10 July 1989.

Victim Support
Introduced in Chelmsford division as Victim Support Scheme, March 1979. Extended throughout Essex by 1982. Now known as 'Victim Support'.

Video Magazine
First issue of 'Focus' prepared in June 1989.

Welfare Officer
Mr. A R Sorrell appointed first police and civilian welfare officer June 1967.

Departments and Sections

Air Support
Helicopter trials began July 1990 with Aerospatial Twin Squirrel helicopter piloted by qualified pilot. Observers are police officers from section headed by Inspector Mike Walker, with one sergeant, four constables and reserve of six trained constables.

Cadets
In 1951, 12 male cadet clerks appointed and paid under local government pay scale. Issued with uniform greatcoat, battledress, beret, mackintosh, jacket and trousers. No powers and not police officers, but many joined force when old enough. Later re-designated police cadets and given insight into police work; received educational training in day-release centre of Mid-Essex technical college. First three female cadets were appointed 1961. By 1965 numbers grown to 80 male and 12 female cadets; generally employed on clerical duties. Cadet training re-organised into two phases in 1966: those between 16-18, and those between 18-19 who were given more responsibility, and attachments to outside organisations and outward bound camps. Residential cadet school officially opened by Princess Anne in 1969, with Chief Inspector John Hedgethorne as commandant. Emphasis changed to providing general education for cadets, with short attachments to police departments in final months before joining force. Cadet school renamed force training school when full-time cadet training ceased in 1978.

Career Development
Superintendent Graham Furnival appointed first career development officer in December 1988.

Communications
Communications department formed 1948, with central control room known as information room (same as in Metropolitan Police). Great Bromley radio transmitter opened 20 December 1948. Private telephone line to New Scotland Yard introduced May 1952, but only operated between restricted hours; full-time line from January 1953. Telex teleprinter introduced 1960, and fully automatic telex 1962. Home Office radio technician stationed at HQ from 1962. Experiments with two-way pocket radios in Chelmsford division in 1965; extended to Basildon 1966; Brentwood, Braintree, Clacton, Harlow, Colchester, Grays in 1967; Saffron Walden, Rayleigh, Maldon and Witham in 1968. Automatic switchboard allowed direct dialling between HQ and divisions from 1968. In 1970 regional teleprinter training school opened at HQ. Police National Computer went live on 1 August 1974; prior to that officers had to visit County Hall to find urgently required registered

owners of vehicles. MIRIAM computer system tested in force from 1981. HOLMES and MIRIAM projects given go-ahead January 1985. IRIS computer system introduced in many police stations from November 1985: terminals gradually installed throughout county. Closed-circuit television installed in classrooms at force training school January 1977. Multi-media section of force training school civilianised August 1985, becoming force television unit.

Community Services Branch
Began work on 1 January 1979, headed by Superintendent Geoffrey Markham and Chief Inspectors Lorna Baker and Ralph Crawshaw. Introduced in response to report commissioned by Robert Bunyard, then Chief Constable, into state of decision-making about juvenile offenders. Essex first force to have coherent policy on dealing with juveniles and elderly offenders; both groups normally cautioned. CSB includes officers of both genders to deal with children at risk and—since September 1979—schools liaison. Branch offices deliberately placed outside police stations to facilitate confidentiality and closer liaison with other welfare organisations. Each office manned by inspector, two sergeants and eight constables. Main thrust of CSB now towards child protection.

Criminal Investigation Department
In 1857 first HMI recommended two or more detective officers be placed at each HQ so that all 'great offences' should have investigating officer 'unfettered by divisional duties'. 'Nothing would add more to the efficiency of the police than the establishment of a good detective system', wrote the HMI, as investigating crime was then responsibility of each superintendent. November 1888 three Essex sergeants and 10 constables employed on detective duty and able to draw plain clothes allowances quarterly. Colchester borough force had Detective Constable Wass before 1869, when he was promoted sergeant; its first detective sergeant was appointed 1878.

Force order dated 28 November 1919, announced creation of detective and enquiry department deployed thus:

Romford: Sergeant 38 Frank Hyde (retired as superintendent on 31 December 1938); Pc 203 Alfred Norman; Pc 525 Charles Clayden.

Grays: Pc 133 William Parrott; Pc 169 Frank Goby

Tilbury: Pc 282 Charles Shelley (retired as chief inspector)

33, 34 & 35.   Some idea of the development of communications can be gained from these photographs of the force information room at various dates.*(Top)* Sergeant Dick Coe operates the sole console in about 1948; *(Centre)* Information room *c*.1971; the four policemen are *(left to right)* Geoffrey Bendall, Peter Bailey, Alan Jipps, and Michael Dunman. *(Above)* Part of the building opened in 1978.

Chelmsford: Pc 220 William Fordham
Brentwood: Pc 143 John Crockford (retired as ACC)
Harwich: Pc 166 William Claxton
Clacton: Pc 287 Orlando Knights (retired as superintendent).

Each applicant for department to be recommended by his superintendent, to have 3-12 years' service, and to serve at least six months' probationary period. Detective to assist with difficult cases, although uniformed constable first involved always to be considered 'officer in case'. Detectives themselves subject to orders of uniformed superintendent at each station. Frank Hyde promoted to new post of detective inspector in November 1921, and given overall responsibility for work of department. George Totterdell took charge 1932; became first detective superintendent. To stop further confusion about department's rôle, name changed to Criminal Investigation Department.

Criminal Intelligence Section Formed 1 January 1964. When regional crime squads began October 1964, became regional crime squad intelligence bureau.

Fraud Squad Formed 1956 with two officers based at HQ. Earliest cases involved enquiries into purchase and re-registration of stolen cars. Renamed 'Fraud and Race Course Squad' 1958, as members had to attend point to point races and deal with fraudulent bookmakers. Reorganised under inspector 1960, with part-time responsibility for investigating major incidents in county. Now consists of detective inspector, two detective sergeants and nine detective constables.

Motor Vehicle Squad Following 1962 working party on thefts of vehicles, one full-time detective sergeant allocated to investigate suspected stolen vehicles.

Crime Prevention Department
Formalised on 1 August 1965 to include one inspector and a sergeant at HQ, and one sergeant specialising in crime prevention at each divisional station. Restructured in 1984 under Superintendent John Deal and Chief Inspector Bob Ward after Home Office circular advocated partnership approach.

Dogs
Some forces experimenting with bloodhounds and mastiffs in early 20th century, but Essex turned down offer in 1908 from man who used bloodhounds to track criminals. Full potential of dogs only realised in 1930s, but experiments in breeding and training ceased at start of Second World War. National working party in 1954 visited Germany, which had used police dogs for many years. German shepherd dogs imported, and allocated to various forces. Central registry maintained by Lancashire Constabulary. Essex purchased two dogs from Surrey Constabulary in September 1953—alsation bitch *Senta* and Doberman pincer *Remoh*; Dan Hare was handler (eventually became dogmaster of Royal Hong Kong Police). Force bought specially designed van equipped with wireless for transporting dogs in 1954; still used some Dobermans. By 1960 two handlers and their dogs based at Harlow, HQ, Brentwood and Colchester; and from 1962 at Grays. By 1970 Essex had 27 handlers, and in the same year purpose-built dog section opened at Sandon.

Fingerprint Branch
Home Secretary's committee appointed in 1900 to find alternative way of identifying criminals; Bertillon system then in use involved measuring their bodily dimensions. Committee decided that identification by fingerprints was more effective; experiments had been carried out since 1883. Fingerprint identification introduced in Essex on 15 July 1901 for prisoners convicted of certain offences, but separate fingerprint branch not formed until 1947; merged with photographic department in 1953 under inspector. Taking of palm prints began 1953. Second fingerprint specialist (title 'fingerprint expert') appointed 1956. Subsidiary fingerprint and photographic offices opened at Romford and Harlow by 1958.

Force Support Unit
Founded May 1973 under command of Chief Inspector Geoffrey Markham, with one inspector, three sergeants and 30 male constables. Formed to deal with public order problems, and to act as mobile reserve to deal with specialist tasks not performed on daily basis, e.g. firearms, large-scale searches, and diving; originally based at Melbourne Park police station in Chelmsford.

Maritime Duties
From 1890 Colchester borough police maintained sergeant and three constables for permanent duty in protecting Colne Fishery. Applicants appointed under 'An Act to Keep the Peace on Canals and Navigable Rivers' (3 & 4 Victoria c.50), but told they would be drafted into borough police if river section ever discontinued; it operated until amalgamation of Colchester and Essex in 1947. In 1914 Port of London Authority suggested that Kent, Essex and Metropolitan Police linked up to provide some policing for the River Thames; no statutory responsibility so Essex declined. In 1949 conference held at Scotland Yard to consider policing of River Thames outside Metropolitan Police boundaries. Essex decided to buy patrol boat

36.   In 1979 three-year-old police dog, Bruce, made veterinary history when he was fitted with rust-proof, nickel-chromium fangs by surgeons at Bristol veterinary college, after he broke his natural teeth while training. The fangs had been weakened by Bruce's habit of biting the wires of his cage. The success of the operation attracted a good deal of media coverage, and Bruce is seen here with his handler, Constable Michael Mercer.

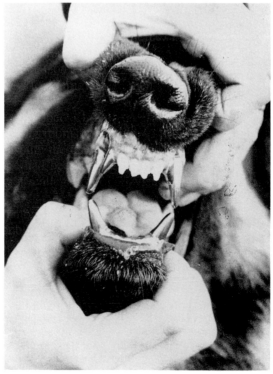

37.   A close-up of the doggie dentures.

38. Sworn to protect oysters. Members of the river section of Colchester Borough Police, on board the cutter, *Prince of Wales*, *c*.1930. From left to right: Ps Elijah Ward, Pc Ted Ward, Pc Jasper Greengrass and Pc Mummery.

for lower Thames: ex-RAF seaplane tender named *Karoo*, bought from Cowes, and fitted-out by Metropolitan Police river branch at Wapping. *Karoo* renamed *Vigilant*. Sidney Cranfield, former constable on Colchester river section, promoted to take charge of *Vigilant* when she began work in September 1949; rest of crew included Constables Bruce Howard, Evelyn Cant, Philip China and William Lemon. *Vigilant II* commissioned August 1959. Built of teak on oak at Shoreham, Sussex; specially designed as police launch, based at Tilbury and designed to patrol whole Essex coast. Crew included George Thurkle and Robert George, both eventually inspectors in charge of Marine Section. *Alert* commissioned 1967 and fitted with radar; she patrolled river estuaries of Blackwater and Crouch. Motor launch *Watchful* commissioned November 1970 to patrol east coast of force area. Southend borough force had part-time sea rescue patrol from 1956; made permanent after amalgamation with Essex in 1969. Boats continue to be updated and replaced. Marine Section now consists of one sergeant and seven constables at Rayleigh, and one sergeant and seven constables at Southminster.

Diving

Diving section began on part-time basis in 1956 when David Van Lennep of Rawreth, friend of Pc Philip China, used own equipment to dive for force when required. Van Lennep later sworn in as special constable; when he retired in 1960 section then included two constables and one sergeant. By 1967 10 trained frogmen; all volunteers. Underwater search team made full-time in February 1976, its officers being part of Force Support Unit. Diving unit now one sergeant and 11 constables.

Motor Vehicles

December 1909 Chief Constable given permission to hire motor car for police purposes, initially for six months from 1 January 1910 at charge not exceeding £50 a year; hiring extended at six month intervals. May 1915 Chief Constable granted £300 a year travelling expenses, and SJC required him to provide and maintain car for use in connection with his police duties; authorised to employ civilian chauffeur, at 30 shillings a week plus livery. April 1917 Chief Constable reported buying 10-12 HP Belsize car for police use at cost of £175; car later used by Braintree superintendent with Pc 422 Herbert W. Bareham as chauffeur. (He transferred from St. Osyth on 15 May 1917, retiring as a sergeant in October 1937.)

From 1932 traffic patrols supervised by Detective Superintendent Totterdell, of Detective and Enquiry Department. By 1935, 21 men based at HQ engaged on traffic patrol duties, with 10 cars and 1 van. Police driving scheme began with grants from Home Office to selected forces that owned their own vehicles. Had to provide cars for experimental scheme whereby police drivers checked dangerous or inconsiderate driving speeding vehicles with dirty number plates or no rear reflectors; police drivers also supposed to be helpful to motorists! Lancashire given grants for 35 cars, Durham 25, Birmingham 16 and Essex 15 cars. Scheme began in Essex on 1 April 1938.

Two Essex officers attended course at Hendon under Lord Cottenham in May 1937, and became force driving instructors. In 1937, 34 vehicles involved in traffic duties; with three inspectors, 10 sergeants and 102 constables. In 1966 HQ traffic department, and divisional traffic patrols formed into Traffic Division. Traffic patrols now part of Support Division.

Mounted Duty
Horses purchased for use in force from 1841 onwards (detailed bills for feeding and veterinary expenses in quarter sessions accounts). By 1885 officers granted what would now be called subsistence payments and 5s. a day lodging expenses for attending race meetings on horseback. Horses also used to escort judges to assizes at Chelmsford. In 1911 Chief Constable authorised to hire horse for mounted patrol in borough of Southend. In June 1922 Essex still had five horses, but by end of 1923 all sold (source: ERO T/P 181/17/19). Colchester borough police hired or borrowed horses for particular incidents, often from cavalry barracks.
Southend borough force (formed 1914) maintained own mounted section, with four constables and three horses; remained in use after amalgamation with Essex in 1969. Section reorganised in 1982 to provide county-wide cover, with five constables under Sergeant Paul Hemmings.

Photographic Department
Established HQ June 1935. Merged with fingerprint department under one inspector, 1953. Scenes of crime department set up at Colchester 1954. Detective Inspector Roy Breaks won Churchill travelling fellowship in 1966 to study police photography and scenes of crime work in USA and Canada. In 1968 department designed and built special camera to photograph fingerprints in either colour or black and white.

School Crossing Patrols
Responsibility for 86 school crossing patrols passed from education department to police on 1 April 1954. Now about 280 patrols throughout county.

Traffic Investigation Unit
Established January 1983 to investigate serious road accidents and draw plans.

Traffic Wardens
November 1935 Romford ratepayers applied to Chief Constable for traffic wardens to operate near schools and busy crossings; no action taken. Traffic wardens first appointed in Leicester in 1961 at instigation of Robert Mark (later Metropolitan Police Commissioner). First ten traffic wardens appointed in Essex on 1 April 1964. Received two weeks training before being posted to Chelmsford and Colchester. Numbers employed doubled in 1965. At first wardens only allowed to give advice and warning before reporting motorists, but powers gradually increased. Currently 137 traffic wardens throughout Essex.

Trophies and Medals

Many cups and trophies have been donated over the years to the various forces now making up the Essex Police. Some of the trophies are no longer competed for, or have been put to other purposes with permission from their donors. Those in the following list (arranged alphabetically by surname) still play an important part in the life of the force.

Bennett Trophy
Awarded to winner of annual competition between probationary constables. First presented October 1959 by Alderman W. J. Bennett, then chairman of Essex County Council.

Betts Trophy
Donated 1968 by Mrs. Edith Betts of Coventry, to traffic warden performing outstanding action while on duty. Donor's son was a Chelmsford traffic warden.

Croker Cup
Awarded annually to division of force gaining highest number of points in competitions for all branches of sport. Donated October 1951 by Mr. A. Croker of Hornchurch.

De Rougemont Cup
Awarded to special constables of division gaining most points in annual competition for drill and police duties. Donated by Brigadier General C. H. De Rougemont, Chief Special Constable, 1950.

Norman Dooley Memorial Trophy
In memory of former special superintendent in Southend. Annually awarded from 1976 to member of special constabulary performing most meritorious act, or one who renders exceptional service to people of Essex.

Long Service and Good Conduct Medal
Instituted by King George VI on 14 June 1951 for regular police officers with 22 years' service.

Millard Trophy
Awarded annually to police officer making greatest contribution to police public relations. Donated 1969 by Alderman S. Woodful Millard, Chairman of Essex Police Authority.

Mitchell Cup
First awarded June 1933 by John Mitchell of Southend for outstanding act of personal courage performed by police, fire, or corporation employee on duty within borough of Southend.

Mitchell Shield
First presented 1976 to team of special constables coming second in De Rougemont Cup competition.

Neville Trophy
First presented 1955 by Donald Neville of Southend, for annual competition between Essex and Southend special constables.

Peel Trophy
First presented December 1962 by Sir Jonathan Peel, retiring Chief Constable, to constable gaining top marks in promotion examination to sergeant. First winner in 1963 Pc 903 Michael Morgan of Braintree division, (resigned 1966).

Salter Cup
Awarded annually since June 1933 to special constables' team gaining highest marks in competition testing knowledge of police duties. Donated by Dr. J. H. Salter, formerly chief special constable for Witham area.

Wilson Trophy
Presented 1960 by Mr. W. W. Wilson of St Clere's Hall, Stanford-le-Hope. Awarded annually to police officer performing most meritorious act in course of duty.

Buildings

The first Essex police stations usually included living accommodation for officers, although some had to find their own lodgings nearby. Houses for married couples were often rented privately by the officer himself, or by the force on his behalf. In December 1881 it was decided to place blue and white enamelled plates with 'County Police' thereon over the doors of private houses occupied by officers. Such plates were later felt to be 'not very dignified for a county such as Essex'. On the instructions of the standing joint committee the blue plates were replaced by a cast metal circular badge, with the county arms surrounded by the words 'Essex Constabulary' and surmounted by a crown. The badges were made by Maldon Ironworks in the 1930s and cost £1 10s. each.

After the Second World War Essex Constabulary made a determined effort to build houses for its officers, and a variety of styles were adopted. That approved in 1963 included for the first time a garage and central heating. It has not proved practicable to compile a complete list of all police buildings in the force area. The following gives opening dates and brief details of a selection of mainly 20th-century purpose-built police stations. The first purpose-built police station in the force was opened at Dunmow in 1843; it is still in use.

Opening Dates Of Some 20th-Century Purpose-Built Police Stations
Basildon: Opened 1963.
Brentwood: Station and court opened August 1937. House known as La Plata left standing on site and adapted for 18 single men with flat for station sergeant. Fourteen police houses built at rear.
Billericay: Opened 1937.
Brightlingsea: Opened July 1985 to replace building occupied since 1908.

39 & 40. The oldest Essex police station *(above)* and the newest. Opened in 1843, Great Dunmow police station was the first in Essex to be purpose-built; now much modernised, it is still in use. Braintree's ultra modern police station, (opened in August 1993), is the third one to stand in the town; the first two were in Rayne Road and Fairfield Road. This photograph shows how far work had progressed in January 1993.

Chelmsford Town: Opened January 1972, replacing original station which was occupied from 1903. Prior to that Chelmsford police operated out of Shire Hall.

Colchester: Opened July 1989, replacing former soldiers' home in Queen Street which housed Colchester borough force from 1938 until amalgamation with Essex in 1947.

Corringham: Opened 1968.

Epping: Opened 1938.

Grays: Opened August 1979 to replace building used since 1929.

Harlow Dog Section: Opened 1968.

Harlow Town: Opened September 1957, replacing building occupied since 1908.

Harlow Traffic: Opened March 1975.

Harold Hill (now in Metropolitan Police area): Opened 1955.

Harwich: Opened February 1915.

Police Headquarters: First police HQ at Old Court, Arbour Lane, Chelmsford, formerly stores depot of West Essex militia; additional living accommodation built there for chief officers. Remained in police use until new HQ—Springfield Court—opened in 1903. Springfield Court still forms centre of present HQ complex. Former chief constable's house now used as offices for chief officers. Filmed by Anglia Television in 1991-93 for television series 'The Chief', based on the fictional force of Eastland.

Dates of alterations and buildings at HQ

Chief Constable's stables converted into married quarters 1920, and orchard into car park 1972. Two new wings costing £31,000 built onto back of main building in 1953; canteen and photographic department in one, traffic and clothing store in other. April 1975 plans approved for new octagonal HQ building with information room in the centre of octagon for security. Octagonal building completed December 1978, and partly taken into use February 1979. Cadet School officially opened 20 October 1969 by Princess Anne. Renamed force training school 1978. Driving school and garage completed 1963. Garage and workshops opened August 1971, after memorial avenue of trees on sports field had to be moved.

Hornchurch (now in Metropolitan Police area): Opened 1955.

Kelvedon: Opened 1966.

Laindon Traffic: Completed 1966.

Maldon: Opened 1913.

Pitsea: Opened 1937.

Rainham (now in Metropolitan Police area): Occupied 1935.

Rayleigh: Opened 1977, replacing building first used in 1960.

Rochford: Opened 1916.

Romford (now in Metropolitan Police area): Building in Main Road first occupied December 1965.

Sandon Dog Section: Opened 1970.

Southminster: Opened 1902.

South Ockendon: Opened 1955.

Southend (then the borough force HQ): Opened 1962.

Stanway Traffic: Opened 1968.

Wickford: Opened 1966.

Witham: Station and court opened 1937. New court built on to existing one, opened 1992.

Social

Essex Police Band

Formed April 1966 by a group of police musicians who gave an impromptu performance on instruments borrowed from Witham British Legion at a dinner at HQ. Junior section formed in 1993.

Essex Police Choir

Inaugural meeting on 2 May 1989. Formed under conductor Norman Eastbrook and accompanist Inspector Josephine Dudley. First concert at Boreham.

Essex Police Comrades Association

Established on 1 January 1924 by Captain John Unett, then Chief Constable, for maintenance of comradeship and good fellowship between retired members of force and those still serving who have more than 15 years' service.

Essex Police Music Society
Founded in 1965. First show *Calamity Jane*, produced February 1966.

Force Library and Museum
Force library committee founded January 1884 under chairmanship of Superintendent Thomas Daunt, with Superintendent William Paterson as vice-chairman and committee comprising Inspector Herbert Ackers, Inspector Charles Robinson, Sergeants James Burrell and William Barnard, Constables David Woodcock and Harry Laver; secretary Sergeant Charles Forbes. Members of force subscribed monthly to fund library, and by May 1884 books for stations and catalogues of books for subscribers were sent out. In 1886 quarter sessions granted £10 towards providing bookcases at police stations so library would be used more. Lasted in reduced form until after World War I. During 1930s moves made to collect artefacts relevant to force history; displayed together in room at HQ. Display dismantled in 1970 because room needed for regional teleprinter training school. Exhibits dispersed to Essex Record Office and Chelmsford Borough Museum.

After success of 150th anniversary celebrations of force in 1990, chief officers felt there was enough support for permanent museum. Space allocated in part of basement at HQ. New force museum set up under committee chaired by DCC Peter Simpson. Officially opened 16 October 1992 by Councillor Geoffrey Waterer, chairman of Essex Police Authority. Applying for charitable status in 1993.

Force Lottery
Introduced May 1976 to support Force Sports Association.

Fun Day
First one held in July 1987 at HQ to make money for charity and involve police and public. First organiser and chairman of committee, Chief Inspector David Bright.

Pensioners Garden Party
First garden party in July 1974 financed by proceeds of 10 mile sponsored walk undertaken by policewomen along Southend promenade.

Appendix VI

It is not practicable in a book such as this to include detailed analyses of recruits who joined the Essex Constabulary and its successors between 1840 and 1990. However, details are given for the first year of the force in 1840; the 150th year in 1990; and 1900, the start of a new century: some basic comparisons can thus be made to see variations over 150 years. Counties of birth have been standardised with the ancient geographical counties recorded in Ekwall's *Concise Oxford Dictionary of English Place Names* (1990 reprint).

Each of the 240 men who joined in 1840 is included, whether he served for one month or 30 years; the same principle applies to the 37 recruits who joined during 1900. Details of the 1840 and 1900 recruits are taken from ERO J/P 2/1 and 2/2. The men and women who joined during 1990 are protected by the Data Protection Act. By the time of publication, 14 out of the total of 173 had either resigned, or chose not to have their details included.

1840 Recruits

Name	Age Joined	Last Job	Collar No.	Birthplace
Abrey Willaim	20	baker	Pc 52	Stow Maries, Essex
Adams Robert	36	servant	Pc 21	Suffolk
Aldridge James	21	labourer	Pc 18	Saffron Walden, Essex
Alford William	31	soldier	Insp	Cooford, Wiltshire
Allen Joseph	21	saddler	Pc 90	Newport, IOW Hampshire
Allingham Samuel	27	servant	Pc 21	Sunbury, Middlesex
Allridge Simon	29	shoemaker	Pc 24	London
Ambrose John	37	butcher	Pc 94	Cavendish, Suffolk
Amey Henry	23	miller	Pc 68	Sudbury, Suffolk
Anderson John	28	army	Supt.	Hawick, Scotland
Anthony Abraham	28	mariner	Pc 88	Cowes, Hampshire
Austin Jonathan	22	labourer	Pc 84	Brinchley, Kent
Bailey Charles	39	soldier	Pc 92	Exeter, Devon
Barker James	42	soldier	Insp.	Not given
Barnard James R	28	soldier	Pc 45	Nayland, Suffolk
Beals Henry	28	miller	Pc 66	Wolsted, unknown
Bedford George	23	shoemaker	Pc 20	Springfield, Essex
Bergin Patrick	33	soldier	Pc 101	Ireland
Berwick Robert	38	soldier	Insp.	Oxford, Oxfordshire
Bickmore Charles	20	labourer	Pc 63	Witham, Essex
Billings John H	38	musician	Pc 61	Westminster, London
Birch Joseph	32	druggist	Pc 8	Cripplegate, London
Bloomfield Joseph	23	grocer	Pc 13	Felstead, Essex
Boltwood Thomas	31	silversmith	Pc 100	Hackney, Middlesex
Bragg Samuel	24	labourer	Pc 82	Bocking, Essex
Burke Walter		Royal Navy	civ.	Mayo, Ireland
Calcraft Charles	32	labourer	Pc 52	Baddow, Essex
Campart Gillery P	28	clerk	Pc 60	Dalston, Middlesex
Cardinal James	27	clerk	Pc 7	Halstead, Essex
Chaplin Joseph	21	weaver	Pc 78	Pattiswick, Essex
Choat William	25	farmer	Pc 65	Haverhill, Suffolk
Church Edward	22	shoemaker	Pc 2	Chelmsford, Essex
Clarke John T	32	soldier	Supt.	Bristol, Gloucester

Clarke Henry	22	butcher	Pc 56	Stoginsey, Somerset
Cobbin William	30	butcher	Pc 46	Essex
Cooke Charles	44	army	Supt.	Churcham, Hampshire
Copland Stephen	27	painter	Pc 95	Greenwich, Kent
Copsey Joseph	22	labourer	Pc 17	Chelmsford, Essex
Cordran Henry	21	clerk	Pc 50	Coggeshall, Essex
Coulson Thomas	43	army	Supt.	Yorkshire
Cousins William	25	servant	Pc 54	Aylesbury, Bucks
Cox James	21	labourer	Pc 79	W. Hanningfield, Essex
Crane Joseph	32	constable	Pc 36	Ramsgate, Kent
Crawley Henry	29	soldier	Pc 75	Middlesex
Cross Henry	22	labourer	Pc 72	Beaumont, Essex
Cullen Edward	28	constable	Pc 64	Nottingham, Notts.
Davey Thomas	37	plumber	Pc 56	Kingston, Surrey
Davis Edward J.	32	solicitor	Supt.	Lambeth, Surrey
Deacon Martin	28	army	Supt.	Hampshire
Digby John M.	22	carpenter	Pc 21	Colne Engaine, Essex
Ditchfield Joseph	27	mariner	Pc 37	Stafford
Dodd Henry	24	baker	Pc 95	Springfield, Essex
Dow Robert	23	weaver	Pc 50	Aberdeen, Scotland
Dowsett William	28	shoemaker	Pc 75	Toppesfield, Essex
Eccles Robert	31	soldier	Pc 18	Ireland
Edmonds Daniel			Supt.	Not given
Edmunds Jonathon	26	groom	Pc 50	Highworth, Wiltshire
Egan Peter	21	surveyor	Pc 55	Roscommon, Ireland
Eldred John	24	shoemaker	Pc 33	Pebmarsh, Essex
Eldridge John	24	clerk	Pc 82	Brompton, Middlesex
Ellis Robert	21	soldier	Pc 25	Knighton, Berkshire
Elsmere Andrew	37	farmer	Pc 22	Shropshire
Ernwright Daniel	32	baker	Pc 81	Limerick, Ireland
Evans Edward S.	21	watchmaker	Pc 16	Totnes, Devon
Everett Charles	20	baker	Pc 86	Braintree, Essex
Fletcher Charles	30	constable	Pc 58	Tillingham, Essex
Flood Henry	32	glassblower	Pc 1	Rockland, Norfolk
Fountain William	31	labourer	Pc 93	Grantham, Lincs.
Fowler James	35	baker	Pc 24	Ramsbury, Wiltshire
Francis Stephen	39		Insp.	Hallingbury, Essex
Fulcher William	23	labourer	Pc 35	Thorpe-le-Soken, Essex
Gager Jonathon	21	tailor	Pc 19	Rye, Sussex
Gallifant Robert	21	butcher	Pc 9	Colne Engaine, Essex
Gallifant William J	20	cooper	Pc 11	Halstead, Essex
Gardley Charles	30	factor	Pc 97	Shoreditch, Middlesex
Garnham Edward	35	servant	Pc 70	Isle of Wight, Hampshire
Godwin Thomas	38	farmer	Supt.	Herefordshire
Gowers John	25	servant	Pc 51	Gt. Waltham, Essex
Gowers William	21	labourer	Pc 81	Leighs, Essex
Gowland John	33	clerk	Pc 63	Knaresborough, Yorks.
Gray Henry	29	servant	Pc 89	Wingham, Kent
Greaves Charles	44	army	Supt.	Wadyley, Berkshire
Greenwood Robert	22	bricklayer	Pc 103	Paulsford, Norfolk
Greygoose James	29	baker	Pc 58	Good Easter, Essex
Griggs Henry	24	carpenter	Pc 57	Chelmsford, Essex
Gunn James	22	servant	Pc 87	Dedham, Essex
Haines Edward	25	gardener	Pc 98	West Molsey, Surrey
Harrington Charles	21	baker	Pc 63	Chignal, Essex
Harrington Frederick	20	silversmith	Pc 22	Colchester, Essex
Harrington Charles	25	butcher	Pc 80	Fryerning, Essex
Harvey John	27	shoemaker	Pc 47	Gestingthorpe, Essex

Hawkins John	43	army	Supt.	Leicester, Leics.
Haydon John	35	glover	Pc 66	Holywell, Dorset
Henwood William	25	soldier	Pc 81	Dorchester, Dorset
Hiatt John	29	waiter	Pc 94	Cork, Ireland
Hindes Abraham	31	clerk	Pc 19	Harwich, Essex
Holby James	38	corndealer	Pc 35	Latchingdon, Essex
Holland John	23	shoemaker	Pc 69	Braintree, Essex
Horan Thomas	32	labourer	Pc 38	Latrim, Ireland
Horsey Charles	24	soldier	Pc 66	Bath, Somerset
Howlett Henry	28	servant	Pc 99	Sudbury, Suffolk
Hoy John	29	mariner	Pc 48	Epping, Essex
Ireland John	32	soldier	Pc 73	Shepscombe, Gloucester
Ixers Benjamin	26	labourer	Pc 53	Springfield, Essex
Jamieson John	31	baker	Pc 74	Halstead, Essex
Johnson Robert	28	army	Supt.	Pattana
Jones John	27	blacksmith	Pc 12	Chelmsford, Essex
Joselyne William	31		Pc 14	Old Sandford
Joyce Charles	39	soldier	Pc 8	Somerset
Kendall John	22	maltster	Pc 40	Suffolk
Kettle John G	23	hairdresser	Pc 61	Minster, Sussex
Keys George	31	shoemaker	Pc 4	Woodham, Essex
Kirk Robert	21	agent	Pc 59	Thornhill, Derbyshire
Knock Francis	24	clerk	Pc 44	Kent
Lambert Frederick	22	cornfactor	Pc 96	Gt. Dunmow, Essex
Leatherdale Elias	21	farmer	Pc 79	Chappel, Essex
Leatherdale John	25	lawyer	Pc 80	Greenstead, Essex
Lee Robert	21	groom	Pc 80	St Maryhay, London
Leich James	33	stonemason	Pc 89	Wellington, Shropshire
Lewsey Charles	33	grocer	Pc 15	Saling, Essex
Low Joseph	25	labourer	Pc 78	Billericay, Essex
Lowe Algernon	26	currier	Supt.	Gt. Burstead, Essex
Luckin Thomas	21	labourer	Pc 62	Gt. Waltham, Essex
Lungley William	29	farmer	Pc 45	Margaretting, Essex
Margerum Jeremiah	25	baker	Pc 8	Weeley, Essex
Marnie Charles	32	soldier	Pc 16	Montrose, Essex
Marsingall Anthony	25	schoolmaster	Insp.	Norton, Somerset
Martin Robert	30	carpenter	Pc 92	Clare, Suffolk
Matthew Spencer	32	glassgrinder	Pc 16	Ospring
Matthews Josiah	25	glover	Pc 70	Maldon, Essex
May John	30	clerk	Pc 55	Middlesex
Mayling Samuel	39	clerk	Insp.	Chelsea, Middlesex
McHardy John B.B.	38	Royal Navy	Chief	Bahamas
McInnis John	41	army	Supt.	Ayr, Scotland
Meade William	25	pig dealer	Pc 58	Rayne, Essex
Moor Thomas H	30	schoolmaster	Pc 8	Cockfield, Durham
Murrell William	26	labourer	Pc 1	Sudbury, Suffolk
Nix James	26	butcher	Insp.	Bury St Edmunds, Suffolk
Noakes Thomas	25	labourer	Pc 29	Springfield, Essex
Norton Albion J.C.	26	farmer	Pc 6	Pebmarsh, Essex
Orridge Thomas	22	farmer	Pc 22	Langford, Essex
Otway James			Supt.	Not given
Pack Robert	30	miller	Pc 97	Suffolk
Page Thomas	27	grocer	Pc 18	Brighton, Sussex
Parr Samuel	24	shoemaker	Pc 39	Colne Engaine, Essex
Parslow James	29	painter	Pc 31	Kingston, Surrey
Perry Thomas	26	labourer	Pc 27	Hildersham, Suffolk
Pettican James	30	corndealer	Pc 41	Thorpe le Soken, Essex
Pettit John	20	smith	Pc 91	Hedingham, Essex

Pilley John	23	shoemaker	Pc 23	Chelmsford, Essex
Pilling George	20	butcher	Pc 10	Stotford, Bedfordshire
Pledger Joseph	22	butcher	Pc 84	Baddow, Essex
Plume Henry	36	constable	Pc 13	Kingston, Surrey
Radley Josiah	24	printer	Pc 1	Castle Hedingham, Essex
Raison Samuel	26	labourer	Pc 44	Dedham, Essex
Randel William	39	soldier	Pc 63	South Brent, Devonshire
Rattigan William	20	farmer	Pc 51	Mayo, Ireland
Redgewell Robert	26	labourer	Pc 88	Sible Hedingham, Essex
Redin Thomas H	25	druggist	Pc 48	Barmer, Norfolk
Richardson William	28	shoemaker	Pc 43	Surrey
Richardson William	25	gardener	Pc 20	Maldon, Essex
Riom Henry	36	proctor	Supt.	Arbroath, Scotland
Rome Andrew	22	teadealer	Pc 64	Dumfrieshire
Rose James	33	labourer	Pc 12	Kingston, Surrey
Roy William	26	farmer	Pc 10	Colchester, Essex
Ryman John	23	saddler	Pc 77	Westminster, London
Sach Edward	32	currier	Pc 81	Coggeshall, Essx
Sams George	28	gardener	Pc 67	Chelmsford, Essex
Scott Robert	23	gardener	Pc 46	Carisbrooke, Hampshire
Seabrook Samuel	27	miller	Pc 83	Stansfield, Suffolk
Seaman Michael	20	farmer	Pc 90	Stanway, Essex
Seers Henry	21	servant	Pc 42	Kingston, Surrey
Sergeant Henry	23	gamekeeper	Pc 85	Stoke, Suffolk
Sergeant John G	25	lawyer	Pc 102	Colchester, Essex
Sherlock Thomas	30	carpenter	Pc 73	Dublin, Ireland
Shiplee William	23	labourer	Pc 73	Wix, Essex
Smith Ethelbert	33	painter	Pc 41	Cheltenham, Gloucester
Smith James	30	labourer	Pc 54	Mersea, Essex
Smith Isaac	21	butcher	Pc 48	Roydon, Essex
Smith William	25	labourer	Pc 2	Ardleigh, Essex
Sparkes Thomas	21	butcher	Pc 48	Maldon, Essex
Spiller Samuel	20	carman	Pc 50	Billericay, Essex
Spurgeon William	34	shoemaker	Pc 34	Bury St Edmunds, Suffolk
Staden John	33	servant	Pc 60	Sundridge, Kent
Steer Richard	26	engineer	Pc 65	Dartford, Kent
Steward Thomas	22	draper	Pc 18	Leigh, Essex
Swoart George	34	tea dealer	Pc 1	Sandwich, Kent
Syer James	22	labourer	Pc 71	Kirby Cross, Essex
Thorogood Charles	34	soldier	Pc 30	Hounslow, Middlesex
Thurston James	32	currier	Pc 2	Bow, London
Tidd Thomas	22	rubber maker	Pc 95	Clerkenwell, Middlesex
Tucker Thomas	32	tailor	Pc 3	Halstead, Essex
Tull John	27	bricklayer	Pc 74	Gosport, Hampshire
Turner George	31	bricklayer	Pc 52	Sittingfleet
Wait Daniel	25	labourer	Pc 43	Bristol, Gloucester
Ward Edward	30	plumber	Pc 58	Ridgewell, Essex
Warnock Alexander	33	Weaver	Pc 5	Paisley, Scotland
Warren James	23	servant	Pc 83	Stanway, Essex
Wheeler Emanuel	25	servant	Pc 6	Frome, Somerset
Wills Samuel	29	baker	Pc 81	Somerset
Woods William	21	labourer	Pc 36	Isle of Wight, Hampshire
Wright Francis	32	shoemaker	Pc 32	Halstead, Essex
Wright Thomas	29	shoemaker	Pc 4	Hatfield, Essex
Yardley Job	32	law and army	Supt.	London

1900 Recruits

Full Name	age on joining	date of joining	last job	place of birth
Alderton Elijah B	21	3 Oct	labourer	Stoke by Nayland, Suffolk
Barton Thomas	26	1 Nov	army & police	St Osyth, Essex
Bell David J	20	10 Sept	gardener	Springfield, Essex
Boast Edward H	20	24 Sept	labourer	Lawford, Essex
Bradfield Joseph	20	6 Dec	labourer	Mildenhall, Suffolk
Clark Alfred J	22	2 April	compositor	Lexden, Essex
Claydon George H	20	5 Jan	labourer	Earls Colne, Essex
Crook Frank	21	23 Oct	labourer	Woodhay, Berks.
Crouch George	20	8 March	ships fireman	Stifford, Essex
Doe Frederick G	20	8 March	labourer	Finchingfield, Essex
Drage Harry	19	7 August	butcher	Hitchin, Herts.
Folger John	21	2 April	railway servant	Grundisburgh Suffolk
French Albert	21	9 March	gardener	Black Notley, Essex
Frost George W	21	15 Jan	ships steward	Tollesbury, Essex
Gamble Harry	22	6 April	police	Broomfield, Essex
Girling William G	21	6 Dec	railway signalman	Foulsham, Norfolk
Gray William H	23	6 Sept	groom	North Benfleet, Essex
Groves Walter	20	7 June	gardener	Ingrave, Essex
Howland Albert E	21	2 April	blacksmith	Felsted, Essex
Ledger Thomas G	24	8 March	police & bricklayer	Hersham, Surrey
Miller Arthur	26	7 July	army & police	Stanway, Essex
Monk Walter	24	24 March	army	Leigh, Essex
Mott Samuel	25	1 Jan	groom	Danbury, Essex
Offord Alfred J	22	4 Feb	grocers asst.	Bury St Edmunds Suffolk
Perry Edward G	22	6 Dec	railway porter	Whittlesford, Cambs.
Peters William J	23	6 Sept.	Met. police	Great Stambridge, Essex
Pettican Albert G	23	1 May	police	Aldham, Essex
Poppy Arthur	22	16 July	printer	Chelmsford, Essex
Rank Alfred	24	1 Feb	police & labourer	Springfield, Essex
Shearman George	21	6 Dec	labourer & militia	Bradfield, Essex
Smith Frederic	21	2 April	baker	Bradfield, Essex
Smith Walter E	21	23 Oct	labourer	Colchester, Essex
Stuckey Charles F	24	7 Dec	labourer & Met. police	Forest Hill, Kent
Thompson Ernest W	22	2 April	labourer	Bocking, Essex
Townsend John	21	1 Feb	yachtman	Tollesbury, Essex
Watson Albert	21	6 Dec	labourer	Alresford, Essex
Wiseman Edwin C	20	20 Feb	game keeper	Burlingham, Norfolk

1990 Recruits

Full Name	Age on Joining	Date of Joining	Last Job	Place of Birth
Ammon Mark W	23	10 Dec	technician	Billericay, Essex
Anderson Paul D	19	22 Oct	student	Barking, Essex
Arthur Karl	26	19 Feb	Royal Navy	Sunderland, Durham
Baird Jacqueline H	19	30 April	police cadet	Braintree, Essex
Banks Keith A	26	10 Dec	baker & special con.	Hockley, Essex
Barber Paul E	32	22 Oct	storeman & special con.	Thundersley, Essex
Barnacle Marina H	23	4 June	hotel management	Stafford, Staffs.
Batchelor Jason P	23	9 July	moulder	Lambeth, London
Battersby Michael J	25	22 Oct	army	Colchester, Essex
Beagle Jane P	24	10 Oct	midwife	St Albans, Herts.
Beer Darren M	19	17 Sept	police cadet	Southend, Essex
Billings Jeanette	22	4 June	secretary	Hammersmith, London
Bourne Robert C	25	10 Dec	army	Birmingham, Warks.
Bowers Sharon E	29	3 June	secretary	Colchester, Essex
Bradley Pauline	21	22 Oct	clerk	Newcastle, Northumberland
Brebner Paul R	25	26 March	blast cleaner	Southend, Essex
Brooking Matthew	19	22 Oct	police cadet	Maldon, Essex
Burey Mark K	23	13 August	warehouseman	Enfield, Middlesex
Burke James L	23	10 Dec	painter	Dublin, Ireland
Byott Neil D	22	22 Oct	salesman	Basildon, Essex
Byrne Paul M	19	26 March	waiter	Wolverhampton, Staffs.
Cakebread Paul J	25	26 March	sales rep	Chelmsford, Essex
Chadwick Peter J	23	4 June	computer consultant	Norwich, Norfolk
Chapple Dean E	22	10 Oct	military police	Not known
Church Victoria J	19	4 June	police cadet	Boreham, Essex
Clark Corrina S	22	17 Sept	clerk	Colchester, Essex
Collett Kevin J	28	22 Oct	shop manager	Bethnal Green, London
Collinson Terence P	24	19 Feb	Royal Navy	Basildon, Essex
Coombs Adrian M	23	26 March	transport manager	Whitechapel, London
Crabb Philip S	20	10 Dec	print originator	Plaistow, London
Crawley Kenneth A	23	13 August	pub manager	Romford, Essex
Crook Angelina S	23	30 April	stock controller	Zambia
Cross Stephen R	30	22 Oct	estate agent	Norwich, Norfolk
Daly Paul B	29	17 Sept	arborist	London
Davies Lee B	25	13 August	technician	Plymouth, Devon
Dear Simon A	25	26 March	shop manager	London
Denney Justin J	19	10 Dec	student	Chelmsford, Essex
Dixon Timothy J	29	19 Feb	civil servant	Rochford, Essex
Drennan Kelly A	22	17 Sept	secretary	Barking, Essex
Easen Joanna S	20	10 Oct	dancer	Maldon, Essex
Eddy Stephen	22	10 Dec	salesman	County Durham
Estall Mark A	19	30 April	estate agent	Reading, Berkshire
Evans Jonathon A	22	9 July	clerk	Wells, Somerset
Ewings Andrew	19	30 April	police cadet	Hadleigh, Essex
Farrer Kevin J	25	9 July	hod carrier	Forest Gate, London
Finch Alison C	21	17 Sept	nurse	Chelmsford, Essex
Finch Michael J	22	13 August	insurance broker	Thurrock, Essex
Fisk Paul M	26	30 April	driver	Chelmsford, Essex
Forrester Kathryn E	24	10 Oct	security officer	London

Foster Sheila	28	17 Sept	security officer	Dulwich, London
Gannon Martin J	26	13 August	supervisor	Balham, London
Gilgan Christopher M	26	30 April	bank clerk	Camberwell, London
Gorbutt Stephen J	21	10 Dec	insurance clerk	Norfolk
Gray-Saunders Deborah J	27	30 April	sales consultant	West Germany
Greaves Michael R	25	17 Sept	sales rep.	London
Griffin Darren T	21	26 March	signwriter	Barking, Essex
Hassinger Jacqueline	24	9 July	shop assistant	Epping, Essex
Hawkins Leslie J	28	17 Sept	storeman & special con.	London
Hearn Karen L	19	9 July	bank clerk	Gravesend, Kent
Heffer Daryl M	23	19 Feb	Royal Air Force	Colchester, Essex
Hibbert Mark A	29	22 Oct	Gibraltar police	Gibraltar
Irvin Sharon Z	28	4 June	sales rep.	Walthamstow, London
Jagger Chloe S	21	22 Oct	clerk	Writtle, Essex
James Neil P	24	4 June	Royal Air Force	Colchester, Essex
Jarman Laura J	21	26 March	sales clerk	Barking, Essex
Jay Gary A	24	13 August	civil servant	Clacton, Essex
Jenkins Susan K	25	19 Feb	console operator	Greenford, London
Jessop Stewart M	29	17 Sept	military police	
Johnson Stephen	19	17 Sept	clerk	Chelmsford, Essex
Jones Darren L	23	10 Dec	army	Cromer, Norfolk
Jose Andrew R	21	17 Sept	student	Romford, Essex
Kalar Sukhvinder	23	30 April	administrator	Barking, Essex
Kemp Andrew C	21	9 July	army	Brentwood, Essex
Knights Barry D	23	13 August	clerk	Ware, Hertfordshire
Lane Nicola	21	10 Oct	secretary	Benfleet, Essex
Langwith Emma L	19	26 March	student	London
Larner Martin D	22	19 Feb	bank clerk	Colchester, Essex
Lawton Amanda J	24	13 August	police civilian staff	London
Layley Christopher D	21	10 Dec	shop manager	Fareham, Hampshire
Leeming Roland G	21	30 April	sales clerk & special con.	Stratford, London
Lewis Darren L	24	19 Feb	design engineer	Hackney, London
Lincoln Rebecca L	19	10 Dec	police cadet	Harlow, Essex
Lindfield Joanne E	23	22 Oct	manager	Walthamstow, London
Littlechild Marie L	19	17 Sept	underwriting asst.	Romford, Essex
Logan John	19	9 July	student	Billericay, Essex
Maleary Glenn E	19	26 March	labourer	Colchester, Essex
Manning Carole J	23	4 June	clerk typist	Brentwood, Essex
Manning Deborah J	22	10 Oct	shop assistant	Colchester, Essex
Marr Gillian E	24	13 August	telecommunications	Ayr, Scotland
Marriner Melanie C	23	10 Oct	secretary	Epping, Essex
Marshall Lee S	23	13 August	army	Kettering, Northampton
McCormack Linda J	22	26 March	police civilian staff	Orsett, Essex
Middleton Geoffrey D	19	26 March	police cadet	London
Middleton Laurence	30	22 Oct	army	Hull, Yorkshire
Morton Paul J	23	4 June	student	Bishops Stortford, Hertfordshire
Mowbray Mairhi E	26	30 April	secretary	Glasgow, Scotland
Neilus Jason O	19	26 March	police cadet	Nottingham, Notts.
Nicholls Keith E	25	9 July	hod carrier	Lewisham, London
Nickerson Joanne L	20	9 July	student	St Albans, Hertfordshire
O'Donnell Brian	29	10 Dec	labourer	Edmonton, London
O'Flaherty Mark C	22	30 April	clerk	Stanford-le-Hope, Essex
O'Mahony Janice	27	13 August	sales assistant	Bishops Stortford, Hertfordshire
Oakes Stephen A	20	10 Dec	bank clerk	Thurrock, Essex
Oldfield Carl	25	10 Dec	military police	Bristol, Gloucestershire

Osborne Mark P	26	10 Dec	army	France
Parker Lawrence	30	10 Dec	army	Dumfries, Scotland
Parkin David A	21	13 August	legal executive	Leeds, West Yorkshire
Payton Susanna	22	26 March	civil servant	Rochford, Essex
Pearce Mark A	29	26 March	coach driver	Tittensor, Staffs.
Penn Karen J	24	17 Sept	clerk	Wickford, Essex
Pettet Peter	22	10 Dec	plastics inspector	Orsett, Esesx
Philpott Derek I	27	22 Oct	Royal Marines	Romford, Essex
Pickles David W	27	4 June	student	Chelmsford, Essex
Poulter Ann	23	9 July	secretary	Halifax, West Yorkshire
Puffett David A	28	19 Feb	sales manager	Billericay, Essex
Quaey Charles E	24	26 March	pensions clerk	Rochford, Essex
Rainbow Paul	29	4 June	technician	London
Raine Martin R	23	26 March	labourer	Chelmsford, Essex
Ralph Wendy	30	22 Oct	hairdresser	South Benfleet, Essex
Restarick Paul	22	9 July	admin officer	Newham, London
Rogers Gary M	28	13 August	police	London
Rogers Paul J	21	10 Dec	bank clerk	Cyprus
Royles Tina M	20	13 August	student	St Asaph, Wales
Sams Andrew D	26	10 Dec	ambulanceman	Brentwood, Essex
Shanahan Dermot J	25	9 July	accounts manager	Hornchurch, Essex
Shaw Lisa J	30	10 Oct	nurse	Plymouth, Devon
Sibley Mark A	28	26 March	security officer	Rochford, Essex
Sims Joanne M	20	22 Oct	police civilian staff	Walthamstow, London
Smith Peter J	24	26 March	sales rep & special con.	Widnes, Cheshire
Smith Joanne L	21	10 Oct	shop asst & special con.	Chadwell Heath, Essex
Smith Mark L	23	26 March	Royal Navy	Romford, Essex
Smith Christopher V	24	4 June	pool attendant	Ilford, Essex
Smith Steven	22	10 Dec	electrician	Wanstead, Essex
Smithers Patrick M	23	22 Oct	draughtsman	Ilford, Essex
Snell Alison D	21	9 July	computer operator	Hoddesdon, Hertfordshire
Snellgrove Kirste L	20	30 April	clerk	Rochford, Essex
Spink Michael B	19	17 Sept	police cadet	Basildon, Essex
Staines Christine A	23	13 August	manager	Rochford, Essex
Staples Robert D	19	10 Dec	student	Harold Wood, Essex
Stoten Daniel	20	30 April	student	Lewisham, London
Strizovic Nikola	26	26 March	technician	Corringham, Essex
Teather Stacy L	19	17 Sept	bank clerk	Romford, Essex
Tyler Susan L	19	19 Feb	student	Chelmsford, Essex
Umfreville Mark P	25	26 March	customs & special con	Chadwell St Mary, Essex
Veal Gary J	25	13 August	postman	Colchester, Essex
Walczak Gary C	29	9 July	HGV driver	Leamington Spa, Warks.
Wall Richard C	22	26 March	factory	Shoeburyness, Essex
Wallace Victor	25	10 Oct	bank clerk	Rochford, Essex
Wheeler Mark	22	26 March	student	Chelmsford, Essex
Whipps Kevin J	22	30 April	consultant	Woolwich, London
Wilson Victoria C	19	26 March	sales assistant	Chelmsford, Essex
Winterbone Martin G	24	4 June	student	Chelmsford, Essex
Wood Nicola L	20	26 March	bank clerk	Westcliff, Essex
Woolf Caroline B	23	6 Sept	clerk	Forest Gate, London
Wright David G	26	10 Oct	prison officer	Ipswich, Suffolk
Zagger Elliot R	19	30 April	salesman	Wanstead, London

Appendix VII

Police Strength Against Population Growth of Essex 1841-1990

Year	Population	Strength	Pol/Pop %	Notes
1840	---	115	---	A
1841	257,929	138	0.05	
1851	269,790	201	0.07	
1861	291,924	246	0.08	B
1871	304,111	285	0.09	
1881	366,387	286	0.08	
1891	336,703	330	0.10	
1901	380,887	393	0.10	
1914	387,143	465	0.12	
1921	416,384	465	0.11	
1931	503,485	513	0.10	
1940	592,000*	770	0.13	C
1951	609,416	1,012	0.17	D
1961	854,044	1,344	0.16	E
1971	1,358,028	2,316	0.17	
1981	1,408,300	2,633	0.19	
1990	1,451,0038	2,859	0.20	

Notes
A   100 Cons. and 15 supts.
B   1 CC; 11 supts. in three classes; 12 insps. in three classes; 10 sgts; 211 cons. in three classes
C   Since 1933 1 CC; 10 supts.; 19 insps.; 66 sgts; 441 cons.D
D.   1 CC; 1 ACC; 2Cs; 11 supts.; 13 CI; 50 insps; 137 sgts; 751 cons; 1 WPl; 3 WPS; 19 WPC
E.   1 CC; 2 ACC; 3 CS; 11 supts; 19 CI; 77 insps; 243 sgts; 1,114 cons; 1 WCI 1 WI; 7 WPS; 34 WPC

Key
*   Estimated figures
CC   chief constable
ACC   assistant chief constable
CS   chief superintendent
supt.   superintendent
CI   chief inspector
insp.   inspector
WCI   woman chief inspector
WI   woman inspector
WPS   woman police sergeant
WPC   woman police constable

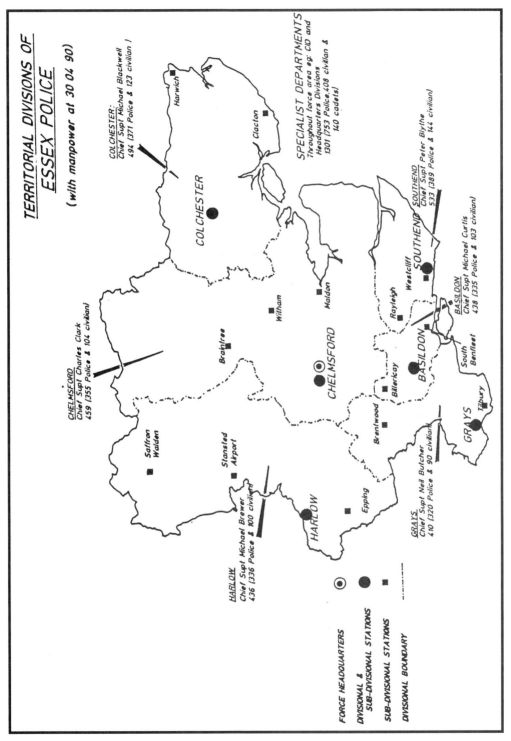

41.   Plan of divisions and manpower in 1990.

Index

Note: where police officers appear in the book more than once with different ranks, they have been indexed under their most senior rank mentioned. The 1990 recruits in Appendix VI have **not** been indexed.